?

Delphi is the   g n   1 International.
Combining th   of int   terfa e design   t   utable Pascal code
and extensive component reusabilty, this product is set fair to be *the* dominant
application environment. This book teaches you the concepts behind Delphi, using
plenty of fully implemented examples. Aimed at programmers who want to
quickly add Delphi to their list of skills, the book treats programmers as
professionals who need no superfluous details. Including help for Pascal and
Visual Basic developers, as well as details of Delphi's database connectivity, this
Instant Guide is the latest of the Wrox Instant series to respond to the real needs
of busy developers who need to migrate quickly from one discipline to another.

What is Wrox Press?

Wrox Press is a computer book publisher which promotes a brand new concept - clear,
jargon-free programming and database titles that fulfill your real demands. We publish
for everyone, from the novice through to the experienced programmer. To ensure our
books meet your needs, we carry out continuous research on all our titles. Through our
dialog with you we can craft the book you really need.

We welcome suggestions and take all of them to heart - your input is paramount in
creating the next great Wrox title. Use the reply card inside this book or mail us at:

feedback@wrox.demon.co.uk
or
Compuserve 100063, 2152

Wrox Press Ltd.   **Tel:** **0101 312 465 3559**
2710 W. Touhy   **Fax:** **0101 312 465 4063**
Chicago
IL 60645
USA

D1146808

Instant Delphi

Dave Jewell

Wrox Press Ltd.®

Instant Delphi

© 1995 Dave Jewell

Published by Wrox Press Ltd. Unit 16, 20 James Road, Birmingham, B11 2BA UK
Printed in the U.S.A

ISBN 1-874416-57-5

Trademark Acknowledgements

Credits

Author
Dave Jewell

Technical Editor
Mike O'Docherty

Series Editor
Luke Dempsey

Technical Reviewers
Jim Shearer
Ewan McNab

Indexer
Ian Wilks

Production Manager
Gina Mance

Book Layout
Eddie Fisher
Greg Powell
Lee Kelly

Proof Reader
Pam Brand

Cover Design
Third Wave

For more information on Third Wave, contact Ross Alderson on 44-21 236 6616

Cover photograph supplied by The Image Bank

About the Author

Dave Jewell is fully employed by his four children as a service engineer. His duties include the repair of broken toys, maintaining model railways and generally fixing things which have been dropped from a great height. In his spare time he poses as a freelance journalist, consultant and Windows developer, writing technical and programming columns for many UK magazines. He has been involved with Microsoft Windows since version 1.0.

Author's Acknowledgements

I would like to express my thanks to Luke Dempsey, Series Editor, for keeping the whole thing on course and for expertly cracking the whip at appropriate intervals. I would also like to thank Mike O'Docherty, Technical Editor, for his expert comments and suggestions on the manuscript. Neither of them realised what a cantankerous, opinionated individual they were dealing with until it was far, far too late ...

Author's Dedication

To Mum, without whom none of this would have been possible. May you find lasting happiness in your new home.

Summary of Contents

Table of Contents

Table of Contents

Table of Contents

Table of Contents

Table of Contents

What Can Delphi Do For Me?

Maybe, like me, you've been feeling rather envious of all those Visual Basic programmers. They have a wonderfully easy-to-use visual development system which enables them to lay out the user interface of a program very quickly. They use an interpreted programming language which means not having to go and make a cup of coffee while your C++ compilation continues chugging along. Best of all, they have access to dozens of top-quality VBX custom controls which can be plugged straight into a program to produce all sorts of professional effects including toolbars, status bars, OLE features, high-speed communications, graphics, multi-media and so on. Some people have all the luck ...

If that's how you feel then I've got great news for you. Borland's remarkable new Delphi gives you everything that Visual Basic has and far more besides. Delphi is going to revolutionize your development work and enable you to build top-quality applications in record time. Here's some reasons why:

 An all new, state-of-the-art visual design system for quickly putting together an application's user interface. Using a 'component' based approach, you merely select reusable components from a configurable palette, and place them onto the forms within your application.

Delphi uses Borland's highly acclaimed object-oriented Pascal programming language with a compiler that runs so fast you'd almost think you're using an interpreter! Better yet, because it's a true compiled language, your programs will execute faster than Visual Basic's interpreted BASIC and you won't need to distribute any monster-sized run-time DLL's along with your application.

Object-oriented programming finally comes of age. Up until now, the OOP promise of easy-to-use, reusable software components hasn't quite been realized - it has been waiting for a development system that makes the promise into a reality. Sure, you can use VBX controls inside Visual Basic, but they're not object-oriented components in the real sense of the word. Delphi creates automatic class definitions for each component you pull onto a form, and every component is itself written in an object-oriented manner. Unlike VBXs, Delphi components are linked in to your application, meaning that you don't have to distribute a lot of extra files with your product. You can use the extensive library of components supplied by Borland and you can develop your own, specialized components and component libraries. Delphi will even let you make use of existing VBX controls, putting an object-oriented 'wrapper' around them.

Delphi represents the easiest, fastest way to build professional, commercial-quality applications with the sort of user interfaces that today's users have come to expect. A 32-bit version is planned for Chicago and Windows/NT so your software investment is assured. Try it - you'll love it!

How to Use This Book

On the understanding that you can't wait to try out Delphi, Chapter 1 provides a whirlwind tour of the development environment and leads you through the step-by-step development of your first application. The next five chapters cover the fundamentals of Delphi program development in more detail, together with useful implementations which show you how to apply the concepts you have learned. At the end of this, you should be very comfortable with Delphi and able to handle a wide variety of programming projects with some ease.

Part two of the book covers more advanced topics, such as how to utilize Delphi's advanced exception handling routines to create robust applications, working with graphics, and how to build your own reusable components. Once you've got this stuff under your belt, you should be well on the way to being a real expert!

A word about the end of chapter exercises: do please take the time to work through this material. It is there to reinforce what you've already learned, and to provide a spring-board for your own experimentation with Delphi.

What You Should Know

To get the most from Instant Delphi, it helps to have some familiarity with the Pascal programming language. This book isn't a tutorial on Pascal, nor on object-oriented programming - it's assumed that you have used Pascal previously, and have some familiarity with the basic concepts of object-oriented programming. If you have absolutely no knowledge of Pascal, a good introductory text is *The Revolutionary Guide to Turbo Pascal* by Borodich, Valvachov and Leonenko, Wrox Press, 1992. This book covers Pascal fundamentals and also serves as an introduction to OOP programming and the object oriented extensions that Borland have built into the Pascal language.

It would also help to have some familiarity with Visual Basic, but this is far less important. Existing Visual Basic users will already be very familiar with the idea of forms, properties, event procedures and of course VBX controls. However, this material is covered in Instant Delphi for the sake of Pascal developers who have no previous exposure to Visual Basic.

Existing Pascal developers can quickly get up to speed with Delphi by reading Appendix A. This concentrates on the language differences between 'Delphi Pascal' and previous versions of the language and also covers reusability of old code in the Delphi programming environment.

In the same way, Appendix B is aimed at existing Visual Basic developers. It compares Delphi with the Visual Basic environment and discusses reusability of VBX files, and so on.

Conventions Used

To enable you to find your way around this book easily, we have used various different styles to highlight different references.

Program Code

All programs in the book are highlighted with a gray background so you can find them easily.

```
var
    f: File;

begin
    AssignFile (f, 'MYFILE.DAT');
    Reset (f, 100);
    {— etc —}
```

When we use extracts from this code we also shade it so you can spot it quickly.

When code features in the middle of sentences, we write it in **this_style**.

In some instances, we repeat parts of the code in an example in various places. This is deliberate, so that you can see the program develop. We have shaded lines which are new additions to the program, and left the lines that are repeated unshaded. This will enable you to see immediately where new stuff has been added:

```
This is repeated code.
This is new code.
This is repeated code.
This is new code.
This is new code.
```

Important Bits, Font Conventions

Bits that you really must read are in this style.

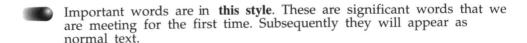 Important words are in **this style**. These are significant words that we are meeting for the first time. Subsequently they will appear as normal text.

- File names are in **THIS_STYLE**. All file names appear like this in the text, even when they are conventionally written in lower case inside a program.

- Keys that you press are in *this style*, such as *Enter* or *Ctrl*.

- Components are in this style

- Their properties are in `this style`

- Things that appear on screen are in this style

Tell Us What You Think

One last thing. We've tried to make the book enjoyable and accurate. The programming community is what we're here to serve, so if you have any queries or suggestions, or comments about this book, let us know, we will be delighted to hear from you. You can help us ensure that our future books are even better. Return the reply card at the back of the book, or contact us direct at Wrox. You can also use e-mail:

**feedback@wrox.demon.co.uk
Compuserve: 100062,2152**

Chapter

Introducing Delphi

The aim of this introductory chapter is to get you up and running with Delphi as fast as possible and to give you a 'feel' for what Delphi development is about. This chapter doesn't attempt to answer all your questions. Indeed, after working through it, you may find that you've got more questions than you had to start with, but don't worry - that's what the rest of the book is for!

You'll learn why Delphi represents one of the most exciting and productive development systems currently available for Windows programming. You'll be introduced to the major concepts behind Delphi and to fundamental parts of the Delphi interface, including:

- The Main Delphi Window
- The SpeedBar
- The Component Palette
- The Form Window
- The Object Inspector
- The Code Editor
- The Interactive Tutors

Most importantly, this chapter concludes with a step-by-step tutorial in the *Implementation* section, which leads you through the development of a genuinely useful program, showing you how to develop your application's user interface and how to code event handlers which respond to user activity. At the end of the tutorial, you'll have a complete, professional looking application and a good understanding of how it all hangs together.

Delphi: Concepts

The diagram below illustrates the four architectural foundations upon which Delphi programming is based. Let's look at the meaning of these different concepts and see how they relate to program development using Delphi.

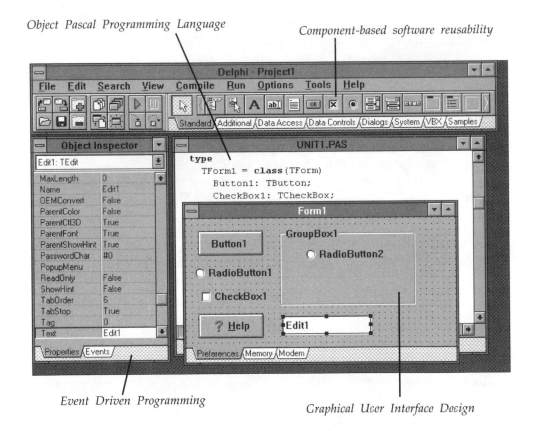

Object Pascal Programming Language

Component-based software reusability

Event Driven Programming

Graphical User Interface Design

Event Driven Programming

Back in the old days, before graphical user interfaces came on the scene, an application required very little user interface code. It was only necessary to get keyboard input from the user one line at a time, process the data and programming - the program code always follows a predetermined sequence of instructions. It always begins at the beginning, executes one or more routines in a set order and then ends at the end!

With Windows, things are somewhat more complicated. In a painting program, the user might drag the mouse across the screen to draw a line, click the mouse to select a new drawing tool, resize the window of the drawing program, enter some text from the keyboard, or even use *Alt-Tab* to 'switch away' from the drawing program altogether.

How are you going to handle all these eventualities inside your program code? You can't possibly know in advance which actions the user is going to take and in what order they will be taken, therefore it isn't possible to lay out your code in a simple, sequential manner.

The answer is to use **event driven programming**. Each of the above user actions (mouse dragging, mouse clicking, window resizing, and so on) can be referred to as an 'event'. With event driven programming, an application spends a lot of time simply waiting for events to take place. When an event occurs, the application decides what action to take (based on the type of event) and then goes back to waiting for another event.

From Switch Statements to Event Handlers

This idea should be very familiar to existing Windows developers who have programmed in C, C++ or Pascal. Conventional Windows programming refers to an event as a 'message', and there are potentially a very large number of Windows messages that can come your way. A program written in C or Pascal is often structured as an enormous `switch` statement, with different blocks of code being executed according to the message that's been received. There will be one of these `switch` statements, embedded in a window procedure, for each type of window defined by the program.

Of course, anyone will tell you that this idea of using enormous `switch` statements isn't a good one. It leads to messy, difficult to maintain code. More recently, it has become fashionable to divide up a conventionally written C or Pascal program into a number of bite-sized routines, each of which is responsible for handling one specific message such as a mouse click, a key press and so on. This is just what happens with Delphi and Visual Basic programming. The emphasis is on writing small, easily maintained routines, each of which has a specific, well-defined purpose.

> Incidentally, if you're a 'classic' Windows developer, you might be wondering where this leaves the message loop - the small chunk of code which waits for Windows messages and then dispatches them. The answer is that it's still there, but you don't have to write it. Both Delphi and Visual Basic implement their own 'behind the scenes' message loop, leaving you to get on with the job of writing the event handling routines.

Each of these event handling routines is called an **event handler**. In Delphi, event handlers are normally specific to a particular window or control. As you learn about the Delphi development system, you'll see that much of the time Delphi will create the shell of an event handler for you, leaving you to fill in the specific code that's unique to your application.

Component Based Software Reusability

Developers who have spent many years writing Windows applications in 'conventional' C or Pascal can become very jealous of Visual Basic programmers. They have a wonderfully simple visual development system which allows them to lay out the user interface of a program very quickly. They use an **interpreted** programming language, which means not having to go and make a cup of coffee while the latest compilation grinds along. Best of all, they have access to dozens of top-quality VBX custom controls which can be plugged straight into a program to produce all sorts of professional effects such as toolbars, status bars, OLE features, high-speed communications, graphics, multi-media and so on. Some people have all the luck.

But now, Delphi developers also have access to a rich set of reusable components that are every bit as good as the ones supplied with Visual Basic. In some ways, Delphi controls are superior, because they are directly linked into your application, becoming a part of the **.EXE** file. This means that you don't have to worry about unscrupulous people 'extracting' proprietary components from your shipped application and building them into their own programs - it's just not possible to do that. This makes Delphi attractive not only to application developers, but also to third party component writers. There's bound to be a thriving market in Delphi components before long.

Delphi has a **component palette** (similar to the control palette in Visual
Basic) from which you can select components and use them to build up the
user interface of your application. The component palette is illustrated
below.

Unlike Visual Basic controls, Delphi components are true 'objects' in the
object-oriented programming sense and are written in the Object Pascal
language - Borland's object-oriented dialect of Pascal.

Delphi provides all the necessary tools and documentation for you to write
your own reusable components which may then be incorporated into your
programming projects, or made available to other developers. Any
component you purchase or develop yourself can be added to the
component palette which organizes all available components into different
categories. Delphi can even make use of your existing VBX custom controls
by putting an object-oriented 'wrapper' around them (although such controls
can't be linked into your **.EXE** file).

Graphical User Interface Design

Like Visual Basic, Delphi allows you to lay out your application visually,
choosing reusable components and adding them to the **form** (window)
you're currently working on. An application can be made up from any
number of forms, which can be turned into reusable modules for
incorporation into other applications.

Some development systems have built-in resource editors which can be used
to lay out controls inside dialog boxes. Unfortunately, these tools are of little
use if the window you're designing doesn't happen to be a dialog box.
Delphi, in contrast, makes relatively little distinction between dialog boxes
and ordinary application windows, allowing you to add components to both
with equal ease.

More importantly, perhaps, is the tight integration between the visual design phase and the actual coding of the application. At any time while you're laying out the user interface code, you can add event handlers for specific components, change the properties of the form, and so on. Delphi provides facilities for aligning controls, grouping them together, and you can also arrange for controls to be created and deleted at run-time as needed.

Object Pascal Programming Language

Delphi uses Borland's highly acclaimed object-oriented Pascal programming language with a compiler that runs so fast you'd almost think you were using an interpreter! Better yet, because it's a true compiled language, your applications will generally run faster than Visual Basic's interpreted BASIC, and you won't need to distribute large run-time DLL's along with your application.

TPW Versus OBJ

Aside from speed of compilation, there's another big benefit to using Borland's Pascal compiler technology. The Pascal compiler generates object files with the suffix **.TPW**, rather than the more common **.OBJ** files generated by C/C++ compilers. **.TPW** files contain far more information than their **.OBJ** equivalents, meaning that Borland's linker can easily strip unreferenced procedures, functions, methods and even global variables from your program. The end result is an **.EXE** file which is often smaller (and therefore faster to load) than its C/C++ equivalent.

Delphi is the first development system which fulfills the object-oriented programming promise of easy-to-use, reusable software components. This is because the idea of component reusability has been built right into Delphi itself. To get you up and running as soon as possible, Delphi takes care of as much of the 'grunt work' as possible, automatically updating class definitions each time you add a form to a control, creating event handler templates as required, and so on. All you have to provide is the application-specific code. In this way, you're spared from rewriting the same old user interface code with each new application you build.

Pascal programmers who have used previous versions of Borland Pascal and Turbo Pascal will want to know about the new language extensions introduced with Delphi such as class definitions and exception handling. These issues are covered in detail in Appendix B.

The following figure sums up the pivotal position Delphi holds between its four key elements of event-driven programming, component based software reusability, Object Pascal and graphical user interface design. (The bomb, of course, is about to generate an event!)

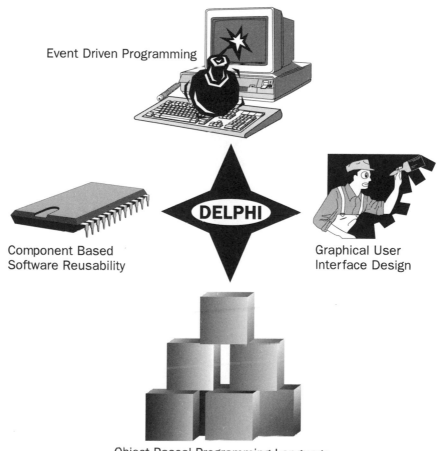

Event Driven Programming

Component Based
Software Reusability

DELPHI

Graphical User
Interface Design

Object Pascal Programming Language

Terminology Time

Throughout this book, we'll be using certain terms extensively, so it's a good idea to ensure that you understand exactly what we mean when we use them. The most commonly occurring terms are defined below. You'll see that each has an equivalent 'classical' phrase for the benefit of those who have developed applications using conventional C/C++ or Pascal development systems.

Delphi Name	Traditional Name	Meaning
Form	Window	The basic building block of a Windows application. A form is generally set up as a dialog box or as an application window. The form is the 'parent' of any controls that may be placed on it.
Component	Control	A component is what conventional Windows programmers would usually refer to as a control. In this sense, controls are actually child windows of the form, but such terminology is confusing. See Note 1
Event	Message	A Windows message generated by the underlying Windows system and converted into a call to an event handler. See Note 2.

Note 1: You need to realize that not all components are visual. For example, push buttons, listboxes and the like have a direct screen representation, but what about a Timer component? Timers are invisible and the user of your application is completely unaware that there's even a Timer component on the form. Some components, such as menu items, do have a visual representation, but not one that's directly related to their appearance at design time. Therefore, components are often child windows - but not always.

Note 2: If you're at all worried that using Delphi will 'lock you in' to 16-bit Windows, then don't be. Borland are committed to releasing a 32-bit version which will run under (and create executables for) Windows NT and Windows 95. If you've previously programmed for Windows using C or C++, you'll know that under 32-bit implementations of Windows, the layout of various Windows messages has changed. C programmers use 'message cracker' macros to write portable code which will compile cleanly for both 16-bit and 32-bit Windows. As a Delphi developer, you don't have to worry about this - the 32-bit version of Delphi will automatically translate incoming Windows messages into event handler calls which look just the same as their 16-bit counterparts. If you want to do 32-bit programming, Delphi will make it easy for you to do so.

The Main Delphi Window

Let's begin our tour of Delphi facilities by starting it up from the Program Manager. If you've just installed Delphi, you should end up with a screen layout similar to the one below, otherwise, select New Project from the File menu.

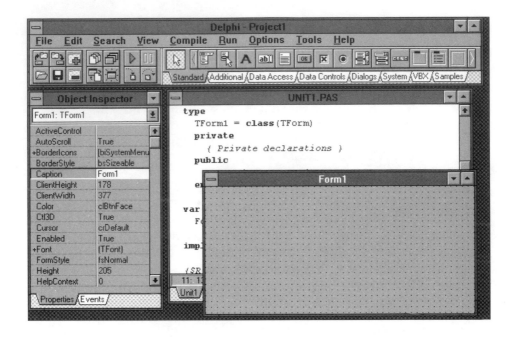

You can see that, like Visual Basic, the Delphi development environment comprises several different windows, each of which can be resized and rearranged to suit your current needs. The most important window in Delphi is the main window (the one with the title Delphi). Closing the main window will terminate Delphi, while iconizing it will cause all the other Delphi windows to temporarily disappear.

Below the menu bar, the main window is divided into two distinct parts: the SpeedBar on the left and the Component Palette on the right. Let's take a look at each of these in turn.

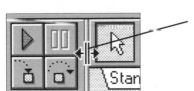

If you slowly move the mouse from the SpeedBar to the Component Palette, you should see the cursor change to a double-ended arrow. You can then hold down the mouse and drag it to the right or left so as to change the relative widths of the SpeedBar and Component Palette.

The SpeedBar

The SpeedBar contains a number of 'SpeedButtons' which are used to perform common actions within Delphi, such as opening and saving files, running the program, and so on. As installed, your SpeedBar should contain the fourteen SpeedButtons shown below:

Reading from left to right and top to bottom, the meaning of these SpeedButtons is as follows:

Open a project.

Save all open files in the current project.

Add a file to the project.

Display a list of units in the current project, so that you can select one.

Display a list of forms in the current project, so that you can select one.

Compile and execute the current application.

Pause execution of the current application.

Open a file.

Save current file.

Remove a file from the project.

Toggle between the current form and Code Editor window.

Create a new form and associated unit.

Step into the next routine. (Disabled if symbolic debugging turned off.)

Step over the next routine. (Disabled if symbolic debugging turned off.)

In addition to the standard **SpeedBar** layout described above, you can customize the **SpeedBar** to your own needs, reflecting the way you work. If you click the right-hand mouse button on the **SpeedBar**, you'll see a popup-menu whose **Configure** option lets you drag new buttons onto the **SpeedBar** and remove buttons that you don't often use. This is explained more fully in Chapter 11: *Customizing Delphi*. It's probably best not to modify the **SpeedBar** configuration at this point - wait until you're thoroughly familiar with the fundamentals of using Delphi. For clarity, we'll be sticking with the standard **SpeedBar** layout throughout this book.

The Component Palette

The other half of Delphi's main window is the Component Palette. In a sense, this is the most important part of Delphi, since it sums up what the development environment is all about - reusable software components.

Along the top of the Component Palette, you can see a number of icons corresponding to each of the available components. You can simply click on one of these components to select it and then click on the current form window to add the component to the form. Let's say, for example, that you wanted to add an edit box to the current form. Click on the edit box icon and then on the form, and you'll have an edit box, created at its default size.

A faster approach is to just double-click a component on the Component Palette. This will immediately place a component onto the form. Yet another way is to click once on the component in the Component Palette and then drag the mouse over the form, creating a component of the desired size. You can also resize or reposition any component that's already been placed onto the form by manipulating the edges and corners of any selected component. Positioning and manipulating components is discussed more fully in the next chapter. Until then, there are just a few special things to note about the Component Palette.

Hints and Allegations

You can get a 'hint' about any component on the Component Palette by moving the mouse cursor over the component's icon and leaving it there for a second or two. A small hint window will be displayed showing the name of the component. This is particularly useful where you don't immediately recognize what a particular component does. You can even add the same hint facilities to your own applications.

Hidden Surprises

The second thing to note is that tabs appear along the bottom of the Component Palette. The palette actually contains a surprisingly large number of components. In order to make the Component Palette easier to use, Borland have divided up all the components into different categories. Each category page is accessed by a tab - as you click the tabs, you'll see different sets of components appear.

> **Notice that no matter which category page is selected, there's always a large cursor shape at the left-hand end of the Component Palette. This isn't actually a component at all - it's just a way of deselecting the currently selected component and returning to the normal cursor function. Having selected a component to place on the form, clicking this part of the palette lets you change your mind.**

You'll also see an arrow symbol at either end of the Component Palette. These arrows can be used to scroll through a large number of components when they won't all fit in the window. In the picture above, the left hand scroll arrow is disabled (grayed out), while the right hand scroll arrow is enabled, indicating that there are more components available to the right.

The Form Window

The **Form window** corresponds to the currently selected form. You build up the user interface of your application by placing components onto the form. By default, the form window is configured so that any components placed on it will 'snap' to a grid, ensuring visual consistency. The size of the grid can be adjusted and you can also decide whether or not you want the grid points to be displayed. By default, the grid is displayed, as shown here. We won't be saying much more about the Form window here, but it will become the focus of our attention soon.

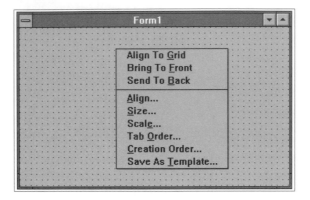

Like many parts of Delphi, the Form window has a **SpeedMenu**, shown above. The **SpeedMenu** will appear when you click the right mouse button on any part of the form. The Form window **SpeedMenu** is described more fully in the next chapter.

Inspecting Properties

Property Names

Property Values

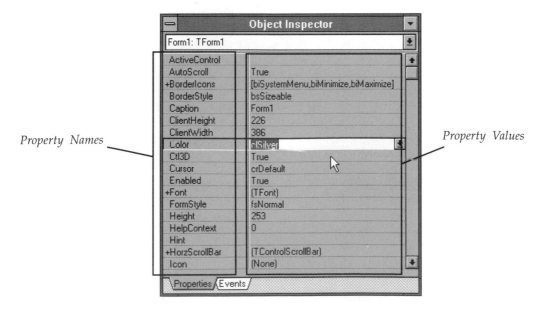

Here's what the Object Inspector window looks like. The name is perhaps somewhat misleading - the Object Inspector isn't just for inspecting, it's also used for altering the characteristics of objects and more besides. Like Visual Basic, Delphi uses the idea of 'properties' to describe the various characteristics of an object. A listbox might have properties such as its name, which font to use, whether items are sorted, and so on. Typically, a particular object can have quite a large number of properties and, as you become more adept at Delphi programming, familiarity with the available properties will enable you to get the best out of the system.

> **Incidentally, you might be wondering why we're suddenly using the word 'object' rather than 'component'. A component is something that can be placed on a form. By definition, this means that a form can't be a component. When we're talking about both components and forms together, we have to use the collective term 'object' to describe both. This is why Borland called this window an Object Inspector rather than a Component Inspector - it's used to manipulate forms as well as components.**

As you can see, the Object Inspector contains a list of all the different properties available for the currently selected object. Not all objects have the same properties - as you select different components on a form, you'll see the list of available properties change. You can immediately tell which object is selected by looking at the contents of the box immediately below the Object Inspector's title bar. This box is called the Object Selector.

The Object Selector

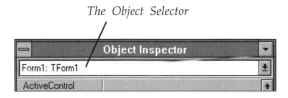

The Object Selector lists all the objects on the currently selected form and can be used to select a new object without switching over to the form window.

Note that the **Object Selector** combo box string is made up of two parts separated by a colon. The first part is the *name* of the currently selected object while the second part is the *type* of the currently selected object. In the example shown here, the form named **Form1** is selected. This form is of type `TForm1`. Whenever you have an object selected whose type or name you're unsure of, just look here for clarification.

The left hand side of the properties list gives the names of all the properties, while the right hand side shows the current value of that property. In the earlier example, the `AutoScroll` property is `True`, the `Color` property is `clSilver` and so on. To change the value of a certain property, you can click on the property of interest and then type in a new value such as `200` for the `Height` property. Some properties are enumerated, which is just a fancy way of saying that they can only have certain values. Boolean properties are enumerated - if you double click on the value part of a Boolean property, it will change from `True` to `False` or vice versa. Try it - double click on the value of the `AutoScroll` property and watch it toggle between `True` and `False`. While an enumerated property is selected, it will also display a drop-down list button immediately to the right of the current value. (Look at the `Color` property above.) If you click this button, you'll see a list of values that the property can take. You can then select one of these using the mouse. For enumerated properties with a large number of values, this is faster than cycling through all the possible values by double-clicking.

Some properties, notably the `Font` property, will display a small ellipsis button when selected. Clicking this button will pop up a configuration dialog box from where you can set up details of the font you want to use. The `Font` property is also an example of a 'nested property'. This means that it encompasses a number of sub-properties which determine the font that is actually used. To see this, double-click on the name part of the `Font` property, rather than the value part. You'll see an expanded list of sub-properties, as shown below. As you might expect, a font is made up of a color, font height, point size and so on.

Enabled	True
- Font	(TFont)
Color	clWindowText
Height	-13
Name	System
Pitch	fpDefault
Size	10
+Style	[]
FormStyle	fsNormal

You can distinguish a nested property from non-nested properties by looking for the small '+' sign immediately to the left of the font name - this changes to a '-' sign while the nested property is displaying its sub-properties. In the above picture, you can see that the **Style** sub-property is also a nested property - an example of one nested property inside another!

Event Handlers

Up until now, you've only seen the Object Inspector's role in viewing and changing an object's properties. However, in Delphi, an object possesses not only properties, but event handlers as well. (These correspond to methods in object-oriented terminology.)

Event handlers are discussed more fully in Chapter 3. Suffice it to say that an event handler is a special routine that's invoked in response to some event such as a mouse click, mouse movement, a key press, and so on. Broadly speaking, properties control the appearance of an object, while event handlers control the behavior of an object. There are very definite exceptions to this, as we shall see. For example, the **OnPaint** event handler has got a lot to do with the appearance of a form.

To view a component's event handlers, click on the Events tab at the bottom of the Object Inspector window to select the Events page. You'll see something like the event handler list shown here.

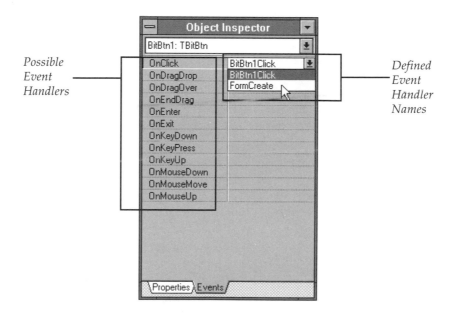

Possible Event Handlers

Defined Event Handler Names

As with the Properties page, the top of the window is occupied by the Object Selector which can be used to choose either the currently selected form, or any of its components.

Each entry in the left hand column represents a possible event for the currently selected object. Of course, you won't want to set up an event handler for every possible event. For example, if you look through the list of handlers in the diagram, you'll see a handler called **OnKeyUp**. As you might expect, this is called in response to a key being released on the keyboard - not something that you'd normally care about. The important thing to emphasize is this: the left hand column displays a list of possible events, not a list of all the events for which you have written an event handler.

If a particular event has a blank field to the right of the event name (such as the **OnClick** event), no event handler has been defined for that particular event. If an event handler has been defined, the name of the event handler routine is displayed in blue. Clicking on the routine name causes a small drop-down list button to appear. Clicking this button will display all the compatible, defined event handlers for all the components on the form (event handlers taking the same number and type of parameters). Selecting an existing event handler in this drop-down list allows you to associate more than one event with the same event handler, as we'll see in Chapter 2. In the diagram, an **OnClick** event handler has been defined for the **BitBtn1** object, but the drop-down list indicates that there is at least one other compatible event hander - **FormCreate**, the **OnCreate** hander of the form itself.

> Note that just because an event handler is compatible with regards to number and type of parameters, it doesn't necessarily make sense to use the same event handler for more than one event. However, Delphi's compatibility checking mechanism is very useful in filtering out incompatible event handlers.

The Object Browser makes it very easy to create a new event handler. Simply choose the event that you want to handle and double click the blank field to the right of the event name. Delphi will open the Code Editor, create a template for your new event handler and position the cursor at the appropriate point within the source.

Editing an existing event handler is just as simple - just double-click on the existing handler name and once again, the Code Editor window will be opened and the cursor positioned at the location of the clicked-on handler code.

> As with the Form window, the **Object Browser** has its own **SpeedMenu** accessed by clicking the right-mouse button. This is fully described in the next chapter.

The Code Editor

Let's try creating an event handler now. Make sure that the current component is **Form1** (using the Object Selector if necessary). Double click on the empty field to the right of the **OnPaint** event in the Object Browser window. This is what you should see. Delphi creates a new routine called **TForm1.FormPaint**, adds the **begin** and **end** statements and places the cursor immediately after the **begin** statement ready for you to start filling in the code.

Delphi places the I-beam cursor here

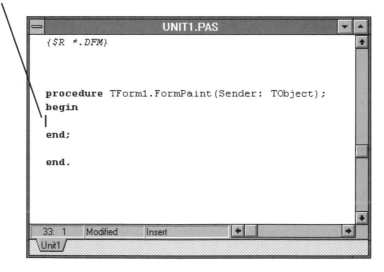

```
{$R *.DFM}



procedure TForm1.FormPaint(Sender: TObject);
begin
|

end;


end.
```

33: 1   Modified   Insert

Unit1

The window that you're looking at now is the Code Editor. Although Delphi is a very productive, visual development environment and does a great deal of behind-the-scenes work for you, you have got to start writing code sooner or later! When you do, you'll be using the Code Editor window.

In Delphi, Code Editor windows are used to edit Object Pascal code. As you can see, Pascal reserved words are highlighted to make the structure of your object code clearer. The colors used for highlighting, the special key codes used for editing functions and many other aspects of the editor are customizable.

> **Chapter 11,** *Customizing Delphi*, **discusses the many ways in which you can alter the editor to suit your needs. If you don't feel comfortable with the default editor settings, in Chapter 11 you'll see how to tinker with them until you are happy.**

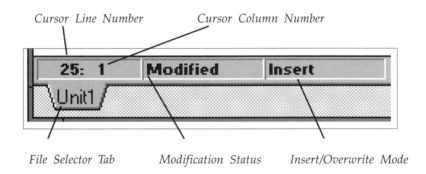

Cursor Line Number   *Cursor Column Number*

File Selector Tab   *Modification Status*   *Insert/Overwrite Mode*

The diagram above shows the important components of the Code Editor status bar. As you move the cursor around within an edit window, the line number and column number are continually adjusted to show you exactly where you are in the file. The Modification status indicator shows whether this particular file has been altered and the Insert/Overwrite indicator will tell you whether characters will be inserted at the current cursor position or overwrite what is already there. (You can toggle between these two modes in the usual way by pressing the *Ins* key on your keyboard.)

The file selector tab provides a mechanism for quickly moving between the various source files that you have open. In the diagram above, there's only one file open, which happens to be called Unit1. Any Delphi project will typically consist of several source files or units, but they won't all show up automatically as Code Editor tabs - only open ones will have corresponding tabs.

The Code Editor SpeedMenu

Like other SpeedMenus in Delphi, the Code Editor SpeedMenu is accessed by using the right mouse button. It looks like this:

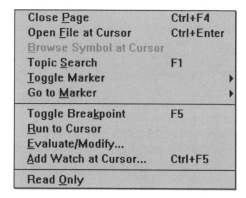

Let's take a closer look at this menu now. The following options are available:

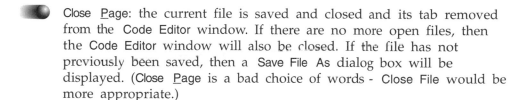

Close Page: the current file is saved and closed and its tab removed from the Code Editor window. If there are no more open files, then the Code Editor window will also be closed. If the file has not previously been saved, then a Save File As dialog box will be displayed. (Close Page is a bad choice of words - Close File would be more appropriate.)

Open File at Cursor: if you place the cursor within a filename, or double-click on a filename to highlight it, selecting this option will cause Delphi to try to load the indicated source file. This is particularly useful when used with the Pascal **uses** statement. For example, double-clicking on the Excepts unit name and then selecting Open File at Cursor will immediately load up the **EXCEPTS.PAS** source file into the Code Editor.

> Note that successful use of the **Open File at Cursor** option
> assumes that you have used the **Options/Project.../Directories/
> Conditionals** dialog box to set up the directories for units and
> include files, otherwise Delphi will simply open a file
> selection dialog for you.

Browse Symbol at Cursor: this option opens the Symbol Inspection
window for the symbol that's currently highlighted in the Code Editor
window. The symbol can be any unit, object or variable that's
defined in the current project. To use this option, you must compile
the project with the Local Symbols and Symbol Information options
enabled (in Options/Project.../ Compiler).

Topic Search: searches the Delphi on-line help file for a topic which
matches the word at the cursor position in the source file. This is
very useful for quickly looking up information on Pascal reserved
words, Windows API calls, and so on.

Toggle Marker: this command toggles a marker at the current cursor
position. A marker is rather like a bookmark, allowing you to mark
a place in a large source file, and then find your way back to it
easily. You can set up to ten markers in any one file. A
marker appears as a small symbol in the left margin of the
marked line. To remove the marker, simply select the Toggle
Marker option again and choose the same marker number. Note that
markers only exist while the file is loaded - once you close the file,
all marker information is lost.

Go to Marker: moves the cursor to a marker that you've set up (as
described above).

Toggle Breakpoint: toggles a debugger breakpoint on the current cursor
line. If there is no breakpoint for the current line, then one is set. If
there's already a breakpoint, then it's removed. The *F5* key performs
exactly the same function. When a breakpoint is set on a
particular line, the line is highlighted in red and a symbol
appears on the left margin of the line in question. (You can
also click the left mouse button in the left-hand margin of the line
for the same effect.)

Run to Cursor: uses the built-in debugger to execute your application
up to the current cursor position. If the code has been modified
since the last compile, you will be asked if you want to recompile
the code first.

- Evaluate/Modify... opens up the Evaluate/Modify dialog box, allowing you to evaluate an expression in your code or modify the value of a variable as your program executes. Application debugging is discussed more fully in Chapter 6.

- Add Watch at Cursor... pops up the Watch Properties dialog box, allowing you to set watch expressions in the integrated debugger. Again, this is covered more fully in Chapter 6.

- Read Only: marks the current file as read only.

Getting a Helping Hand

Like most Windows applications, Delphi includes a comprehensive on-line Help system which can be accessed in a variety of ways. As mentioned earlier, it's particularly useful when coding to be able to use the Topic Search facility in the Code Editor's SpeedMenu to look up key words and API routines in the help file.

In addition to the main Help file, Delphi includes a set of interactive lessons to get you started with Delphi development. These lessons are called Interactive Tutors and can be accessed from the Help menu. When you select this option, you should see a screen similar to that below. Like the Component Palette, this is a form of paged display. You select different category pages by choosing one of the category bars on the left hand side. The right hand side of the window will then display a list of interactive lessons which are available for that category.

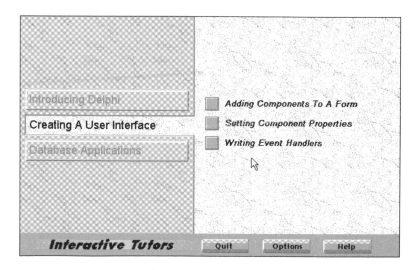

As you work through the various Interactive Tutors, you'll often see information displays like the one below. These provide important information as you work through the various lessons. The bottom part of the information display shows how far you are through each lesson and the four buttons allow you to obtain help, cancel the lesson, return to the previous part of a lesson or move on to the next part of a lesson.

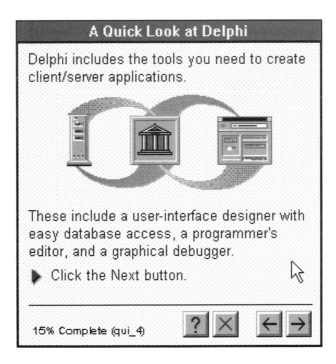

We recommend that you work through all the Interactive Tutors available. They give you a good insight into the power of the Delphi development environment, and they're fun to use too!

Delphi Basics: Implementation

Up until this point, we've been looking at the various facilities available in Delphi, but we haven't really seen how these different parts work together. It's a bit like seeing a set of jig-saw pieces and wondering what the finished picture looks like. Having laid some foundations, we're going to get a lot more practical now and proceed step-by-step through the creation of a useful application.

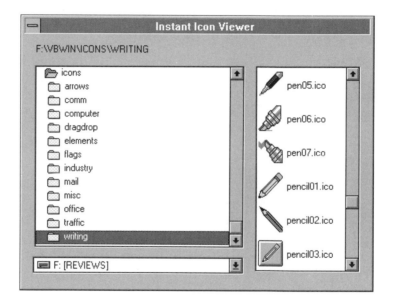

Here's what the application looks like - it's called the Instant Icon Viewer. You can use this program to browse your hard disk, looking at all the icon files (files with an extension of .ICO) which you have available. Many development systems are shipped with a large number of attractive icons that you can incorporate into your own programs. Unfortunately, it can be really tedious to find an appropriate icon, since Windows doesn't have a built in program for viewing large numbers of icons at the same time.

The list box to the right-hand side of the Instant Icon Viewer window
provides a graphical scrolling display of all the icons in the current
directory. In this way, you can quickly find one that meets your needs.

OK, let's begin work on this application. Firstly, start up Delphi and you'll
find yourself looking at an empty form window. It might surprise you to
know that this is a complete working application as it stands! Just click the
Run button in the SpeedBar and Delphi will compile and run the application,
displaying an empty window. Close the window and return to the form
window.

Creating the User Interface

The first step in creating any Delphi application is to lay out the user
interface. If you tried running this skeletal application a moment ago, you
may have noticed that we got a regular, resizeable application window.
What we actually want is a dialog box, so move over to the Object Inspector
window and click on the **BorderStyle** property. Double click the value part
of the property once and you should see it change to **bsDialog**.

+BorderIcons	[biSystemMenu,biMinimize,biMaximize]
BorderStyle	bsDialog
Caption	Form1

We also want to change the caption in the title bar of the window. Click on
the **Caption** property and type in the title Instant Icon Viewer.

BorderStyle	bsDialog
Caption	Instant Icon Viewer
ClientHeight	273

Saving the Project

Now is also a good time to save the new Delphi project. Pull down the
Save Project option on the File menu, select a directory where you want the
project to be located and type **ICONVIEW** as the name of the Pascal unit.
You'll then be asked to name the project itself. Type **IVIEW** and press the
OK button. You can now return to this project at any time by loading it
from Delphi's File menu.

A project can't have the same name as a unit. You should also
realize that if you create a form and set the **Name** property to
Dave, for example, and you also save the unit as **DAVE**, there
will be a problem. If you then create a new form that loads
Dave (that is it uses **DAVE**), you can't then reference the form,
that is, **Dave.Create** is invalid. This is because when you
name a form, Delphi creates a variable with the same name
in the unit, that is, **Dave: TDave**, which is accessible by all
units which use **Dave**.

Adding the Components

At this stage, we're ready to add the various components to the form
window. We'll begin by selecting a Label component from the Component
Palette. Click once on the form window to create a component at the default
size. If you happened to be watching in the Code Editor, you might have
seen things change as the Label component was added. Here's what the
Code Editor window should look like now:

Adding a Component to a Form

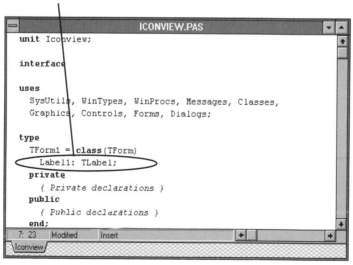

As you can see, a member field has been automatically added to the
TForm1 definition. If you were to delete the **Label** field, the member field
would disappear again! Similarly, if you were to rename the **Label** field,
you'd see its name change in the class definition for the form. It's this
synergy between the Code Editor and the visual form layout that helps to
make Delphi so productive.

In the same way, add a Listbox to the form, and then switch over to the System page of the Component Palette. Now add a DriveComboBox, a DirectoryListBox and finally a FileListBox. The form should now look something like this:

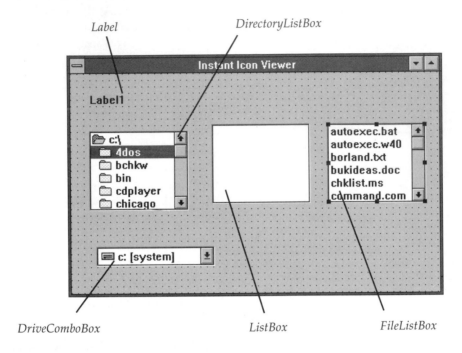

Label   DirectoryListBox

DriveComboBox   ListBox   FileListBox

You might be wondering why we've added a FileListBox - there doesn't seem to be one in the screenshot of the finished application. In actual fact, the FileListBox *is* present in the final version of the Icon Viewer, but it's hidden from view, as we shall see.

Setting up Properties

That's really it as far as constructing the user interface is concerned. The next step in developing an Delphi application is to set up the properties of each component.

You can set some properties directly from the form by dragging components around and resizing them. Try moving and resizing the various components so that they appear in approximately the positions that they'll occupy in the completed application (put the FileListBox somewhere off to the right for now, we'll deal with it later).

Now, let's assume that we don't much care for the standard system font that's used by dialog boxes and would prefer to use a finer-looking Sans Serif font. One way of getting this effect is to individually set up the **Font** property of every component on the form. Doing this, however, would be very tedious, especially if we had a large number of components.

The ParentFont Property

A better approach is to make use of the **ParentFont** property. If you look at this property, you should find that it's set to **True** for each of the components on the form. This is the default value for a newly created component. When **True**, the **ParentFont** property tells a component to use the parent's font settings. In our case, the parent is the form, so we only need to alter the form's **Font** property and, hey presto, all the components will end up using the new font too. Try it out: set the form's **Font** property to a font of your choice (the one shown above is MS Sans Serif, 10 point - but, you may have different fonts installed).

Naming Components

One of the most important properties an object has is its name. You use the name when referring to it in the code of a program. Rename the other components as follows:

Component	Name
FileListBox1	HiddenFileBox
ListBox1	IconList
DirectoryListBox1	DirectoryPicker
Label1	CurrentPath
DriveComboBox1	DrivePicker

In addition, rename the form itself to **IconViewForm**. By renaming the components in this way, we've given them more meaningful names which helps in the process of coding the application. Having done all this, the class definition for the form (as seen in the Code Editor) should look much like the one on the next page (the order of fields is unimportant):

```
TIconViewForm = class(TForm)
  CurrentPath: TLabel;
  IconList: TListBox;
  HiddenFileBox: TFileListBox;
  DirectoryPicker: TDirectoryListBox;
  DrivePicker: TDriveComboBox;
private
  { Private declarations }
public
  { Public declarations }
end;
```

Setting a FileListBox Mask

Because this is an icon viewer, we only want to process **.ICO** files. Select the **HiddenFileBox** component and alter its **Mask** property using the Object Inspector. This will ensure that only icon files are visible to the icon viewing program.

Left	352
Mask	*.ico
MultiSelect	False

Using Owner-Draw ListBoxes

Now select the **IconList** component. You'll notice from our original picture of the finished program that we want to display a list of icons along with the name of each file. Ordinary list boxes can't do this - they only display strings. In order to get the functionality that's required, we have to use an owner-draw list box. You may already be familiar with this concept from conventional programming work in C/C++ or Pascal. An owner-draw listbox doesn't perform any drawing itself. Instead, each time an entry needs to be drawn, the list box calls a special routine inside the application. It's this routine which does the application-specific job of drawing each entry in the listbox.

To turn the **IconList** component into an owner-draw listbox is simple - just change the **Style** property to **lbOwnerDrawFixed**. This tells Delphi that we want each cell to be the same height. At the same time, set the **IntegralHeight** property to **True**. This will cause the size of the list box to be automatically adjusted at run-time, so that an exact number of cells fits into the listbox.

At this stage, you can save the project and then try running the program to see how it's looking.

Adding the Application Code

The third and final step in creating a Delphi program is to add the application-specific code. You may have noticed that changing the current disk drive has no effect on the directory list box, so let's begin by putting that right.

Double-click on the **DrivePicker** component. Delphi will immediately create a new event handler called **TIconViewForm.DrivePickerChange**. You'll need to add a few lines of code to this new routine to arrive at the state of play shown below:

```
procedure TIconViewForm.DrivePickerChange(Sender: TObject);
begin
    { Point DirectoryPicker at wanted drive letter }
    DirectoryPicker.Drive := DrivePicker.Drive;
    { Update Caption of CurrentPath to reflect drive change }
    CurrentPath.Caption := DirectoryPicker.GetItemPath
            (DirectoryPicker.ItemIndex);
end;
```

Whenever the current drive selection is changed, this routine updates the Drive field in the DirectoryPicker component and adjusts the caption of the CurrentPath label. If you compile and run now, you'll see that the DrivePicker control is working properly. However, clicking the mouse around in the DirectoryPicker control doesn't seem to have any effect on the CurrentPath label. Let's fix that too.

Double-click on the DirectoryPicker component. Once again, Delphi will create a new routine, this time called TIconViewForm.DirectoryPickerChange. There's only one line of code that needs to be added to this procedure, like this:

```
procedure TIconViewForm.DirectoryPickerChange(Sender: TObject);
begin
    { Update display to reflect directory change }
    UpdateDisplay (DirectoryPicker.Directory);
end;
```

OK, so what's the UpdateDisplay routine, I hear you cry! This is a routine that we'll write ourselves (we'll make it a separate procedure so that we can call it from elsewhere). First, add the following procedure declaration to the list of procedures in the TIconViewForm declaration. Don't add it to the private or public part of the class.

```
procedure UpdateDisplay (const NewDir: String);
```

Now add the actual procedure anywhere in the implementation part of the unit. Here's what it should look like:

```
procedure TIconViewForm.UpdateDisplay (const Newdir: string);
begin
   { Update CurrentPath's Caption with new directory pathname }
   CurrentPath.Caption := NewDir;
end;
```

With these changes, clicking the mouse in the directory list box will properly update the CurrentPath caption but there's one last problem with the directory changing logic. If you use the cursor keys to change the selection highlight in the directory list box, you'll see that once again, the CurrentPath caption isn't being updated.

We can easily fix this too. Select the DirectoryPicker component, switch over to the Events page of the Object Inspector and double-click the mouse to the right of the OnClick event entry. This will create another event handler for the DirectoryPicker, and place you at the beginning of the routine. Add a couple more lines of code like this:

```
procedure TIconViewForm.DirectoryPickerClick(Sender: TObject);
begin
   { Update display according to current selection on DirectoryPicker }
   UpdateDisplay (DirectoryPicker.GetItemPath(DirectoryPicker.ItemIndex));
end;
```

Running the program now, you'll find that the cursor keys correctly update the CurrentPath caption.

Using the FormCreate Event

You've probably noticed that when the program is first started, the CurrentPath caption stays set to CurrentPath until you do something with the mouse in the DrivePicker or DirectoryPicker components. This is obviously not very useful and should be fixed.

This raises the question of initialization. How can we arrange for code to be executed when the Form is first created? We need something that's equivalent to the **WM_CREATE** message familiar to most Windows programmers. Fortunately, Delphi comes to our rescue in the shape of the **FormCreate** event. This is a special event (with its own event handler) that's generated when a form is first created, but - crucially - before the form is first displayed on the screen.

> If you have an application that wants to hide or disable components under certain conditions, you can use the **FormCreate** event handler to do the work. Since this all happens before the form is made visible, the hidden components will never be seen.

Use the Object Selector at the top of the Object Inspector to select the form. Double-click the mouse to the right of the **OnCreate** event entry. This will create a **FormCreate** handler and place you at the beginning of the routine. Add the following code:

```
procedure TIconViewForm.FormCreate(Sender: TObject);
var
    D: String;
    I: Integer;
begin
    { Set up initial drive for DrivePicker }
    GetDir(0, D);
    DrivePicker.Drive := D[1];
    { Set initial CurrentPath caption }
    CurrentPath.Caption := DirectoryPicker.GetItemPath
                     (DirectoryPicker.ItemIndex);
    { Set cell height for IconList }
    IconList.ItemHeight := GetSystemMetrics (sm_cyIcon) + 10;
end;
```

The last line of code in this routine sets the cell height of the owner-draw listbox. It's a convenient place to do this here. The **GetSystemMetrics** API routine is used to set the cell height equal to the vertical height of an icon plus ten pixels. This allows for a gap above and below each icon - without it, every icon would be right up against the next one and things wouldn't look so nice.

By the way, you may be wondering why you can't 'see' any icon files in the **HiddenFileBox** component. That's because we haven't told this component where to look for the icons. Add the following code to the end of the **UpdateDisplay** routine now.

```
{Fill file box with current directory's icons }
HiddenFileBox.Directory := NewDir;
```

Save the project again, and with all these changes, you should find that the program now looks something like this when it's running:

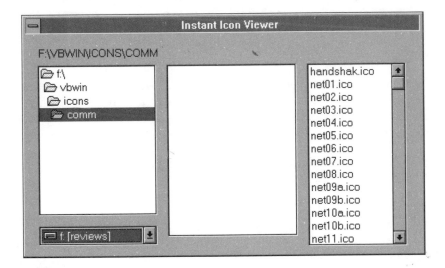

Implementing the IconList Code

Our Icon Viewer is now almost finished. The last part of the program is the implementation of the owner-draw listbox. There are two things we need to do here. Firstly, we want to copy the names of all the icon files from the **HiddenFileBox** component into the **IconList** box. Secondly, we need to write the application-specific code that's responsible for drawing each item.

In order to improve performance, the Icon Viewer will load all the icons into memory each time that the directory is changed. These icon images will be stored into the list box along with the filename information. This means that there may be a small delay when switching to a directory with a large number of icons but, once there, you'll be able to scroll very rapidly through the icon list.

Add the following variable declarations to the **UpdateDisplay** routine:

```
var
    I: Integer;
    S: String;
    p: TPicture;
```

Next, add the following code to the existing body of the routine:

```
{ Clear contents of the icon list }
    for I := 0 to IconList.Items.Count - 1 do
        TPicture (IconList.Items.Objects [i]).Free;
    IconList.Items.Clear;

    {Now refill with new stuff }
    for I := 0 to HiddenFileBox.Items.Count - 1 do
    begin
        s := CurrentPath.Caption;
        if s [Length (s)] <> '\' then s := s + '\';
        s := s + HiddenFileBox.Items [i];
        { Create a TPicture and load from file }
        p := TPicture.Create;
        p.LoadFromFile (s);
        IconList.Items.AddObject (HiddenFileBox.Items [I], p);
    end;
```

This code takes care of deleting any previous information in the **IconList** and then adds a set of filenames to the **IconList**, along with the actual picture information from each icon file.

The last-but-one job is to add the drawing code for the list box. Select the **IconList** component and switch to the Events page of the Object Inspector. Double-click to the right of the **OnDrawItem** event and Delphi will create a new routine called **IconListDrawItem**. Add the following code to the routine.

```
procedure TIconViewForm.IconListDrawItem(Control: TWinControl;
  Index: Integer; Rect: TRect; State: TOwnerDrawState);
var
    s: String;
    x, y: Integer;
    Pic: TPicture;
begin
    IconList.Canvas.FillRect (Rect);
    { First draw the icon }
    Pic := TPicture (IconList.Items.Objects [Index]);
    IconList.Canvas.Draw (Rect.Left + 2, Rect.Top + 5, Pic.Graphic);
```

```
   { Then draw the string }
   s := IconList.Items [Index];
   x := Rect.left + GetSystemMetrics (sm_cxIcon) + 7;
   y := Rect.Top + (IconList.ItemHeight - abs (Font.Height)) div 2;
   IconList.Canvas.TextOut(x, y, s);
end;
```

If you execute the application now, you'll find that the **IconList** component has sprung into life, displaying a colorful graphical list of all the icons in each directory (assuming you've found a directory with some ***.ICO** files in it!). Once the excitement of this has worn off, remember that there's one final thing to do. Change the **Visible** property of the **HiddenFileBox** component to **False**. Visually, it isn't a part of the user interface and it's used here only as a lazy way of getting a list of icon names. Once you've made the component invisible, you can resize it to a very small size and just forget about it. Resize the other components as you want and don't forget to save the project when you're through.

Summary

In this introductory chapter, you've become familiar with the various elements of the Delphi development environment and built a useful icon viewing utility. You've seen how the Code Editor, Object Inspector and Component Palette work together as part of a three-step development process:

1   Design your user interface and lay out your chosen components on a form.

2   Set up the properties of each component as required.

3   Glue it all together with event handlers which implement the wanted behavior.

As promised, you've probably got more questions than you started out with! We'll begin to answer those questions in the next chapter by taking a more in-depth look at those first two steps - laying out your user interface and setting properties. In Chapter 3, it'll be the turn of events and event handlers to come under the microscope.

Exercises

1   Try experimenting with the various properties used in the icon viewer. Change them one at a time and see what effect they have on the program.

2   Suppose you wanted something to happen when the user clicked on an icon in the viewer program - what event handler would you need to provide? How could you use this to give extra functionality?

3   How would you go about modifying the icon viewer to display the bitmaps (`*.BMP` files) in a given directory rather than icons? Hint: it's a lot easier than you might think!

Chapter

Developing a User Interface

No matter how good your application is, it won't succeed without an intuitive, modern, straightforward user interface. This is one of Delphi's great strengths - it gives you all the tools you need to put together a great looking user interface in far less time than would be required with conventional programming techniques. Some of the main benefits of using Delphi include the graphical design process tightly integrated with the Code Editor, a large library of reusable software components including state-of-the-art tabbed dialogs, and the ability to use your existing investment in VBX controls within Delphi projects.

The previous chapter was devoted to a whirlwind tour of Delphi in which you learned the three principal steps of Delphi development: creating the user interface, setting up properties and writing the code to glue it all together. In this chapter, we're going to cover those first two steps again in a lot more detail, concentrating on the things you weren't told about earlier! Along the way, you'll learn about:

- The most useful form properties
- Component positioning and grouping
- The most useful component properties

We'll round off the chapter by building a better Windows Task Manager utility. This program includes an innovative facility for making any Windows application stay on top.

Form Properties: Concepts

At this stage, you should already be feeling very comfortable with forms. A form is essentially just a window onto which you can place one or more components. In this section, we'll be looking at how you can change various aspects of a form's appearance and behavior, the differences between dialogs and application windows, and so on.

Getting a '3D' Look

When you create a form, you'll notice that by default, the form has the **Ctl3D** property set to **True**. Here's what a typical form might look like in this case.

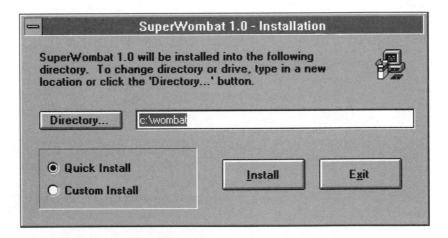

By way of contrast, the screenshot below shows exactly the same form again, but with the **Ctl3D** property turned off. You can see that there's quite a difference between the two. Instead of the up-to-date 3D look that characterizes modern applications, you just get a flat 2D box with an ordinary white background.

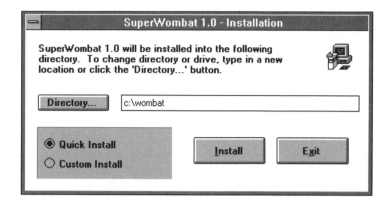

The **Ctl3D** property is a very simple way of giving a modern, attractive look to your application, but there are a couple of important things that you need to bear in mind if you're going to use it.

Firstly, don't forget that the 3D effect is created by a Microsoft dynamic link library called **CTL3DV2.DLL**. Although this file isn't a standard part of the Windows 3.1 distribution, you will have it lurking somewhere on your hard disk (perhaps in your **C:\WINDOWS\SYSTEM** directory) because it's installed and used by Delphi itself. However, the situation may not be the same for the user of your application. If you plan to ship programs which use the **Ctl3D** property, then you should ideally include the Microsoft **.DLL** on the installation disks and set up your install program to load it onto the destination disk.

> If **CTL3DV2.DLL** can't be found, the program will still run successfully, but the user simply won't see any 3D effects. If you want to study the code responsible for loading the DLL yourself, have a look at the **InitCtl3D** routine in the **FORMS.PAS** source file.

The second point to make concerns a related property, **ParentCtl3D**. This is a property that many components possess. When the **ParentCtl3D** property is set to **True** (the default), the control looks at the **Ctl3D** property of its parent (normally the form) to determine whether or not it should take on a 3D appearance. If **ParentCtl3D** is **False**, the component uses its own **Ctl3D** property to make the decision.

The advantage of this property is one of visual consistency - by changing the **Ctl3D** property of the form, all controls on a form will change to match. Thus it's very easy to toggle a form and all it's associated components between 3D and 2D.

Giving a Form Some Style

There are several different properties that affect the 'style' of a form. The first of these, **BorderStyle**, you've already encountered. This property is used to set the type of border which the form has at run-time. You've already used the **bsDialog** setting to get a dialog box. The default setting - **bsSizeable** - will give you a standard, resizeable application window while the other settings are less often used. You could use the **bsNone** settings (for example) as the basis of a screen saver application which takes over the entire screen and whose client area is exactly the same as the window area.

BorderStyle	Result
bsDialog	Standard dialog box border - can't be resized.
bsSingle	Single-line border - can't be resized.
bsNone	No border whatsoever - can't be resized.
bsSizeable	Resizeable border.

BorderIcons is the name of another important property. This is a nested set property, meaning that it's made up of a set of sub-properties - three in this case. These three sub-properties determine whether the form has a system menu, minimize button and maximize button. If you tell Delphi that you don't want a system menu, then you won't get a close box in the top left-hand corner of your window, and you'll need to provide some other mechanism for terminating your program, such as a button or a menu selection.

AutoScroll	False
- BorderIcons	[biSystemMenu,biMinimize,biMaximize]
biSystemMenu	True
biMinimize	True
biMaximize	True
BorderStyle	bsDialog

Note that if while experimenting with these techniques you
find yourself with an application that can't be terminated -
don't panic! It's not necessary to shut down Windows to get
rid of it. Just double-click on the desktop to start up the Task
Manager, select the name of the 'runaway application' and
then press the <u>E</u>nd Task button to get rid of it.

Minimizing and Maximizing

The **Icon** property of a form is used to determine which icon is displayed
when the form is minimized. To set up the icon for a form, select the **Icon**
property in the Object Inspector and click on the little ellipsis control that
appears to the right of the value field. You should see a Picture Editor dialog
box appear as shown below. You can then use the <u>L</u>oad... button to select
the desired icon and it will appear in the Picture Editor window. The icon
will be linked into your executable file when you next build the project. If
you don't set up an icon for your form, Delphi will use a standard form
icon.

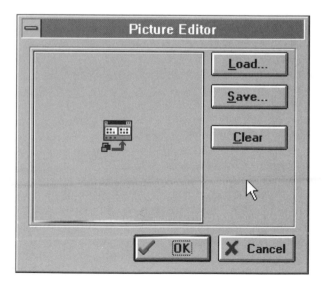

Using the **LoadFromFile** method, it's even possible to set up
the minimized icon of a form dynamically, so that the icon
can be changed at run-time.

Most Windows applications display their initial window using default values for the size and position of a window. This is achieved by passing the **CW_USEDEFAULT** parameter to the **CreateWindow/Ex** API function. There will be times, however, when you'll want to build applications that start up in a zoomed state occupying the whole screen area, or even start as a minimized icon. The Windows Print Manager is a good example of the latter type of program.

You can control the initial state of the form with the **WindowState** property. This can have three possible values, as outlined below:

Value	Meaning
wsNormal	The form appears with default size and position, taking into account the current value of the **Position** property.
wsMaximized	The form appears maximized (zoomed to the full screen area).
wsMinimized	The form appears minimized (as an icon).

Manipulating Components

Having dealt with form properties, let's turn our attention to the individual components of a form.

Adding Components to a Form

In Chapter 1, you discovered how to add components to a form by first clicking on the desired component in the component palette and then clicking on the form window. This will create a component at its default size. As pointed out earlier, you can also double-click directly on a component on the Component Palette - this will add a component to the form with the default size at some system-defined position.

> If you want to add a component to the form using some non-standard size, just click once on the Component Palette to select a component, then hold the mouse down on the form and drag the mouse across the window. A 'rubber band' outline of the component will be displayed, and releasing the mouse at any time will create a component of that size.

Go ahead and experiment with these facilities until you're happy with the different ways of adding components to a form. You may have noticed that once you've added a component to a form, you can't add another component (not even one of the same type) unless you go and click once more on the Component Palette. Think of it as being like a real artist's palette - when you click on the palette, you've loaded your brush with paint and you're ready to 'paint' a control onto the form. Once done, you need to go and get some more paint before you can do anything else.

> Suppose you've clicked on a control in the **Component Palette** and you then change your mind - how do you cancel the operation without having to draw a control? The answer is to click on the Cursor Selection tool in the **Component Palette** (the arrow symbol to the left). This 'unloads' your paint brush and restores the status quo.

This all sounds fine, but what if you want to add several components of the same type to a form? It's a bit tedious having to go back to the Component Palette each time. The trick here is to use the *Shift* key. Hold down the *Shift* key when you click on the required component in the palette. Now, you'll find that you can add as many components as you like to your form, and, as if by magic, your paint brush will stay loaded. To return to normal operation, just click on the Cursor Selection tool.

All the above possibilities are summarized in the table below.

Action	Result
Click on a component on the palette and click once on the form.	Adds a component (default size).
Double click on a component on the palette.	Adds a component (default size and position).
Click a component on the palette and drag the mouse over the form.	Adds a component of the desired size and position.
Hold down the *Shift* key and click a component on the palette.	Adds multiple components of the same type.

Under the Hood: Component Default Sizes

Incidentally, if you're wondering where the default size for a component is defined, you have to look inside the source code of a particular component. For example, here's part of the source code for a **SpeedButton** component. This routine, **TSpeedButton.Create,** is called each time a control is created. You can see that the bounds of the control are set to **(0, 0, 25, 25)** in the code. This defines the default size of the control.

```
{ TSpeedButton }
constructor TSpeedButton.Create(AOwner: TComponent);
begin
  inherited Create(AOwner);
  SetBounds(0, 0, 25, 25);
  ControlStyle := [csCaptureMouse];
  FGlyph := TButtonGlyph.Create;
  ParentFont := True;
  FSpacing := 4;
  FMargin := -1;
  FLayout := blGlyphLeft;
  Inc(ButtonCount);
end;
```

Deleting Components

Removing components from a form is just as easy as adding them. To delete a component, just click once with the mouse on whatever you want to remove. This will select the component and you can then remove it by pressing the *Del* key or selecting Cut or Delete from the Edit menu.

If you want to remove several components in one operation, just use shift-clicking - the standard Windows way of selecting more than one thing at a time. Select the first component by clicking on it and then, holding down the *Shift* key, click on all the additional components you want to remove. You can then release the *Shift* key and pressing Del (or selecting Cut or Delete) will then delete all the selected components.

As an alternative to clicking the mouse on components to select them, you can try holding down the mouse button and dragging it over everything that you wish to select. This will select all the components over which you've dragged and, again, you can then delete them all in one operation.

Note that if you've had the **Code Editor** window open while placing components on a form, you'll have noticed that Delphi adds an object to the form's class definition for each new component. In the same way, deleting components from a form will automatically delete the corresponding references from the class definition.

If you accidentally create an empty event handler for a component, don't worry about manually deleting it. The next time you recompile your application, the event handler will silently disappear, providing that you haven't added anything between the initial **begin** and **end** statements.

The example class definition below includes a radio button, standard push button and edit box. If you generate this code and then watch while you delete the components, you'll see the various objects disappear from the class definition too.

```
type
  TForm1 = class(TForm)
    RadioButton1: TRadioButton;
    Button1: TButton;
    Edit1: TEdit;
  private
    { Private declarations }
  public
    { Public declarations }
  end;
```

Moving and Resizing Components

To move a component on a form, you only need to drag it to its new location using the mouse. If you want to move several components at the same time, you can just shift-select them (as described under '*Deleting Components*') and then drag them around together. This is especially useful for groups of related components.

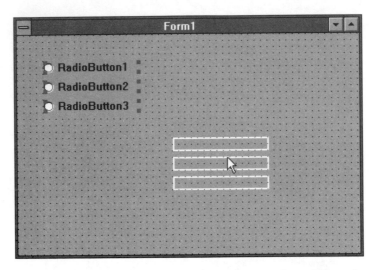

In the picture here, three radio buttons have been selected together and the mouse is being used to drag their outlines to a new position. When the mouse is released, the radio buttons jump to their new location.

Sizing Handles

If you look closely at a selected component (assuming it's the only one selected), you'll see that it's surrounded by eight little black squares or sizing handles. As you move the mouse over these sizing handles, you'll see the cursor change shape to indicate the direction in which the component can be resized. You can 'stretch' a component to the left, right, up or down or you can pull a corner in any direction.

Sizing Handles

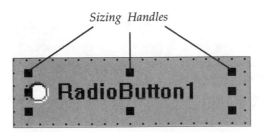

You might have noticed that when you have more than one component selected at the same time, the sizing handles appear to be gray, rather than black. This is Delphi's way of telling you that the sizing handles are disabled - you can only use sizing handles when a single component is selected. In this case, the sizing handles simply indicate which components have been selected.

As it happens, there is a way to alter the size of several components at the same time. To try it out, put several push buttons onto a blank form and then deliberately resize them so that they're all different sizes. They look horrible, don't they? Now pull down the Edit menu and select the Size... menu item. You should see the following dialog box appear.

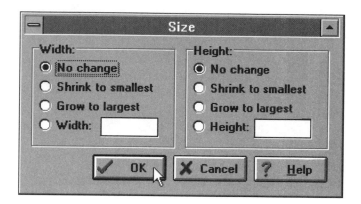

Using this dialog, you can easily resize multiple components so that they all have the same width or height. For example, to make our push buttons all the same size again, just select Shrink to smallest for both the width and height and then press the OK button.

Using the Form Grid

While moving and resizing components, you probably spotted the fact that they appear to 'jump' as you move them around. This is because, by default, components will 'snap' to the form grid. The form grid is an imaginary grid of points on the form window. It's used to align components, making it easy, for example, to place one push button directly below another.

You can change the grid spacing and you can decide whether or not you want components to snap to the grid. Turning off grid snapping allows you to use the mouse to place components *exactly* where you want them or to give them an *exact* size. You can also choose whether or not Delphi will display the grid.

All these options are controlled via the Environment Options dialog which is reached via the Options menu. You may find it best to leave the grid settings as they are, but in special circumstances you may want the flexibility of placing components in precise pixel positions, or you may wish to turn off the grid display when working with an intricate form layout.

> If you prefer to work with grid snapping turned off, you can still align a selected component to the grid by selecting **Align to Grid** from the **Edit** menu. This saves you from having to turn on grid snapping, align the component and then turn grid snapping off again.

Aligning Components

There will often be times when you want to align components precisely. You might, for example, want the left hand edges of some buttons to line up, or you might want to arrange for a number of push buttons to be equally spaced in a dialog box. In the following example, the three push buttons are equidistant from one another and horizontally centered in the dialog box.

There are a number of ways to do this. The first is to make use of the form grid that we discussed earlier. You can use the grid to precisely align components and set component spacing. Provided that your grid spacing is sufficiently large (the default spacing is eight pixels) you should be able to do this fairly easily.

A faster technique is to make use of the Alignment dialog. To try this out, shift-select a number of components on a form and then select the Align... item from the Edit menu. You'll see a dialog like the one below.

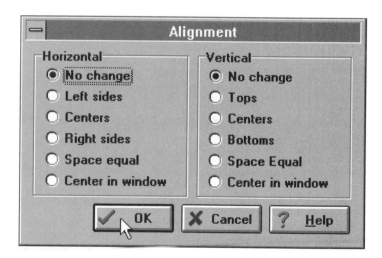

This looks very much like the Size dialog that we saw earlier, but it's concerned with component position rather than with component size. Using this dialog, you can center one or more components horizontally or vertically on the form window, space them out equally along either axis and align components along any of their four sides or their centers.

Yet another technique is to use the Alignment Palette shown here.

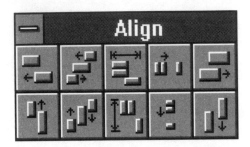

If you select Alignment Palette from the View menu, a small window will appear. Unlike the Size and Alignment dialogs, this is a '**modeless** palette', meaning that you can leave it on the screen while you do other work, using it as and when necessary. At first sight, the ten alignment icons look a little cryptic, but are explained fully below.

Icon	What it Does
	Aligns to left edge of first selected component.
	Aligns centers of components horizontally with first selected component.
	Centers the selected component(s) horizontally in the window.
	Spaces components out equally horizontally.
	Aligns to right edge of first selected component.
	Aligns to top edge of first selected component.
	Aligns centers of components vertically with first selected component.
	Center the selected component(s) vertically in the window.
	Spaces component(s) out equally vertically.
	Aligns to bottom edge of first selected component.

> Note that when using the **Alignment Palette** to align multiple components, it's important which component you select first. Delphi will remember the first selected component and use it as a reference for aligning other components.
>
> Also, when centering one or more component horizontally or vertically, bear in mind that the phrase 'in the window' implies centering within the innermost container object. For example, if you try to horizontally center six buttons on a form, they'll be centered with respect to the form. If those buttons are in a Panel component, then they'll be centered with respect to the Panel.

The Alignment Palette and the Alignment dialog complement each other and in conjunction with the form grid provide a powerful set of facilities for placing components exactly where you want them.

The AutoSize Property

On the subject of component properties, you need to be aware of the **AutoSize** property. For text-based components, this property causes the size of the component to vary according to the amount of text and the font size in use. For graphical controls, such as the Image component, it causes the component to vary in size to match the width and height of the displayed bitmap. By default, **AutoSize** is **True**.

- In the case of Label components, the size of the component automatically increases or decreases depending on the length of the component's caption and the font size.

- For Edit box components, the size of the component varies only according to the font size.

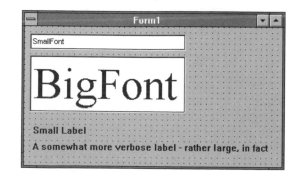

This is illustrated graphically in the picture above. Selecting a large font for the second Edit box automatically increased its height, just as selecting a smaller font would have reduced it (we reduced the width of the larger box manually after resetting its font).

As for the labels, they both started off at the same size. The bottom one grew steadily larger as more characters were typed into the **Caption** property.

It can sometimes be useful to turn off the **AutoSize** property, especially for label components. For example, suppose you have a label which is going to hold a variable-sized text string, such as the **CurrentPath** label in our icon viewer program from Chapter 1. In such a circumstance, turning **AutoSize** off will 'freeze' the size of the component so that it won't run into some other component or even off the end of the form altogether!

Specifying Size and Position

In general, whatever size you specify for a form will be the size used at run-time. However, this isn't always going to be what you want. For example, you might wish to display a bitmap in a form and have the form automatically re-size itself to suit the size of the bitmap that's being displayed - just like the picture below.

Achieving this sort of effect is quite simple - add an Image component to your form, set its **AutoSize** property to **True**, set its **Left** and **Top** properties to zero and double-click the component to set up the bitmap which you want to be displayed.

You can then add other components to the form which will appear in front of the background bitmap. To make the form resize itself to the size of the displayed bitmap, just add a couple of lines of code to the form's **FormCreate** event handler like this:

```
procedure TForm1.FormCreate(Sender: TObject);
begin
    ClientWidth := Image1.Width;
    ClientHeight := Image1.Height;
end;
```

As an alternative to the above, you could arrange for a picture to be loaded at run-time rather than design time, as below:

```
procedure TForm1.FormCreate(Sender: TObject);
begin
    Image1.Picture.LoadFromFile ('C:\WINDOWS\ARCHES.BMP');
    ClientWidth := Image1.Width;
    ClientHeight := Image1.Height;
end;
```

> **Although we've hard-coded a bitmap file name here, you could (for example) arrange to load a different, user-specified bitmap when the form is created.**

Incidentally, when dealing with forms, it's important to understand the difference between the **ClientHeight**/**ClientWidth** properties and the similarly named **Height**/**Width** properties. The **Width** and **Height** properties refer to the **total** width and height of the form, including any scroll bars, caption bar, frame and so on. On the other hand, **ClientWidth** and **ClientHeight** relate only to the client area of the window - that part of the window which contains the application-specific text or graphics. If you were to replace **ClientWidth** and **ClientHeight** with **Width** and **Height** in the **FormCreate** procedure above, you'd find that there'd be no room to display the right edge and bottom edge of the bitmap.

Note that when you design a form, take care that it doesn't exceed 640 pixels wide by 480 pixels high - the size of a VGA screen. Nowadays, many people use higher-resolution displays such as super-VGA, but your software will be unpopular if you don't cater for standard VGA screens as well.

The run-time position of a form is dictated by the **Position** property. This property can take several values, as given in the table below.

Position	Result
poDesigned	The form has the same position and size that was set at design time (this is the default case).
poDefault	The form appears with a default position and size. This option is equivalent to using **CW_USEDEFAULT** for both position and size in a call to **CreateWindow** or **CreateWindowEx**.
poDefaultPosOnly	The form has the design time size, but a default position. This option is equivalent to using **CW_USEDEFAULT** for position.
poDefaultSizeOnly	The form has the design time position, but a default size. This option is equivalent to using **CW_USEDEFAULT** for size.
poScreenCenter	The form has its design time size, but is centered on the screen.

For dialog boxes, the most appropriate value to use is generally **poScreenCenter**, since this will center the dialog box on screen. The same warning applies for form position as for form size - take care not to use a form position that will be off-screen on a 640*480 display.

Keeping Tabs on Your Components

An important consideration with user interface design is the idea of **tab order**. Although you may be very comfortable with using a mouse, not everyone feels the same way. You need to cater for those users who get on much better just using a keyboard. The *Tab* key represents the standard way of moving between the various controls in a dialog box.

Each time you press the *Tab* key, the Windows dialog manager will move you from the currently selected control to the next one in the tab order. If you hold down the *Shift* key while pressing Tab, you'll move from one control to another in reverse order. This is illustrated here using a hypothetical dialog box from earlier in this chapter.

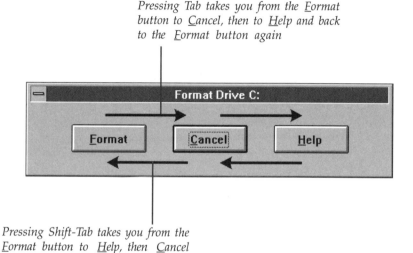

Pressing Tab takes you from the Format button to Cancel, then to Help and back to the Format button again

Pressing Shift-Tab takes you from the Format button to Help, then Cancel and back to the Format button again

When you build your program's user interface in Delphi, the tab order used depends on the order in which you add controls to the form. If you were to add the Format button first, then the Cancel button and finally the Help button, you'd get the situation shown above. The tab order is dependent on a component property called (not surprisingly) **TabOrder**. Each time you add a component to a form, it gets a **TabOrder** value that's one greater than that of the last component added. In the diagram above, the Format button has a **TabOrder** of zero, the Cancel button has a **TabOrder** of one, and so on.

Of course, you won't always add components to the form in the 'right' tab order. You can alter the tab order in one of two ways. The first way is simply to go through all the components on your form and edit the **TabOrder** property as appropriate.

> Note that `TabOrder` should always bear some relationship to the spatial position of the components. For example, if you have a horizontal row of buttons, pressing the *Tab* key should move the selected button one place to the right each time it's pressed. Hopping around all over the place in a haphazard manner will confuse and frustrate users of your application.

The alternative, and easier, way of rearranging tab order is to make use of Delphi's Edit Tab Order dialog. To see this dialog box, choose Tab Order... from the Edit menu.

The list box shows all the components in the current form which have the **TabStop** property set (see below for an explanation of the **TabStop** property). By selecting individual components in the list box and pressing the blue up and down arrows, you can very easily rearrange the form's tab order to get it the way you want.

OK, so what's the **TabStop** property? This is a simple Boolean property that determines whether or not a component appears in the tab order. If a component doesn't appear in the tab order, then you can't tab to it. Components which respond to the mouse or keyboard such as edit boxes, push buttons, radio buttons and the like have their **TabStop** property set to **True** by default. By setting their **TabStop** property to **False**, you can exclude them from the tab order (and they won't then appear in the Edit Tab Order dialog).

> Some components, such as labels, don't have TabOrder and
> TabStop properties because it wouldn't make sense to be able
> to tab to them!

Grouping Components

Up until now, it's seemed as if each component on a form has been
completely independent of all the other components. However, it's possible
to organize form components into one or more **groups**. As a practical
example, look at the form window shown below. Four radio buttons are
used to specify the size of a floppy disk and all four radio buttons are
grouped together into the Specify Disk Size group box. The Specify Disk Size
group box is referred to as the 'container' of the radio buttons - it
effectively becomes their parent. Just as the form window is the parent of
the two push buttons and the group box, so the group box becomes the
parent of the four radio buttons that it contains.

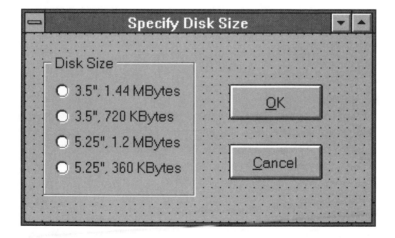

So, how do you group components together? To try this out, put a group box
component onto a form and make it big enough to accommodate a number
of other controls. Now *with the group box still selected*, add another control to
the form in the usual way. If you double-click on the Component Palette, the
new component will automatically appear inside the selected group box.
Otherwise, you must explicitly place the new component into the group box.
Provided that the group box was selected when the component was created,
you'll find that the new control is now 'owned' by the group box.

Grouping components together in this way has several advantages. Suppose you wished to rearrange the layout of your dialog box in the above example. Dragging the Specify Disk Size group box around will cause all the 'child' components to follow it around as well. This obviously makes things much more convenient when reorganizing complicated forms.

In addition, since the group box has now become the parent of those four radio buttons, any changes that you make to the **Font** or **Color** properties of the group box will be reflected in the child components, provided that they have the **ParentFont** and **ParentColor** properties set to **True**. If you leave the group box's **Color** and **Font** properties alone, then it will continue to shadow the **Color** and **Font** properties of its parent (the form window in this case) and will in turn be shadowed by its children. Effectively a 'pecking order' has been established within the form!

Delphi provides several types of component which can serve as containers, including group boxes, panels, scroll boxes and note books. Surprisingly perhaps, you can nest one container inside another, putting panels into group boxes, group boxes into note books and so on. It's therefore possible to create a complex hierarchy of components within a single form. If you're feeling adventurous and you go down this route, be sure to heed the following warning:

Take care when you delete a container component - all child components belonging to the container component will also be deleted.

What happens to tab order within a container component? The answer is that each container component has its own 'child-level' tab order. Another example of a real-life dialog box should serve to make this clear:

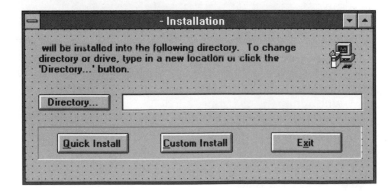

In this dialog box, the bottom three push buttons belong to a container component - the panel that surrounds them. The edit box has a **TabOrder** of zero, followed by the Directory... push button with a **TabOrder** of one. The panel component itself has a tab order of two, but the three child push buttons have a tab order of zero, one and two.

This might seem odd at first, but you need to think of the container's internal tab order as distinct from that of the form. When you press the *Tab* key with the Directory... button selected, the form's tab order dictates that the panel component will receive the focus. The panel then passes the focus on to the first component in *it's* tab order - the Quick Install button - and then to the Custom Install button the next time *Tab* is pressed, and so on.

If this still isn't clear, the diagram below shows another way of looking at it. Bear in mind that since Delphi container objects such as panels and group boxes can be nested to many levels, you can end up with a hierarchical 'tree' of tab ordering information. We've shown this here with a three level arrangement.

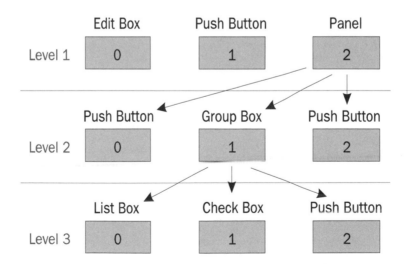

Using Hints

As you know, pausing the mouse over a specific component on the Component Palette will cause a little 'hint' window to appear, giving you the name of that particular component type. We promised you in Chapter 1 that Delphi could be used to build similar hint windows into your own applications. Let's look at how you'd do it.

Firstly, try adding one or more buttons to a form in the usual way. Now set the **Hint** property of each button to some plain-English description of what you want that button to do. Set the **ShowHint** property of each button to **True** and run the application.

When you compile and run the program, you should find that pausing the mouse over one of the child push buttons will cause a hint string to pop up as shown. Normally, of course, you'd choose a hint string which gives the user a little more help than is the case here!

Of course, this doesn't just work for buttons. Most Delphi components have **Hint** and **ShowHint** properties. Panel components can have hints and even the form itself can be given an associated hint string. The majority of components also have a **ParentShowHint** property which determines whether they 'inherit' their parent's **ShowHint** value. This works like the **ParentCtl3D** and **ParentFont** properties.

> The **TApplication** component is a special, predefined object which collects together a number of useful properties. These include the **HintPause** and **HintColor** properties. They let you control the mouse delay before a hint is shown and also the background color of the hint box. You may want to avoid changing the color since pale yellow (the default value for **HintColor**) has become something of a standard. It's used, for example, by Delphi and by many of Microsoft's applications.

Task Manager: Implementation

We've covered a lot of ground in this chapter. Delphi provides a rich set of facilities for building great looking user interfaces and, in order to fix all this stuff in your mind, we're going to spend the rest of this chapter working through the development of a new, improved Windows Task Manager program.

In case you're not familiar with the Windows Task Manager, it's the small program that gets executed whenever you double-click on the desktop or select the Switch To item on the system menu. If you've not used it before, try it now. As it stands, the Task Manager provided with Windows is perfectly workable, but it doesn't have a particularly interesting user interface and there's one important feature that it lacks - more on that soon.

Creating the User Interface

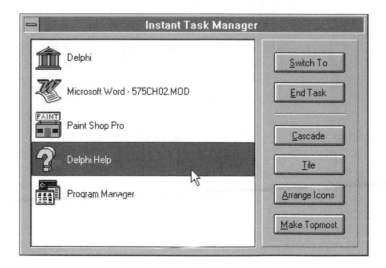

Our replacement Task Manager is shown here. As you can see, it has a much nicer user interface implemented using an owner-draw listbox, a concept that you should already be familiar with from the example in Chapter 1. This Task Manager will do everything for you that Microsoft's Task Manager does and it has an important little bonus in the shape of the Make Topmost button. Using this button, you can select any running application window and specify that it remain on top even when it isn't active. This is particularly nice when used with Windows utilities such as the calculator and the calendar. Microsoft built a 'stay on top' facility into the Windows Clock, but they didn't go the whole way and build the same capability into their other applications. Using the Instant Task Manager, you can easily turn any application into a stay on top utility!

Right, let's roll up our sleeves and make a start. Open a new project and then immediately save it as **TASKMAN** and its associated Pascal unit (containing the source code for the form) as **TMFORM.PAS**. Now change the form's **BorderStyle** property to **bsDialog** and change the **Caption** property to Instant Task Manager (or whatever you prefer to call it). Change the **Position** property to **poScreenCenter** so that the dialog is centered on the screen.

Add a list box component on the left hand side of the form and a panel component on the right hand side. Since we're going to be using an owner-draw list box, change the **Style** property of the list box to **lbOwnerDrawFixed** and change its name to **IconList**.

With the Panel component selected, double-click six times on the button component of the Component Palette. This will add six push buttons to the form as child components of the panel. You can verify this by moving the panel around and you'll see that all six buttons move with it.

> **Note that when you use multiple double-clicks in this way to place many components at once, they all 'stack' on top of one another. Don't be put off by this - you can easily move each component to where you want it after you've finished with the Component Palette.**

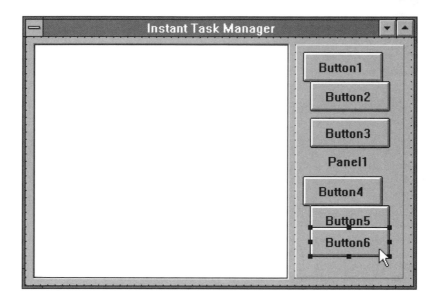

At this stage, your form should look something like this. All the buttons are still at their default size and we've made no attempt to align them properly. However, you'll see that we've arranged the buttons from top to bottom, in the order that they were created. This is important since, as explained earlier in the chapter, the tab order depends on the order of component creation. By arranging the buttons in the order that they were created, the user will be able to tab down from the top button to the bottom one in a natural way.

Setting up the Properties

Select the form (Form1) in the Object Inspector and change the **Font** property to MS Sans Serif, 8 point, regular. (Of course, you can use an alternative font if you want to, but this is good one to use in dialog boxes.) You should see the font of all six buttons change to reflect the new font.

Now use the **Name** property to rename all the buttons in the form, starting with **Button1** and working down to **Button6**. The new names should be as follows (note that there are no spaces allowed between the parts of a component name because it is used directly as an Object Pascal identifier).

Old Name	New Name
Button1	SwitchTo
Button2	EndTask
Button3	Cascade
Button4	Tile
Button5	ArrangeIcons
Button6	MakeTopmost

> Note that as stated in Chapter 1, it's always a good idea to name components so as to reflect their particular purpose, since this makes for more reusable code. In the case of captioned components such as buttons, always name them *before* setting their **Caption** properties. Doing so will cause the captions to change to reflect the new component names and - if you choose the component names carefully - you'll then find that your captions are almost what you want them to be, reducing the amount of typing required.

Now go through the six buttons again, altering the captions slightly to agree with our earlier screenshot of the finished Task Manager.

> The ampersand (&) character can be used in the **Caption** property to make the following character underscored for 'hot-keying'. For example, a **Caption** of '**F&red**' will appear as '**Fred**'.

Now, those push buttons look a little tall and one or two are a little narrow for their captions. To rectify this, resize just one of the buttons (it doesn't matter which one) to a smaller height and widen the last two buttons so as to accommodate their somewhat lengthier caption strings. Now use the Shift-click technique to select all six buttons and select the Size Dialog from the Edit menu. Select Grow to largest (Width) and Shrink to smallest (Height) and press OK. All your buttons should now be the right size.

See if you can align the buttons inside the panel component and, at the same time, replace the panel's caption with an empty string.

> **Hint:** Use the **Align** palette to center the buttons horizontally in the panel and to space them equally in a vertical direction. You can then pull the four lower buttons down a little lower.

If you look again at the screen shot of the finished application, you'll notice that the first two buttons are separated from the other four by a small, 3D line. You can achieve the same effect by placing a bevel component onto the form (look on the Additional page of the Component palette). Changing the bevel component's **Shape** property to **bsTopLine** makes it into a single line (at the top of its selection area) and its width can then be adjusted as required.

To complete the user interface, you should rename the form itself to **TaskManForm** and the panel to **ButtonPanel**.

Adding the Application Code

Now it's time to start adding the application-specific code via the Code Editor.

Initializing the Task List

Select TaskManForm in the Object Inspector window, swap over to the Events page and double click on right hand side of the **OnCreate** field. This will create a new routine called **TTaskManForm.FormCreate**. This procedure is executed when the form is first created - it gives us an opportunity to perform any required initialization.

Add the following code to the procedure.

```
procedure TTaskManForm.FormCreate(Sender: TObject);
var
    Wnd: hWnd;
    buff: array [0..127] of Char;
begin
    { Set height of icon list to accommodate icons }

    IconList.ItemHeight := GetSystemMetrics (sm_cyIcon) + 10;
```

```
{ Now iterate over all top-level windows }

Wnd := GetWindow (Handle, gw_HWndFirst);
while Wnd <> 0 do
begin
    if  (Wnd <> Handle) and
        IsWindowVisible (Wnd) and
        (GetWindow (Wnd, gw_Owner) = 0) and
        (GetWindowText (Wnd, buff, sizeof (buff)) <> 0) and
        (lstrcmpi (buff, 'TaskMan') <> 0) then
            IconList.Items.AddObject (buff, GetPicture (Wnd));

    { Step to next }

    Wnd := GetWindow (Wnd, gw_hWndNext);
end;

{ Select first item in the listbox }

IconList.ItemIndex := 0;
end;
```

Analyzing the Procedure

The first thing this procedure does is to set the vertical cell height of the owner-draw list box so that it's large enough to accommodate an icon. This is similar to the code used for this purpose in the icon viewer of the previous chapter. The procedure then iterates through all the top level windows it can find, checking whether or not they should be added to the current task list. If the window text of a particular window is **TaskMan**, then the window is ignored, because we obviously don't want to include the Task Manager itself in the list of running programs. If the window is suitable for adding to the list box, then the **AddObject** method (of the **Tstrings** class) is called to add the window caption, at the same time calling the **GetPicture** function (defined below) to obtain an appropriate icon handle. Finally, the first item in the list box is selected.

The GetPicture Routine

Here's the code for the **GetPicture** routine. This should be included in the source code before the **FormCreate** procedure (alternatively, you could include the function heading at the start of the implementation section).

```
function GetPicture (Wnd: hWnd): TIconListRec;
var
    ilr: TIconListRec;
    buff: array [0..127] of Char;
begin
    ilr := TIconListRec.Create;
    with ilr do
    begin
        TheWindow := Wnd;
        TheIcon := GetClassWord (Wnd, gcw_hIcon);
        if (TheIcon = 0) and
           (GetModuleFileName (GetClassWord (Wnd, gcw_hModule), buff,
           sizeof (buff)) <> 0) then
             TheIcon := ExtractIcon (hInstance, buff, 0);
        if TheIcon = 0 then TheIcon := LoadIcon (0, idi_Question);
    end;

    GetPicture := ilr;
end;
```

The AddObject Method

If you look at the definition of the **AddObject** method, you'll see that it takes a **TObject** parameter as its second parameter. This is rather awkward for us, since we want to store both an icon handle and a window handle in the listbox.

The solution to this sort of problem is to define a new object of our own, called **TIconListRec**. Here's what the definition of **TIconListRec** looks like:

```
type TIconListRec = class
                    TheIcon: hIcon;
                    TheWindow: hWnd;
               end;
```

This definition must appear before the **GetPicture** routine, preferably immediately after the **implementation** keyword of the unit. With this object definition in mind, you can see that the **GetPicture** routine first tries to get the class icon for the specified window. If this fails, it then uses the Shell API routine, **ExtractIcon**, to locate the first icon in the executable file. If this also fails, then the procedure gives up and uses the standard Windows 'question mark' icon. The '**TheWindow**' field of the **TIconListRec** data structure is filled with the window handle and the result passed back to the **FormCreate** procedure and thus to the **AddObject** method.

Because we're using `ExtractIcon`, one of the `SHELL.DLL` routines, it's necessary to also include `ShellAPI` in the `Uses` clause of the unit.

Try running the program now and you should see something like the figure below. Although the list box is being correctly set up, we haven't yet provided the code which tells it how to draw each item. This is just the same situation that we had with the icon viewer in Chapter 1 - the default behavior of an owner-draw list box is simply to display the string items if no owner-draw procedure has been provided.

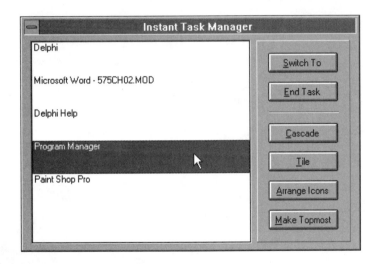

Drawing the List Box

With the `IconList` component selected, double click to the right of the `OnDrawItem` in the Events page of the Object Inspector. This will create another new routine, whose inner workings you must provide! Add the following code to the routine.

```
procedure TTaskManForm.IconListDrawItem(Control: TWinControl;
   Index: Integer; Rect: TRect; State: TOwnerDrawState);
var
    s: String;
    x, y: Integer;
    ilr: TIconListRec;
begin
    with IconList.Canvas do
    begin
```

```
        FillRect (Rect);
        { First draw the icon }
        ilr := TIconListRec (IconList.Items.Objects [Index]);
        DrawIcon (Handle, Rect.Left + 5, Rect.Top + 5, ilr.TheIcon);
        { Now draw the window title }
        s := IconList.Items [Index];
        x := Rect.left + GetSystemMetrics (sm_cxIcon) + 12;
        y := Rect.top + (IconList.ItemHeight - abs (Font.Height)) div 2;
        TextOut (x, y, s);
    end;
end;
```

Using Icon Handlers

Again, you'll notice that this is much like the Icon Viewer's custom item drawing code. The main difference is in the use of icon handles. The icon viewer used a **TPicture** object so this could be drawn immediately using Delphi's built-in polymorphic **Draw** routine. Since, this time, we've stored an ordinary Windows icon handle in the list box, we need to use the **DrawIcon** API routine to show it. With this code in place, you should find that the program looks just like our initial task manager screenshot - but we're not quite finished yet!

Adding the Mouse Click Routines

The final job is to add the code that deals with the various mouse clicks that can take place while the application is running, including double-clicking on the listbox itself. Firstly, add the following four procedure definitions after the **implementation** keyword of the unit. These routines have never been fully documented by Microsoft, but they're necessary in order to write a Task Manager program like the one we're developing. These definitions make the procedure names known to the Pascal compiler and tell the Pascal linker which run-time DLL each is located in.

```
procedure TileChildWindows (Wnd: hWnd; Flags: Bool);
far; external 'USER';
procedure CascadeChildWindows (Wnd: hWnd; Flags: Bool);
far; external 'USER';
procedure SwitchToThisWindow (Wnd: hWnd; Flags: Bool);
far; external 'USER';
function IsWinOldApTask (Task: THandle): Boolean;
far; external 'KERNEL';
```

Now add the following routine to the **implementation** part of the unit. This is the real heart of the Task Manager program - the code that's responsible for switching to a specified window, thereby making another application active. Because this routine has been defined as a method of the form, you will need to add a corresponding procedure declaration to the form's class definition. Just add it in the same place as the existing declarations.

```
procedure TTaskManForm.SwitchToWindow;
var
    ilr: TIconListRec;
    SwitchWnd: hWnd;
    style: LongInt;
begin
    ilr := TIconListRec (IconList.Items.Objects [IconList.ItemIndex]);
    with ilr do
    begin
        if not IsWindow (TheWindow) then MessageBeep (0) else
        begin
            SwitchWnd := GetLastActivePopup (TheWindow);
            style := GetWindowLong (SwitchWnd, gwl_Style);
            if (style and ws_Disabled) = 0 then
                SwitchToThisWindow (SwitchWnd, True);
        end;
    end;
end;
```

Adding Event Handlers

With this code in place, we can begin adding the various event handlers. Let's start with the IconList window itself. Use the Object Inspector to add a double-click handler for the list box. It should look like this:

```
procedure TTaskManForm.IconListDblClick(Sender: TObject);
begin
    SwitchToWindow;
    Close;
end;
```

A very simple routine this time   what it does is to switch to the requested window and then terminate the Task Manager dialog using the Close method. If you run and compile the code now, you'll find that double-clicking an item in the list box will indeed switch you over to that application.

So far, so good. Here are the event handlers for the Tile, Cascade, ArrangeIcons and EndTask buttons. Install them in the usual way, using the Object Inspector.

Note that double-clicking on a button is a short cut technique
for installing a button's OnClick event hander.

```pascal
procedure TTaskManForm.TileClick(Sender: TObject);
begin
    Hide;
    TileChildWindows (GetDesktopWindow, TRUE);
    Close;
end;
```

```pascal
procedure TTaskManForm.CascadeClick(Sender: TObject);
begin
    Hide;
    CascadeChildWindows (GetDesktopWindow, FALSE);
    Close;
end;
```

```pascal
procedure TTaskManForm.ArrangeIconsClick(Sender: TObject);
begin
    Hide;
    ArrangeIconicWindows (GetDesktopWindow);
    Close;
end;
```

```pascal
procedure TTaskManForm.EndTaskClick(Sender: TObject);
var
    ilr: TIconListRec;
    taskStyle: LongInt;
begin
    ilr := TIconListRec (IconList.Items.Objects [IconList.ItemIndex]);
    with ilr do
    begin
        taskStyle := GetWindowLong (TheWindow, gwl_Style);
        if not IsWindow (TheWindow) then
        begin
            MessageBeep (0);
            Close;
        end
        else if (taskStyle and ws_Disabled) <> 0 then
        begin
            MessageBeep (0);
            Close;
            SwitchToWindow;
        end
        else
        begin
         Close;
            SwitchToWindow;
            if not IsWinOldApTask (GetWindowTask (TheWindow)) then
                SwitchToWindow;
```

```
        if IsWindow (TheWindow) and
        ((TaskStyle and ws_Disabled) = 0) then
    PostMessage (TheWindow, $10, 0, 0);
        end;
    end;
end;
```

Why do some of these event handler's hide the Task Manager window before doing anything else? The reason, of course, is that if we were to call **CascadeChildWindows** (for example) with the Task Manager dialog still active, the Task Manager window would itself get tiled, which is unlikely to be what's wanted!

Reusing an Existing Event Handler

That's almost it. There are just two more buttons to implement. The first of these, SwitchTo, has exactly the same effect as if we double-clicked on the icon list. Wouldn't it be nice if we could avoid the necessity of duplicating an existing event handler and just use the existing code? As it happens, Delphi will allow us to do just that.

Select the SwitchTo button in the form and then move over to the Object Inspector. Select the Events page and click **once** on the **OnClick** field. You should then see a small drop-down combo button appear. Click this button and scroll through the list of defined event handlers, as shown on the previous page. Select the existing **IconListDblClick** handler and you're through - this hander will now be called when the **SwitchTo** button is clicked **and** when a double-click occurs in the list box.

Making a Program Stay on Top

The final button is **MakeTopmost** and here's its event handler.

```
procedure TTaskManForm.MakeTopmostClick(Sender: TObject);
var
    ilr: TIconListRec;
    style: LongInt;
begin
    ilr := TIconListRec (IconList.Items.Objects [IconList.ItemIndex]);
    with ilr do
        if not IsWindow (TheWindow) then MessageBeep (0) else
            SetWindowPos (TheWindow, hWnd_TopMost, 0, 0, 0, 0,
                swp_NoMove or swp_NoSize);
    Close;
end;
```

If (for whatever reason) the window handle isn't valid by the time this procedure is executed, then the **MessageBeep** routine is called. Otherwise, **SetWindowPos** is called with the magic **hWnd_TopMost** parameter. This has the effect of bringing the specified window to the top 'layer' of the screen and it will stay there even when deactivated - an invaluable feature.

The only other decision we have to make is how to install the new Task Manager. Well, to make it a permanent addition to your Windows setup, you can copy the existing **TASKMAN.EXE** in your Windows directory to **TASKMAN.OLD** (so that you won't have to retrieve it from the installation disks if you change your mind!). Then, you can just copy **TASKMAN.EXE** from the directory you've been working in to your Windows directory. This will replace the existing Task Manager.

Summary

In Chapter 1, the emphasis was on familiarization with the Delphi environment, whereas the current chapter has focused on form and component properties and placement - how to build the user interface of your application. In the next chapter, we're going to take a much more in-depth look at events, including a discussion of all the different event types available, how to respond to mouse and keyboard events in your application, and so on. Armed with this information, you'll be in good shape to take on even more challenging Delphi programming projects.

Exercises

1   You may have noticed that the original Windows Task Manager program will automatically close down if you click on a different application while it's active. How would you go about adding similar functionality to our Task Manager?

Hint: have a look at the `OnActivate` and `OnDeactivate2` events.

2   If you were to accidentally make a particular application 'stay on top', how might you go about rectifying the situation? What's really needed, of course, is a way of toggling particular applications between stay on top mode on the one hand, and ordinary, overlappable windows on the other. How might you implement this in the Task Manager program?

Hint: take a look at the `SetWindowPos` routine

Chapter

Event Handling

The sample programs developed in the previous two chapters have used events and event handlers - procedures which respond to different events. In this chapter, we're going to look in more detail at the different types of events that are available, how you'd use them in an application and how you'd go about writing event handlers for the most common types of event.

When programming in Delphi, you won't be able to do anything useful without mastering event handlers - a graphical development system such as Delphi can only take you so far. Event processing is the 'glue' which turns a form and its otherwise passive collection of components into something that behaves as you'd want it to. You've already seen this in Chapter 1, where a **FileListBox**, **DirectoryListBox**, **DriveComboBox** and **ListBox** were glued together so as to form a cooperative whole. Without the event handlers, the program would look pretty, but it would be no more use than a chocolate teapot.

In this chapter, we'll cover the following topics:

- What an event is.
- How traditional Windows programs deal with messages.
- Writing portable Delphi applications.
- The relationship between Windows messages and Delphi events.
- Which events are available.
- Managing event handlers, keyboard events, and mouse events.

Event Handling: Concepts

Events are the life-blood of a graphical user interface such as Microsoft Windows. Every time that you move the mouse, click the mouse button, or type a keystroke, you're generating an event or message. These are examples of what we'll call low-level events - they have a very obvious connection to the action that the user performs.

If all we had was these low-level events, then Windows programming would be extremely tedious. For example, suppose you want something to happen when the user double-clicks on a particular control. To determine when a double-click takes place, you'd have to remember the time and position of the previous mouse click. Then, next time you got a mouse click, you'd have to see if it was in approximately the same location and relatively soon after the previous click - if it was, you'd know that you'd just received a double-click event.

As another example, consider what happens when the user is using your application and then clicks on a window belonging to another application. You'd have to intercept the mouse click, determine that it wasn't intended for your own application and then, somehow, you'd have to transfer control to the other program, at the same time passing on the mouse click so that the newly activated program could take the appropriate action.

If you've previously done any Windows programming, you'll know that it's actually much simpler than this. The Windows system itself takes care of determining when a double-click takes place and automatically sends an appropriate message to the application. Similarly, when you click on an inactive application, Windows figures out what's happened and sends a high-level **WM_ACTIVATE** message to the window involved. These higher-level messages make life a lot easier for the application programmer, who would otherwise have to write a large amount of code just to determine what the user was trying to do.

Traditional Event Handling

Classic Windows development is built around the notion of a **window procedure**. Each new type of window that you define in your application has to have an associated window procedure. For example, if you create a drawing application, your main program window will have its own special window procedure; if you define a floating toolbar window, you need to provide a window procedure for that too.

The job of a window procedure is to respond to all the different Windows messages that the window can receive. Window procedures are frequently organized as enormous 'switch' statements which execute different chunks of code according to the message that's currently being processed - repaint the window if we get a **WM_PAINT** message, re-size the window contents if we get a **WM_SIZE** message, and so on.

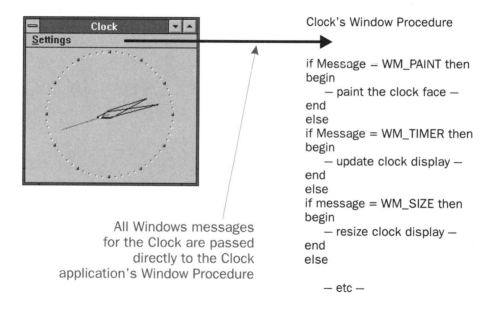

Clock's Window Procedure

```
if Message - WM_PAINT then
begin
    - paint the clock face -
end
else
if Message = WM_TIMER then
begin
    - update clock display -
end
else
if message = WM_SIZE then
begin
    - resize clock display -
end
else

    - etc -
```

All Windows messages for the Clock are passed directly to the Clock application's Window Procedure

Maintenance Disadvantages

Note that the traditional Windows approach has some maintenance disadvantages. A window procedure is often hundreds, even thousands, of lines long. Making changes to an application with such procedures in it is a nightmare.

Often, those developers who try to write well-structured programs will split a window procedure into many different routines, called from the main window procedure according to the message received. This allows them to write one small, modular routine for each different Windows message that the application is interested in. This approach, while good, isn't obligatory. With Delphi, on the other hand, you typically **must** write a separate event handler for each event that a particular component or form needs to handle. A modular, more easily managed, programming style is forced upon you.

Under the Hood: Portability Considerations

With traditional Windows programming, the developer must pay special attention to portability of source code, especially with the current emphasis on the 32-bit future of Windows.

Message Formats

When passed to a window procedure, a Windows message has three distinct parts.

- The message number
- The **wParam** field
- The **lParam** field.

(There are actually other components to a message, but these aren't passed directly to the window procedure.) Here's what a typical window procedure looks like in Pascal terms:

```
function WProc (Wnd: hWnd; Msg, wParam: Word; lParam: LongInt): LongInt;
begin
    — lots of code goes here —
end;
```

The window procedure always receives the window handle (in case the procedure is used by more than one window of the same class) followed by the message number and the **wParam** and **lParam** fields. The meaning of **wParam** and **lParam** are completely dependent on the message number. For example, when receiving the **WM_ACTIVATE** message, the **wParam** and **lParam** fields have the following meanings:

- **wParam**: a 16-bit Boolean 'activation' flag,

- **lParam** (high word): a 16-bit Boolean 'minimized' flag,

- **lParam** (low word): the handle of the window being activated or deactivated.

As you can see, Microsoft have chosen to pack a Boolean flag and a window handle into the **lParam** field of this particular message. This is where the problems start: under Win16 (the generic term for the 16-bit Windows API specification), there's no problem with this arrangement. Under Win32 (the generic term for the 32-bit Windows API, whether implemented under Windows/NT, Windows95 or Win32), this packing arrangement just isn't possible, because a window handle is 32-bits wide. The window handle would take up the whole of the **lParam** field, leaving no room for the minimized flag.

This is what the message layout for **WM_ACTIVATE** looks like under Win32.

- **wParam** (low word): a 16-bit Boolean 'activation' flag,

- **wParam** (high word): a 16-bit Boolean 'minimized' flag,

- **lParam**: the handle of the window being activated or deactivated.

As you can see, the new message layout capitalizes on the fact that **wParam** and **lParam** are both 32 bits wide under Win32. This allows Microsoft to move the minimized flag into the spare high word of the **wParam** field, leaving the window handle to have **lParam** all to itself.

That's all very well if you're writing a 16-bit or a 32-bit Windows application, but what if you want your source code to be portable between both environments - a reasonable design objective? In this case, it seems that you have no choice but to clutter up your code with messy **#ifdef** statements, like this:

```
#ifdef WIN32
    fMinimize = HIWORD (wParam);
#else
    fMinimize = HIWORD (lParam);
#endif
```

This sort of approach - like the monster-sized switch statements mentioned earlier - is guaranteed to reduce anyone who tries to write neat and tidy source code to a nervous wreck.

Message Crackers to the Rescue

To be fair, Microsoft largely solved the portability problem by introducing 'message crackers' - a set of macros defined in the **WINDOWSX.H** header file. The message crackers work by pulling a message into its individual components - cracking it open, as it were - and then calling a routine which handles the actual message processing. For instance, the line of code below would form part of the **switch** statement of a portable windows procedure written in C:

```
HANDLE_MSG (hwnd, WM_ACTIVATE, MyApp_OnActivate);
```

This tells the compiler to generate a **case** clause for the **WM_ACTIVATE** message. The macro automatically cracks apart the important parts of the message and calls the programmer-supplied routine **MyApp_OnActivate**, with each message component as a parameter. Here's how the **MyApp_OnActivate** procedure would be declared, again in C.

```
void MyApp_OnActivate (HWND hwnd, UINT state,
                       HWND hwndActDeact, BOOL fMinimized);
```

As you might guess, the various macro definitions do 'the right thing' for both Win16 and Win32, allowing you to write portable window procedures and portable message handling routines.

> It's also interesting to note that the message cracking approach provides the same modular, one-routine-per-message approach that we get in Delphi.

Application Frameworks

So far, we haven't said anything about C++ and so-called **application frameworks** - Borland's OWL and Microsoft's MFC are good examples. An application framework is a class library which provides the essential facilities for every C++ Windows application, written so as to provide maximum portability between Win16 and Win32. With application frameworks, a carefully written application need only be recompiled when moving between the two different environments - the 'message cracking' is performed behind the scenes in the class library.

Portability in Delphi

While we're on the subject of portability, we should give you some tips for writing portable Delphi applications.

As far as portability to Win32 is concerned, it's all good news. Provided you 'do things the Delphi way', you should have few problems in moving your application between the 16-bit and 32-bit versions of Delphi.

What do we mean by 'doing things the Delphi way'? Here are a few golden rules for coding your Delphi programs in a portable way:

- Avoid using Windows API calls whenever possible. For example, rather than using the **GlobalAlloc** and **GlobalFree** routines, you should use Delphi's **GetMem** and **FreeMem** equivalents.

- When drawing graphics, use the routines provided by the VCL (Visual Component Library). When using icons, bitmaps and so on, try to use the VCL representations of those objects, rather than going direct to the Windows API.

- Don't make any assumptions about the size of the **Integer** type. When compiling for Win16, an integer is 2 bytes long. When compiling for Win32, it's four bytes - the same as a **LongInt**. If you need to define common data structures that will be used by 16 and 32-bit versions of your application, use the **ShortInt** and **LongInt** types explicitly to define the size of each field of the structure, rather than **Integer**.

- Take great care when sending or receiving messages. As explained above, the format of many Windows messages differs between Win16 and Win32. When receiving messages, use Delphi's event handling mechanism. When sending messages, avoid using the **SendMessage** or **PostMessage** API calls. Rather, call the target's event handler for the event you want to send.

- If you find that you do need to issue Windows API calls, remember that handles are now 32-bits wide. For example, with Win16, passing the **GWW_HINSTANCE** index to the **GetWindowWord** routine will return the instance handle associated with a particular window. Under Win32 this isn't possible because instance handles are now 32 bits but **GetWindowWord** still returns a 16 bit value - you need to use **GetWindowLong** with an index of **GWL_HINSTANCE** instead.

91

Event Handling in Delphi

Unlike traditional Windows development, Delphi insulates the application program from 'raw' Windows messages. When an event occurs, the appropriate event handler belonging to the component that's receiving the event is simply executed.

You can think of it as a layered architecture. At the lowest level, Windows receives low-level mouse and keyboard notifications from its various device drivers. Windows then analyses these messages to determine the intended destination window. At the same time, low-level messages may be converted to high-level messages such as **WM_KILLFOCUS**, **WM_ACTIVATE**, and so on. The appropriate messages are constructed and sent to the Delphi application. Within the Delphi run-time library, each message is 'cracked' and converted into an event handler call to the appropriate component. For this reason, in Delphi programming, we talk about events rather than messages. The general idea is shown below.

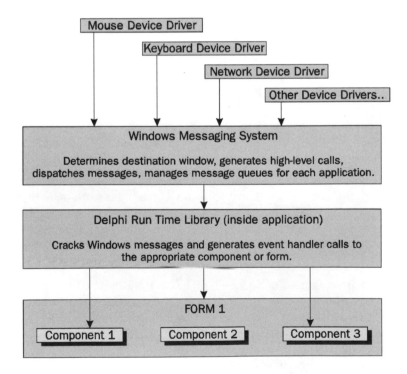

Bear in mind that this diagram is something of a simplification. For example, what happens to all those events for which you haven't defined an event handler? The answer is that they're processed inside Delphi's run-time library, ultimately being sent to the **DefWindowProc** (default window procedure) API routine if there's nothing else to do with them. Bear in mind also that, unlike Visual Basic, Delphi is a true, object-oriented system. If you look at the source code to the run-time library, you'll see that many component types are derived from more general object definitions. Thus, even though a particular component that you've defined may not handle a specific event, the event may be handled by a class higher up in the inheritance hierarchy.

Available Events

The following table lists some of the Delphi events which have equivalent Windows messages. If you've programmed for Windows before, this table will show you under what circumstances a particular event is generated and what can be gained by writing an handler for that event.

Delphi Event	Windows Message
OnActivate	WM_ACTIVATE (wParam <> WA_INACTIVE)
OnClick	WM_COMMAND
OnClose	WM_CLOSE
OnCloseQuery	Similar to the WM_QUERYENDSESSION message
OnCreate	WM_CREATE (or WM_INITDIALOG for dialog boxes)
OnDblClick	WM_LBUTTONDBLCLK
OnDestroy	WM_DESTROY
OnDragDrop	Similar to (but more general than) WM_DROPFILES
OnDragOver	WM_QUERYDRAGICON
OnDrawCell	WM_DRAWITEM
OnDrawItem	WM_DRAWITEM

Continued

Delphi Event	Windows Message
OnDrawTab	Similar to WM_DRAWITEM
OnDropDown	CBN_DROPDOWN (combo box notification message).
OnEndDrag	Similar to (but more general than) WM_DROPFILES
OnKeyDown	WM_KEYDOWN
OnKeyPress	WM_CHAR
OnKeyUp	WM_KEYUP
OnMeasureItem	WM_MEASUREITEM
OnMeasureTab	Similar to WM_MEASUREITEM
OnMouseDown	WM_LBUTTONDOWN, WM_RBUTTONDOWN
OnMouseMove	WM_MOUSEMOVE
OnMouseUp	WM_LBUTTONUP, WM_RBUTTONUP, WM_MBUTTONUP

As you can see, there isn't always a direct, one-to-one correspondence between a Delphi event and a Windows message. Some Delphi events are specific to particular component types - for example, OnApply and OnDrawTab - while others are specific to the Delphi implementation itself, notably the OnMessage event. Some events, such as OnMouseUp and OnMouseDown, correspond to more than one Windows message.

Creating Event Handlers

When creating an event handler for a particular component, always remember to perform the following three step procedure. Step one is especially important, because it's easy to forget this step. You'll end up creating an event handler for the wrong component or form which can produce some unexpected results!

Firstly, select the component to which you want to add an event handler. You can do this by single-clicking in the form window or by using the drop-down list at the top of the Object Inspector window.

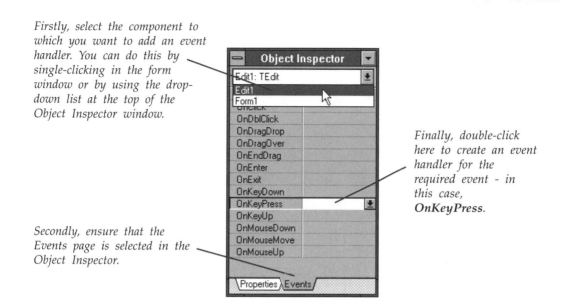

Finally, double-click here to create an event handler for the required event - in this case, OnKeyPress.

Secondly, ensure that the Events page is selected in the Object Inspector.

> **Note that you can use the same procedure to locate an existing event handler for a component. If the event handler procedure already exists, you'll be taken to that point in the Code Editor.**

Try it for yourself: create an empty form and add a single edit box to it. Now, using the steps outlined above, create a new **OnKeyPress** handler for the edit box. You should end up inside the Code Editor with things looking like this:

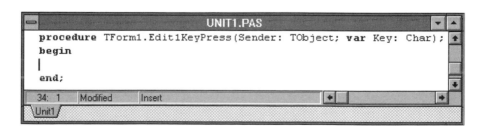

You'll notice that Delphi has already written the procedure declaration for you and added the **begin** and **end** statements - all you have to do is type in the body of the procedure! If you look back to near the beginning of the Pascal source file, you'll see that Delphi has also added the same procedure declaration to the class definition for the form window, making the procedure a method of the form.

```
type
  TForm1 = class(TForm)
    Edit1: TEdit;
    procedure Edit1KeyPress(Sender: TObject; var Key: Char);
  private
    { Private declarations }
  public
    { Public declarations }
  end;
```

> Note that if you compile or run the application at this point, your new event handler will disappear! Delphi assumes that if you don't provide a body for the event handler before the next compile, you intend to discard it.

Event Handler Naming Conventions

The name of the event handler requires a little explanation. It's made up of three distinct parts as shown in the diagram on the next page:

- The form name, (followed by a period)
- The name of the component
- The name of the event to which this handler relates.

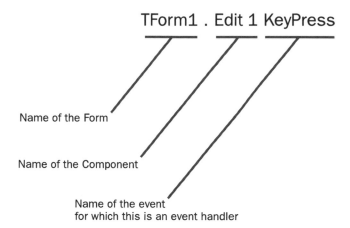

TForm1 . Edit 1 KeyPress

Name of the Form

Name of the Component

Name of the event
for which this is an event handler

When setting up event handlers for forms, rather than for components, the component name is replaced by the string **Form**, so that (for example) **FirstForm.FormCreate** would be the name of the **OnCreate** event handler for the form called **FirstForm**.

A couple of things to notice: firstly, the event name isn't prefixed by **On**. In other words, the name of the event handler is **TForm.Edit1KeyPress**, rather than **TForm.Edit1OnKeyPress**.

Secondly, the form name is always preceded by the letter **T**. This specifies that the form name is actually a type, rather than a variable. This is an important distinction - Delphi allows you to set up forms which you can then use as new types in other applications. Just as Delphi's components may be used in many different programs, your own custom forms become reusable building blocks too. This is something that we'll be covering in more detail in later chapters.

If you find this confusing, here's another way of looking at it. You only need to define a form and its components once, but more than one copy of the same form can be created within the same application. The classic example of this is the MDI (Multiple Document Interface) style of program, such as the Windows 3.1 Program Manager. For such an application, you'd need to create a form to use as the basis for the group window. Naturally, the users of your application would want to be able to have more than one group window at the same time. A form definition, along with its components and event handlers, constitutes a reusable object in the true object-oriented sense of the word, so it can easily be plugged into other applications.

Automatic Event Handler Renaming

Suppose you wanted to rename a form - would you have to rename all the event handlers that relate to that form? Or, imagine that you wanted to rename a component - would you have to rename all the event handlers you've defined for that particular component?

Thankfully, the answer to both these questions is no! Delphi automatically tracks the names of forms, components and related event handlers. As you rename the forms and components, the event handler names change too.

Try it out! Have a go at altering the name of the form and the edit box. If you watch the Code Editor window, you'll see the event handler name change. Here's what our event handler finished up looking like:

```
procedure TDavesForm.TextEditorKeyPress(Sender: TObject; var Key: Char);
begin
end;
```

Deleting an Event Handler

Inevitably, there will be times during the course of application development when you wish to delete an event handler that you no longer need. One way to do this is to delete the event handler procedure from the Code Editor window. At the same time, you'll need to remove the procedure declaration from the form class definition. At this point, the event handler will still appear in the Object Inspector window. The next time you try to build the application, you'll get a message like that below:

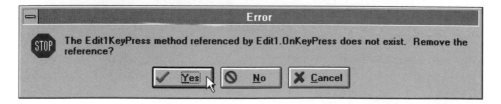

If you click the Yes button to continue building the application, you should find that the event handler has disappeared from the Object Inspector.

Handling Keyboard Events

Get back to the stage you were at earlier - a form with just a single edit box component on it. Set the **Text** property of the edit control to an empty string. Now create an **OnKeyPress** event handler for the edit box and add a couple of lines of code to the event handler so that it looks like this:

```
procedure TForm1.Edit1KeyPress(Sender: TObject; var Key: Char);
begin
    if (Edit1.SelStart = 0) or (Edit1.Text [Edit1.SelStart] = ' ') then
        Key := UpCase (Key);
end;
```

Code Analysis

This fragment of code uses the **SelStart** and **Text** properties of the edit box - **SelStart** specifies the beginning of the current text selection (or the insertion point if there's no selection) and **Text** specifies the actual contents of the edit box. So, the condition checks whether we're typing at the start of the edit box or immediately to the right of a space; if we are, the character just typed is mapped to upper case.

If you run the application and try typing in the edit box, you should see that the first letter of each word automatically becomes upper case. (You might wish to add such functionality to an application which, for example, asks for a user's name or address.)

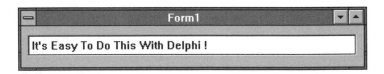

What's interesting about this example is the ease with which we got the desired result: the code is extremely simple. How would you go about doing this in a conventional language such as C? The answer is that you probably wouldn't bother because it's too much hassle. The Windows edit box gives you styles such as **ES_UPPERCASE** and **ES_LOWERCASE** which cause the **entire** contents of an edit box to be forced to upper or lower case. However, there's no magic style which provides the effect we've got here. To do that, you'd probably need to start subclassing the edit box or do something equally unpleasant.

By using a **with** statement, it would be possible to make the code even simpler, like this:

```
procedure TForm1.Edit1KeyPress(Sender: TObject; var Key: Char);
begin
    with Edit1 do
          if (SelStart = 0) or (Text [SelStart] = ' ') then
            Key := UpCase (Key);
end;
```

Notice that you need to explicitly refer to the **Edit1** component every time you reference one of the edit box's methods or properties (as in the first version of the code) or else use a 'with' clause (as in the second version).

> **This is an important point - just because this is the edit box's event handler doesn't automatically mean that the edit box is 'in scope'. The event handler is a method of the form, so only the form's methods and objects are immediately accessible inside the event handler. This might seem like a weird way of arranging things but it is sensible - by making all event handlers methods of the form, each has access to the form's methods and thus to *all* other components of the form and *their* methods. If the event handler was merely a method of the edit box, it would be more difficult to access the form and other components.**

You'll notice that, other than the **Sender** object, the **OnKeyPress** event handler takes only one parameter, the key that's been pressed. (Since **Key** is a **var** parameter, the event handler is at liberty to change the key code in any way it wishes.) Like the routines associated with the SDK's message cracker macros, the number and type of parameters to an event handler is dependent on the type of the corresponding event we're dealing with. To illustrate this, let's take a look at another common event.

Using Modifier Keys

The **OnKeyPress** event is a relatively high-level way of dealing with key strokes. It conveniently presents the key to you in the form of a character which can be easily modified. The price you pay for this ease of use is a lack of flexibility. Using **OnKeyPress**, you can't take account of any modifier keys that were held down at the time the key was pressed. Modifiers might include any or all of the *Shift*, *Alt* and *Control* keys, or even the buttons on

the mouse. To do that, you need to use either the **OnKeyDown** or
OnKeyUp event.

Here's the procedure declaration for the **OnKeyDown** event which, as you can
see, provides greater control than **OnKeyPress**.

```
procedure TForm1.Edit1KeyDown(Sender: TObject; var Key: Word;
                     Shift: TShiftState);
begin
         { insert your code here.... }
end;
```

(The **OnKeyUp** event looks just the same as for **OnKeyDown**.) The
TShiftState type used by the **Shift** parameter is defined as below:

```
TShiftState = set of (ssShift, ssAlt, ssCtrl, ssRight,
                     ssLeft, ssMiddle, ssDouble);
```

Because it is a set, any combination of these modifiers may be active when
the key was pressed.

Using the KeyPreview Property

Suppose you want to perform some special key processing which applies to
the whole form, rather than to just a specific control. Let's say, for the sake
of argument, that you want to give your users the ability to easily type the
© (copyright) character into a form. This might be necessary, for example,
when creating a front-end to the Microsoft Help Compiler - you want the
users to be able to embed their own copyright information into the form
they're creating.

An easy way of doing this would be to write a **OnKeyPress** event handler
like the one we saw earlier, maybe replacing every occurrence of the @
character with a ©. But what if you had several edit boxes and wanted
them all to have this ability - you wouldn't want to write a special event
handler for each.

The easiest way to do this sort of thing is to use a form's **KeyPreview**
property. This allows a form to examine all key presses **before** they are
passed to the currently selected component. To enable the **KeyPreview**
feature, just set it to **True** in the Object Inspector window.

101

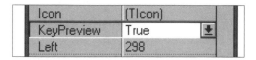

Now create an **OnKeyPress** handler for the form, **not** for any component on it. Once you've done that, all key strokes will be sent to this new event handler first. Try using an event handler like the one shown below:

```
procedure TForm1.FormKeyPress(Sender: TObject; var Key: Char);
begin
    if Key = '@' then Key := '©'
end;
```

If you now create one or more edit boxes and run the application, you'll find that typing @ always results in the © character being displayed - it works for all the edit boxes.

There are obvious advantages with this technique. If you want to do something out of the ordinary with keyboard input, you can centralize all your special code into the form's **OnKeyPress** event handler rather than putting similar code into the event handler's for each component. Of course, another way to do this would be to use a shared event handler, but the **KeyPreview** is often easier.

The ActiveControl Property

What if you wanted one or more controls to be treated as a special case? How would you get round the fact that the form's key handler affects all the controls on the form? Once again, there's a simple solution - the **ActiveControl** property. You can use this property to determine which control is currently active and modify the event handler's behavior accordingly, like this:

```
procedure TForm1.FormKeyPress(Sender: TObject; var Key: Char);
begin
    if (Key = '@') and (ActiveControl <> Edit2) then
           Key := '©'
end;
```

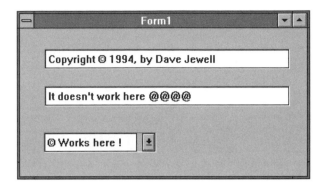

Event Handling: Implementation

Building a Better Mouse Trap

So much for keyboard events - now let's turn our attention to mouse events. In order to put things on a practical footing, we'll devote the rest of this chapter to the development of a 'Doodle' style application that lets you use the mouse for drawing.

This will give you a good grasp of how to handle mouse events handling and it will also serve as an introduction to the Delphi graphics API (which is covered in more detail in Chapter 7).

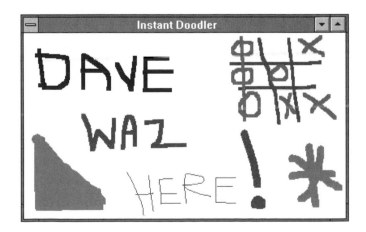

The finished application is shown on the previous page. You can draw onto the form window by simply holding down the left mouse button and moving it around within the window. Pressing the right mouse button momentarily will erase the current image. You'll also be able to modify the pen width and the current drawing color.

Start a new project by selecting New Project from Delphi's File menu. Change the form's caption property to Instant Doodler, or whatever you want to call it. Now save the project as **DOODLE** and the Pascal unit code as **DUDLEFRM.PAS**.

Handling the Mouse-Down Event

The first job is to take care of what happens when the user presses the left mouse button down on the form. Let's create an event handler for this in the usual way. With the form selected (you can't really select much else as this form has no components yet!) change over to the Events page of the Object Inspector and double-click the right-hand value field beside the **OnMouseDown** event name.

Double-Click here

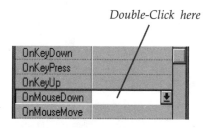

```
procedure TForm1.FormMouseDown(Sender: TObject; Button: TMouseButton;
                Shift: TShiftState; X, Y: Integer);
begin

end;
```

Here's the event handler that gets created. As you can see, there are some similarities with the key event handlers that we saw earlier. We've already encountered the **TShiftState** type, but **TMouseButton** is new. It's declared as follows:

```
TMouseButton = (mbRight, mbLeft, mbCenter);
```

> Note that you can also get this information from the `Shift`
> parameter, but because `TMouseButton` is an enumerated type
> rather than a set, it represents a more convenient way of
> determining which button has been pressed.

In addition, as you might expect, the `OnMouseDown` event handler receives
the X and Y coordinates of the location where the mouse was pressed.

Now add the following code to the `OnMouseDown` handler so that it looks
like this:

```
procedure TForm1.FormMouseDown(Sender: TObject; Button: TMouseButton;
                    Shift: TShiftState; X, Y: Integer);
begin
    if Button = mbLeft then
    begin
        Canvas.MoveTo(X, Y);
        fMouseDown := True;
    end;
end;
```

This moves the drawing position of the form to the mouse's current location
and sets a variable, `fMouseDown`, to `True`. This variable tells us that the left-
hand mouse is down and we're currently drawing.

Add the `fMouseDown` variable to the form's class definition like this:

```
type
  TForm1 = class(TForm)
    procedure FormMouseDown(Sender: TObject; Button: TMouseButton;
                      Shift: TShiftState; X, Y: Integer);
  private
    { Private declarations }
  public
    { Public declarations }
    fMouseDown: Boolean;              { True if mouse is down }
  end;
```

The Canvas Property

The demo programs developed in the first two chapters of this book have
both used the `Canvas` property of an object, but we haven't explained it up

to now. Suffice it to say at this point that the **Canvas** represents the drawing surface of an object - hence the name. Both forms and components have an associated **Canvas** property which you can access at run-time to draw your own graphics onto that object. In traditional Windows programming terms, the **Canvas** is something like a device context, but rather easier to use. We'll be talking a lot more about the **Canvas** object in Chapter 7.

Tracking Mouse Movement

With the **OnMouseDown** code completed, let's turn our attention to the code that deals with tracking mouse movement. We obviously need to follow the mouse as it's moved over the form, so that we can make it leave a 'paint trail' behind itself.

As with a lot of things in Delphi, the code to do this is extremely easy. Add an **OnMouseMove** event handler to the form in the usual way and then add the following code to it:

```
procedure TForm1.FormMouseMove(Sender: TObject; Shift: TShiftState;
                           X, Y: Integer);
begin
    if fMouseDown then Canvas.LineTo (X, Y);
end;
```

The table of equivalent Windows messages and Delphi events shown earlier in the chapter indicated that the **OnMouseMove** event corresponds to a **WM_MOUSEMOVE** message. Every time that you move the mouse over an active window, a stream of **WM_MOUSEMOVE** events is generated. In a Delphi application, the **OnMouseMove** event handler is called each time the mouse moves.

As you can see, the **LineTo** method of the **Canvas** property (which is itself an object) is called to draw a line from the previous mouse position to the new position. This is why it was necessary to set the initial drawing position in the **OnMouseDown** handler.

> You can also see why it was stated that programming Windows graphics with Delphi is very easy - we don't have to keep referring to device contexts all the time - the device context is inherent in the particular **Canvas** that we're using.

What Goes Down Must Come Up

If you now run the program, you'll find that you can already start doodling with the program - the only trouble is, you can't stop! The mouse will continue to draw all over the form even after it has been released. This is hardly surprising since we haven't told the application to stop drawing when the left mouse button is released - we now need to add the **OnMouseUp** event handler to do that. Here it is in all its glory:

```
procedure TForm1.FormMouseUp(Sender: TObject; Button: TMouseButton;
                    Shift: TShiftState; X, Y: Integer);
begin
    if Button = mbLeft then fMouseDown := False;
end;
```

With this change, the program now works as advertised.

Doodling in Color - Using the TColorDialog Component

As it stands, this program is unlikely to take the world by storm - it's not exactly a state of the art drawing package! Let's see how easy it is to add a few more features to the program using some of the other event handling techniques that we've seen in this chapter.

Firstly, we'll develop a mechanism for changing the color of the pen. Before we do this, alter the **Color** property of the form to **clWhite**. With an application that can draw in any color, white is a more appropriate background color to use than gray.

Now move over to the Component Palette, select the Dialogs page and double-click on the ColorDialog control - a component that we've not previously used before. A ColorDialog component will appear on your form.

> Note that the **ColorDialog** is an example of a non-visual component. Although it's visible on the form at design-time, the **ColorDialog** has no run-time appearance until it's actually invoked, at which time it displays the standard Windows color selection dialog. Another example of a non-visual component is the **Timer**, something that never appears at run -time but is often extremely useful.

In order to get the ColorDialog to appear, we need to call its **Execute** method - like pretty well everything else in Delphi, the ColorDialog component behaves like an object with its own properties and methods. If you've done much Windows programming before, you'll probably have guessed that this component is actually implemented as an object-oriented 'wrapper' around a call to the standard color selection dialog in the **COMMDLG.DLL** library.

The simplest way to invoke the dialog is with a key press. Let's choose to use the *c* key to bring up the color dialog. Create an **OnKeyPress** event handler for the form in the usual way and add the following code to the routine. Notice that we've used the **UpCase** run-time library call so that whether the user types *c* or *C*, the dialog will still get called.

```
procedure TForm1.FormKeyPress(Sender: TObject; var Key: Char);
begin
    if UpCase (Key) = 'C' then
    begin
        ColorDialog1.Execute;
        Canvas.Pen.Color := ColorDialog1.Color;
    end;
end;
```

After typing in this code, select the **ColorDialog1** component and change its **Ctl3D** property to **True**. This will give the dialog a nice, up-to-date 3D look rather than its default 'flat' appearance.

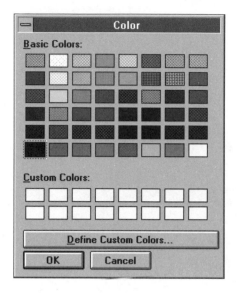

As you can see, setting the current pen color is simply a matter of accessing the ColorDialog component's **Color** property, which is set according to the selection that you make.

Just to add an additional nice touch, try inserting the following code immediately before the ColorDialog's **Execute** method is called:

```
ColorDialog1.Color := Canvas.Pen.Color;
```

This will have the effect of displaying the currently selected drawing color inside the color selection dialog. As you can see - this is really simple stuff! Much easier than setting up those big, complicated data structures that you'd have to use if talking directly to the **COMMDLG.DLL** library.

Painting Vs Drawing

You may have noticed something untoward when using the color selection
dialog. After the dialog disappears from the screen, any part of the drawing
that was behind the dialog has been erased. The same thing happens if any
other window obscures our Doodle application. Again, if you draw a doodle
on the form window and then drag the window to the edge of the screen,
you'll see exactly the same thing happen when the off-screen part of the
window is redrawn. It's as if our application isn't redrawing the contents of
its window.

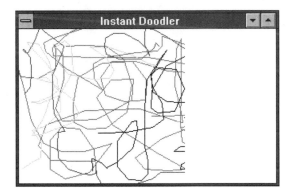

In fact, that's exactly what's happening. A Delphi application won't
automatically redraw any graphics that are placed onto the form's **Canvas**.
Once the drawing surface of the window is obscured or moved off-screen,
whatever was on that part of the window is lost. Up until now, we've been
merely drawing images on the screen. By contrast, painting is the act of
'refreshing' an existing image as and when necessary. This corresponds to
the **WM_PAINT** message in the Windows API.

To get an application 'to remember' the image which has been drawn onto
it, the simplest technique is to create a bitmap at run-time and draw the
image into that bitmap. We'll be demonstrating this technique in the next
chapter when we meet the Image component.

> **You might also want to refer to Chapter 7 which contains more
> material on graphics techniques, and to Borland's GRAPHEX
> demo program which is located in the directory
> \DELPHI\DEMOS\GRAPHEX.**

Changing the Pen Width

A useful feature of any half-way decent drawing program is the ability to vary the size of the pen. Assuming that we want to alter the pen size between 1 and 9 pixels in size, we can easily cater for this by checking for a key press of any number between 1 and 9. Try modifying the form's **OnKeyPress** event handler so that it looks like this:

```
procedure TForm1.FormKeyPress(Sender: TObject; var Key: Char);
begin
    if UpCase (Key) = 'C' then
    begin
        ColorDialog1.Color := Canvas.Pen.Color;
        ColorDialog1.Execute;
        Canvas.Pen.Color := ColorDialog1.Color;
    end
    else if Key in ['1'..'9'] then
        Canvas.Pen.Width := Ord (Key) - Ord ('0');
end;
```

With this simple change, typing the character 5 will set the current pen width to five pixels, 6 will set it to six pixels, and so on. The figure below shows the variation in pen width that you can now achieve.

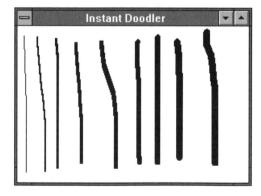

Clearing the Window

At this stage, our doodling program is almost finished, but we need to provide a means of clearing the window and starting another doodle. A simple way of doing this would be to clear the window whenever we get a click of the right mouse button click.

For many years, Microsoft fought shy of using the right-hand mouse button in their software, the assumption being that some people might not have a two-button mouse. In practice, one-button mice are rare (I've never seen one !) and we'd advise you to freely use the right mouse button in your applications since it adds a useful facility to your own programs. For example, Borland use the right mouse button to pop up **SpeedMenus** in Delphi and in their other development systems and Microsoft have recently followed suit - the right mouse button invokes a popup menu in Word for Windows 6.

Edit the form's **OnMouseDown** event handler so that it looks like this.

```
procedure TForm1.FormMouseDown(Sender: TObject; Button: TMouseButton;
                    Shift: TShiftState; X, Y: Integer);
var
    Rect: TRect;
begin
    if Button = mbLeft then
    begin
        Canvas.MoveTo (X, Y);
        fMouseDown := True;
    end;

    if Button = mbRight then
        begin
            SetRect (Rect, 0, 0, ClientWidth, ClientHeight);
            Canvas.Brush.Color := Color;
            Canvas.FillRect (Rect);
        end;
end;
```

This procedure initializes a **TRect** object (a rectangle) to the dimensions of the **Canvas**, sets the **Canvas**'s **Brush Color** to the form's background color, and then fills the rectangle, thus clearing the window. The **FillRect** method is the Delphi equivalent of the Windows API **FillRect** routine but, again, without the need to explicitly specify a device context.

Summary

We've covered quite a bit of ground in this chapter, examining the basics of event handlers and how they relate to 'traditional' Windows messages. We've also looked at key handling, mouse handling, and developed a quick and easy Doodle program that brings these ideas together. You may have noticed that the Doodle program was somewhat contrived - we ended up bending over backwards to avoid the use of menus in the program's user interface! In a real-world, commercial application, you would never rely on assorted key strokes to access the various features of an application without giving some sort of visual cues to the user. The Doodle program, simple though it is, really needs to have a File menu for terminating the application and at least one other menu for changing pen size and color.

Without further ado then, let's move on to the next chapter, and learn about how to incorporate menus into a Delphi applications, for an even more professional look and feel. See you there.

Exercises

1 See if you can modify the Doodle program to fill the window background with different colors, rather than always clearing to white.

Hint: remove the existing code that deals with right-hand mouse clicks and modify the color handling code. You could use the letter *c* to invoke a color selection dialog for changing the pen color and *C* to invoke a color selection dialog for changing the window background.

2 Can you modify the Doodle application to draw straight lines instead of freehand sketches? For example, the user could click and hold down the mouse button to define a line's starting point and then release the mouse at the desired endpoint.

Chapter

Using Menus In Your Applications

Menus have an important role to play in user interface design - a role that's sometimes overlooked. The logical arrangement of program options in a menu can go a long way towards making an application easier to learn and more pleasant to use. In addition, pop-up menus (what Borland call SpeedMenus) offer a lot of scope for providing help and commonly used options right where you need them.

In the exercise at the end of the previous chapter, we suggested enhancing the Doodle program so that the user could draw straight lines between any two points. The obvious way to change over from 'scribble mode' to 'straight line mode' (and vice versa) would be to use a menu, or perhaps a floating toolbar - one of the user interface components that Delphi provides (we'll be discussing them more fully in a later chapter). If you **really** want to make life easier for your users, you could provide a pop-up menu (activated through the right-hand mouse button); this would allow them to select a different tool almost instantly, without having to move away from the area of interest. Details like this can really make or break a program from the user's point of view.

In this chapter, we'll cover the following topics:

- Adding menus to your application.
- The Delphi Menu Designer.
- Writing menu event handlers.
- Pop-up menus, sub-menus and pre-designed menus.
- Modifying menus at run-time.

Menus: Concepts

Descriptions of menu facilities are sometimes confusing because of the vague or ambiguous terminology that's used. So that we don't confuse you, we'll define some important terms now, before we go any further.

The Menu Bar, showing various Menu titles

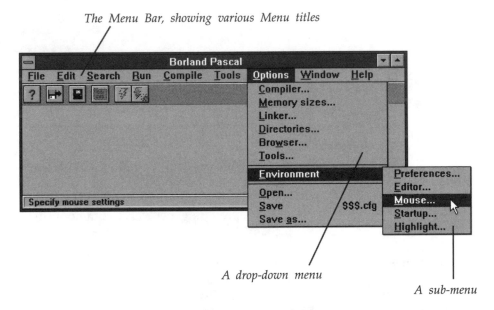

A drop-down menu

A sub-menu

Term	Meaning
Menu bar	The area immediately below the caption bar where the menu titles are displayed.
Menu title	The title of a drop-down menu such as File, Edit, and so on.
Drop-down menu	A menu displayed when you click on a menu title.
Menu item	An item in a menu, whether it be a drop-down menu, sub-menu or pop-up menu.
Sub-menu	A menu attached to a menu item, exposed as you move over the associated item.
Pop-up menu	A menu (such as a SpeedMenu) that pops up in response to some user action and which is not linked to the main menu.

Sub-menus are indicated by the presence of a special triangular marker to the extreme right of a menu item, as shown below. (They can be attached to pop-up menus too.) In practice, sub-menus are rarely used in applications because there's a feeling that they are awkward and cumbersome. If used in moderation they're OK, but some well-known applications employed five or six levels of sub-menus, which gave sub-menus a bad name.

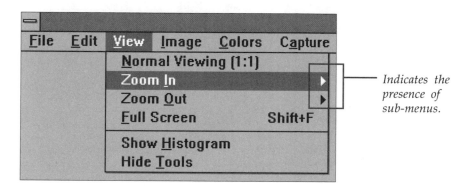

Indicates the presence of sub-menus.

Adding a Menu to Your Application

Let's find out how easy it is to add a menu to a Delphi application. Create a new project and, with the Standard page of the Component Palette selected, double-click on the MainMenu component.

As with the ColorDialog that we used in the last chapter, a MainMenu is a non-visual component (its appearance on the form at design-time bears no relation to its appearance at run-time).

Now, we need to add some items to the menu. To do this, select the MainMenu component on the form and double click on the right-hand side of the **Items** property in the Object Inspector. The **Items** property corresponds to the various menu items contained within the menu. Don't worry about the other properties at this point - we'll be explaining them later. Clicking the **Items** property will start the **Menu Designer**. Alternatively, just double-click on the menu component in the Form Window.

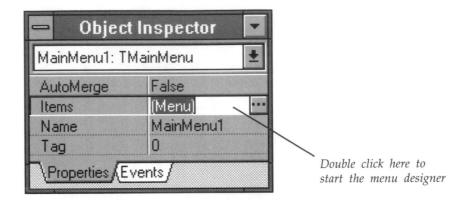

Double click here to start the menu designer

Using the Menu Designer

Having started the Menu Designer, you should see a window like the one below. This is the Menu Designer's main window.

The Menu Designer doesn't look very exciting, but is actually a very powerful facility. The rectangular box within the window is a pictorial representation of the application's menu bar - empty to start with, because we haven't added any items. The shaded box at the left-hand end of the menu bar indicates the currently selected menu item.

The Menu Designer is used in conjunction with the Object Inspector. If you take a look at the Object Inspector, you'll see that no object appears to be selected and yet it is displaying a set of properties. Very odd! What's happening is that the Object Inspector is displaying the properties that relate to the currently selected menu item or menu title; if you enter a name - such as **&File** to specify the caption File - to the **Caption** field, you should see the menu title change in the Menu Designer as soon as you've pressed *Enter*. Having done this, Delphi will be ready for you to enter the **Caption** field of the first menu item in the new File drop-down menu. You can continue building up menu items like this with very little effort.

When you want to create a second drop-down menu, just click on the dotted outline immediately to the right of the first menu title and type a new menu title into the **Caption** property of the Object Inspector. The new menu title will then appear. You can repeat this process as many times as you like to create an arbitrarily large menu structure.

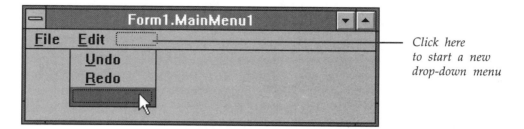

Click here to start a new drop-down menu

At any time, you can click on a menu title in the Menu Designer window and the corresponding drop-down menu will be displayed. You can then click on an item in the menu and it will be selected ready for modification in the Object Inspector.

The easiest way to add a sub-menu is to use the Menu Designer's speed-menu described later.

Menu Item Properties

The function of a menu item's **Caption** property is obvious - it corresponds to the item's displayed text, just like any other component's **Caption** property. But what about the other properties, what do they do? Let's have a look at some of the more important ones.

The Break Property

The **Break** property can take on one of three different values as outlined below. Note that the effect of these settings is not reflected in the Menu Designer itself, but can be viewed in the Form window.

 **mbNone**: This is the value used for normal menu items.

 **mbBreak**: This property value can be applied to both menu titles and menu items. When applied to a menu title, it causes the menu title to be located on a new line. Effectively, the menu bar splits into two or more lines, depending on how many menu titles have **mbBreak** set. You would not normally use this facility unless you wanted to do something very unorthodox with your menu bar!

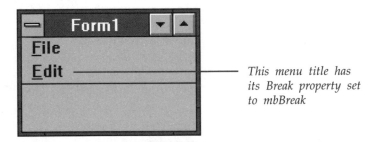

This menu title has its Break property set to mbBreak

When applied to a menu item, **mbBreak** causes that item (and all subsequent items) to begin in a new column. You'd typically use this facility to display a large number of choices under one drop-down menu, but grouped for clarity. (This type of menu was often used under Windows 2.x for making a font selection.)

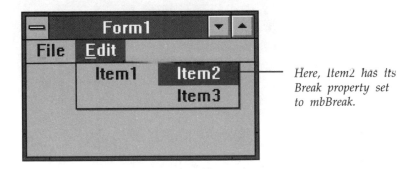

Here, Item2 has its Break property set to mbBreak.

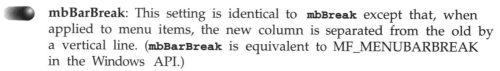

(**mbBreak** is equivalent to the **MF_MENUBREAK** specifier in the Windows API.)

mbBarBreak: This setting is identical to **mbBreak** except that, when applied to menu items, the new column is separated from the old by a vertical line. (**mbBarBreak** is equivalent to MF_MENUBARBREAK in the Windows API.)

The Caption Property

The **Caption** property has already been discussed earlier. However, it does have one useful facility which is worth noting here. If you set the **Caption** of a menu item to a single dash character (-), the item will be treated as a horizontal separator within the drop-down menu. Such items can't be highlighted, grayed or disabled. (This is equivalent to the **MF_SEPARATOR** flag in the Windows API.)

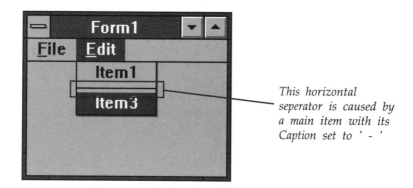

This horizontal seperator is caused by a main item with its Caption set to ' - '

The Checked and Enabled Properties

These properties both have Boolean values (they can be **True** or **False**). The **Checked** property determines whether or not a tick mark appears to the left of the item name. The **Enabled** property determines whether or not an item is usable - when disabled, a menu item takes on a dim, grayed-out appearance and can't be selected. Both properties may be used in combination. (In the Windows API, the **Checked** property corresponds to the **MF_CHECKED** flag and the **Enabled** property corresponds to the **MF_ENABLED** and **MF_GRAYED** flags.)

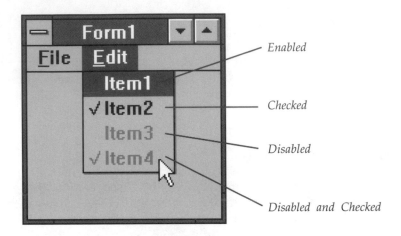

The Name Property

The **Name** property of a menu item corresponds to its variable name in your application's source code. The Menu Designer will automatically set the **Name** property of each menu item based on the **Caption** string you set up. For example, if you give an item a **Caption** of **Open...**, the item will be given a **Name** of **Open1**; if you give an item the **Caption Exit**, then it will be named **Exit1**, and so on. Of course, there's nothing to stop you from naming the item yourself if you wish to do so, but the default name used by Menu Designer will probably save you time and effort.

You might be wondering why a digit is appended to the end of an item name. This is because Delphi automatically assumes that there may be more than one occurrence of a menu item with the same **Caption** string, so that the first **Open...** item is named **Open1**, the second **Open2**, and so on.

> If you're using pop-up menus in your application, then it's likely that you'll have at least two menu items with the same name - one in the main menu and another in the pop-up menu. Remember that pop-up menus should not be used to provide a different set of options to the main menu. Rather, they should provide some of the most-used options at the place where they're most needed.

The Shortcut Property

The **Shortcut** property is used to assign a keyboard shortcut to a particular menu item. For example, many programs adopt the convention of mapping the *Ctrl-S* key combination onto the Save menu item. Unlike some development systems, Delphi makes it a simple process to set up menu shortcuts like this one: just click on the **Shortcut** property of the menu item and select the desired key combination; when your application is compiled, it will automatically recognize those keystrokes.

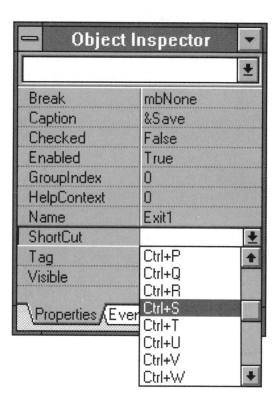

> Delphi does not check for duplicate shortcut combinations. It's your responsibility to ensure that different menu items do not have the same shortcut.

Other Menu Item Properties

Here's a quick run-through of the less frequently used menu item properties:

Property	What it Does
GroupIndex	This can be used to organize related menu items into groups. This is particularly useful when creating MDI (Multiple Document Interface) applications where you want the menu to change according to the type of document window that's currently active.
HelpContext	Used to assign a unique help context number to each menu item. When running Delphi, you can click the *F1* key any time a menu is active - help on the currently selected menu item will appear. This property lets you build the same user-friendliness into your own programs.
Hint	Assigns a 'fly-by' hint string to each item. You can arrange for these to appear in a status bar by responding to the **OnHint** event.
Tag	Can be used for any application-specific purpose. If you want, you can assign a unique number to each menu item using this property.
Visible	Can be used to make a particular menu item hidden or visible as needed. This is a lot simpler than trying to add and delete menu items at run-time.

Inserting and Deleting Menu Items

Deleting menu items is very simple. In the Menu Designer, just highlight the menu item that you want to delete and press the *Del* button or choose Cut from the Edit menu. Bear in mind that if you delete a menu title, then the entire drop-down menu will also be deleted. If you want to delete several items at once, you can use the standard *Shift-click* approach to select multiple items prior to pressing *Del*.

To insert a menu item, use the mouse to select a menu item in a drop-down menu. If you then press the *Ins* key, a new item will be inserted immediately above the selected item. You can then fill in the details of this item in the usual way. The *Ins* key can be pressed repeatedly to insert several new items at once. To insert menu titles, select a menu title on the menu bar and press the *Ins* key - a new drop-down menu and menu title will be added to the left of the current selection.

Rearranging Your Menus

The Menu Designer also supports the popular 'drag-and-drop' mechanism for simplifying the rearrangement of menu titles and menu items.

To move a menu item from one place to another in a drop-down menu, just click and hold down the left mouse button, then drag the item to its new location. The menu item will be inserted before the menu item on which it is dropped. In exactly the same way, you can rearrange menu titles (and their associated drop-down menus) on the menu bar by dragging them to an alternative position.

You can even drag menu titles onto menu items and vice versa! If you drag a menu title onto a menu item, a new menu item is formed - the drop-down menu on the original menu title, if any, becomes a sub-menu on the new item; conversely, if you drag a menu item onto a menu title, a new menu title is formed - any sub-menu is magically transformed into a drop-down menu! This symmetry just reinforces the fact that, as far as menu bars are concerned, menu titles are really just menu items and, as far as menu titles are concerned, drop-down menus are just sub-menus.

None of this is as complicated as it may sound - the whole process is very intuitive. Spend a few minutes familiarizing yourself with the Menu Designer. Try to replicate the menu layouts of some other applications and you'll soon feel comfortable with the facilities.

Menu Event Handlers

No matter how good your menu looks, it won't be much use until you've hooked it up to your application code. This is done by associating an event handler with each menu item. To create an event handler for a specific menu item, just double-click on the menu item in the Menu Designer. In usual Delphi fashion, this will transfer you to the Code Editor with the shell of the code already written and the cursor positioned ready for you to add the procedure body.

The example below shows the event handler for a **SaveAs1** menu item. Other than the **Sender** object, the event handler takes no parameters - it's entirely up to you what happens in response to a particular menu item selection.

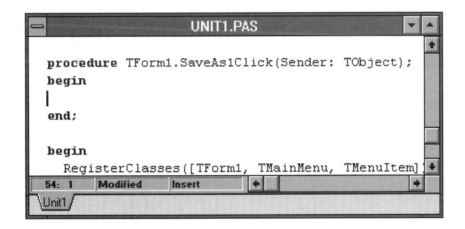

You might think that it's rather inconvenient to have to write an event handler for every single menu item. If you come from a more orthodox Windows programming background, you'll know that the traditional way to implement menu handling is to use a big switch statement, similar to the one used for message processing - the window procedure for a particular window type acts on menu selections as part of its **WM_COMMAND** message processing.

There are advantages and disadvantages to both approaches. A large switch statement for all possible menu selections means that all your menu handling code is centralized, resulting in a possibly smaller program. On the other hand, if you've got a large, complex menu structure with many menu items, it can become unwieldy.

The more modular approach of one event handler per item increases the number of event handlers that you have to fill in, but makes for more maintainable code.

Sharing Menu Item Event Handlers

Although Delphi assumes that you want a menu handler for each menu item, this approach isn't forced on you. If you want to share a common event handler among two or more menu items, you need to point several menu items at the same handler. Even if you prefer each menu item to have its own handler, sometimes you will need a menu item to share an event handler for some other reason (such as when you want to put the same logical item on a pop-up menu and a drop-down menu).

Menu items can share events using the same technique that was explained in Chapter 3 for other component events. To recap, you should first create an event handler for one menu item by double-clicking on it from the Menu Designer window; you can then select another menu item, go over to the Object Inspector's Events page and use the **ComboBox** selector to choose an existing event handler for it:

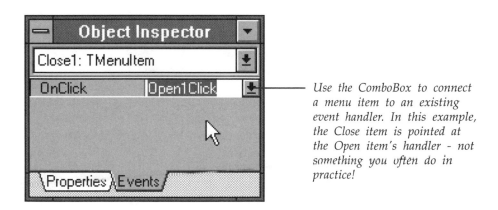

Use the ComboBox to connect a menu item to an existing event handler. In this example, the Close item is pointed at the Open item's handler - not something you often do in practice!

This raises the question of how to discriminate between different menu selections if they are all directed to the same event handler? The key to doing this is the **Sender** parameter that's passed to the event handler by Delphi. We haven't, up to this point, discussed **Sender**. It's really there to resolve situations such as this, where an event handler can be triggered for a variety of different reasons. Look at the following sample handler:

```
procedure TForm1.Open1Click(Sender: TObject);
var
    buff: array [0..127] of Char;
begin
    StrPCopy (buff, 'You chose item ' + (Sender as TMenuItem).Name);
    MessageBox (0, buff, '', mb_ok);
end;
```

This procedure uses the **StrPCopy** function from the **Strings** unit to create a null-terminated string from the menu item's **Name** property. The **as** reserved word is used to cast the **Sender** object to a **TMenuItem** (an exception will be raised at run-time if **Sender** is incompatible with **TMenuItem**). Then, the menu item name is passed on to the **MessageBox** function in the **WinProcs** unit for display on screen:

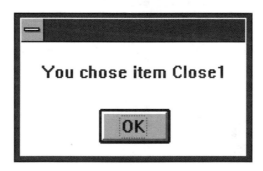

Checking menu items by name isn't particularly efficient. If you want to pursue this avenue of sharing event handlers, then a faster approach would be to directly compare the **Sender** parameter against various menu items:

```
procedure TForm1.Open1Click (Sender: TObject);
begin
    if Sender = Open1 then MessageBox (0, 'You chose Open', '', mb_ok)
    else
    if Sender = Save1 then MessageBox (0, 'You chose Save', '', mb_ok)
    else...... {etc }
end;
```

Alternatively, as previously mentioned, you could use a menu item's **Tag** property. This would allow you to reduce a shared event handler to a simple **case** statement.

The Menu Designer Speed-Menu

In addition to the facilities described above, the Menu Designer contains a number of other, powerful capabilities that are accessed through its speed-menu. To access the speed-menu, simply press the right-hand mouse button in the Menu Designer.

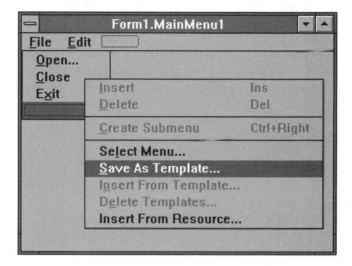

- The first two items (Insert and Delete) correspond to facilities we've already covered for editing the layout of menu items and menu titles.

- The Create Submenu option can be used to create a sub-menu beneath the currently selected menu item.

- Sometimes, you'll write a program that uses several different menus (such as an MDI application) or which displays different menus according to its mode of operation. The Select Menu... option can be used to select one of the defined menus.

- Delphi allows you to save and retrieve **menu templates** describing an entire menu layout. You do this with the Save As Template..., Insert From Template... and Delete Templates... options (see the next section for details).

The Insert From Resource... option is useful if you have menu resources that you want to import from another development system. Clicking on this option brings up a standard File Open dialog box that can be used to load Menu Files (***.MNU**) or Resource Script files (***.RC**) into Delphi. A menu resource - if found - is inserted in front of the currently selected menu item or menu title.

Menu Templates

The template facility allows you to treat entire menus or drop-down menus as reusable components. To retrieve a menu template, select the place in your existing menu where you want the template to be inserted and select Insert From Template.... For example, you might wish to add a standard Edit drop-down menu to the menu bar; the Edit menu normally follows the File menu, so you'd click the gray box to the right of the File menu title, then select the Insert From Template... option to get the dialog shown below - clicking on the name of the desired template would insert it at the current position.

Edit menus, File menus and others often have a standard layout. By exploiting menu templates, you can save yourself some time when putting together a new application menu. Even if a particular pre-designed template doesn't suit your exact requirements, you can use it as a starting point for your own work.

The Save As Template... option can be used to create your own templates by saving the *entire* current menu as a new template for incorporation into new projects. The Delete Templates... option can be used to remove any templates that you no longer want.

The Insert From Template... and Delete Template... options are grayed out on the speed-menu if no menu templates currently exist. Menu templates are held in the file **\DELPHI\BIN\DELPHI.DMT**. This isn't a text file and can't be modified outside of Delphi.

Pop-Up Menus

Up to this point, we've only looked at the **MainMenu** component of Delphi, but what about adding our own pop-up menus? Pop-up menus are implemented using the **PopupMenu** component which, like **MainMenu**, is located on the Standard page of the Component Palette.

Double-click on the PopupMenu component to add one to your form. Like MainMenu, the PopupMenu component is non-visual - its design-time appearance bears no relationship to it's run-time appearance. Double-click on the PopupMenu component on the form and you'll see the familiar Menu Designer window.

> A word of warning when adding multiple menus (of either type) to your form. When double-clicking on a menu component in the **Component Palette**, Delphi will place the new menu in the top left corner of the form. Although this has no relevance to the menu's run-time location, it's easy to think that nothing has happened after a double-click when, in fact, the new menu has been placed right on top of the existing ones! Therefore, it's a good idea to rearrange the menus on the form as you create them.

When working with a PopupMenu, the Menu Designer behaves just as it does for a MainMenu. You can add and delete menu items, move them around in the menu structure, create sub-menus and so on. Like a main menu, a pop-up menu can be as complicated as you want; however, let's emphasize once more that the real job of a pop-up menu is to provide a few, often-used options to the user at the point where they're needed.

Pop-up Menu Properties

The menu items of a pop-up menu have identical properties to their main menu counterparts, so we won't waste time describing them again. The pop-up menu itself, however, has rather different properties, as shown below.

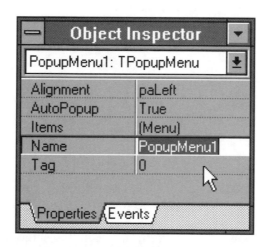

The **Alignment** and **AutoPopup** properties are especially interesting.

The **Alignment** property controls where the pop-up menu will appear in relation to the mouse pointer, assuming that the menu appeared in response to a right-hand mouse click. (It's also possible to force a pop-up menu to appear at run-time without the user having to click the mouse). The possible values for this property and their meanings are as follows:

Value	Meaning
paLeft	Places the top-left corner of the pop-up menu at the mouse location.
paCenter	Places the top-center of the pop-up menu at the mouse location.
paRight	Places the top-right corner of the pop-up menu at the mouse location.

Incidentally, you need to bear in mind that these alignment values are not cast in concrete. For example, if you set the **Alignment** property to **paLeft**, it only means that Windows will *try* to pop up the menu with its top-left corner at the mouse location. This won't be possible if the mouse cursor is near the right edge of the screen or near the bottom edge. In these cases, Windows will choose a more suitable location nearby.

The AutoPopup Property

The second important property of pop-up menus is the **AutoPopup** property. This is a Boolean value that's set to **True** by default. If you want your pop-up menu to pop up when the user clicks the right mouse button, leave it set to **True**. In itself, this isn't enough to make the pop-up menu appear. You also need to set up the **PopupMenu** property of the associated form, specifying the name of the pop-up menu that you wish to appear:

Things are done in this way because it gives your program the opportunity to select from a number of possible pop-up menus depending on the current context. For example, suppose you have a drawing program that handles circles, ellipses, bitmaps, text and other drawing objects - you might decide to provide a user interface that pops up a menu based on the currently selected object. For instance, you might have a pop-up menu that contains options applicable to an ellipse (change width, color, and so on), and a different pop-up menu that relates to a text object (change font, point size, style, and so on). By assigning the **PopupMenu** property of the form at run-time, you can decide which pop-up menu actually appears.

But here's an important point: if you're using a form that has its **PopupMenu** property set to the name of a valid pop-up menu, you won't be able to use right-hand mouse clicks for any purpose other than activating pop-up menus. To illustrate this, try setting up a form with a pop-up menu, initialize the **PopupMenu** property with the menu's name and then add the following event handler to the form:

```
procedure TForm1.FormMouseDown(Sender: TObject; Button: TMouseButton;
                   Shift: TShiftState; X, Y: Integer);
begin
    if Button = mbRight then MessageBeep ($ffff);
end;
```

This event handler causes your speaker to beep at you when it's called. However, you'll find that once you've installed this event, you can click the right mouse button as much as you like, but you won't get a beep on your machine's keyboard. Instead, you'll see the pop-up menu appear each time. At the Windows API level, the **WM_RBUTTONDOWN** message is being filtered out by Delphi and used to pop-up the menu - it never gets as far as the **OnMouseDown** handler.

This has considerable bearing on the way you implement your user interface and program code. Referring again to our imaginary drawing application, we could arrange for the object-selection code to set up the form's **PopupMenu** property: when the user selects an object in the application window with the left mouse button, the form's **PopupMenu** property would be set to the name of the appropriate pop-up menu. Try this out for yourself: add two pop-up menus to a blank form, initialize the **PopupMenu** property to point to one of them and then add the following event handler:

```
procedure TForm1.FormClick(Sender: TObject);
begin
    if Form1.PopupMenu = PopupMenu2 then
       Form1.PopupMenu := PopupMenu1
    else
       Form1.PopupMenu := PopupMenu2;
end;
```

If you now click the left mouse button on the form, you'll find that it alternates which pop-up menu is activated by the right-mouse button.

This approach isn't bad, but why settle for two mouse clicks when you only need one? Wouldn't it be nice if we could just click the right mouse button on any 'not-necessarily-selected object' and have an appropriate pop-up menu appear. To do this, we need to look at invoking pop-up menus directly from the application code.

Activating Pop-up Menus

To get the sort of effect just described, you shouldn't use the form's **PopupMenu** property - just leave it blank. This immediately gives us back the ability to handle right mouse clicks ourselves. All we need do is install an **OnMouseDown** handler that figures out which object has been clicked on and activates the corresponding menu directly. We can use the **Popup** method to do this: **Popup** takes X and Y screen coordinates as arguments and activates the menu at that location. Here's a sample **OnMouseEvent** which suits our purpose:

```
procedure TForm1.FormMouseDown(Sender: TObject; Button: TMouseButton;
  Shift: TShiftState; X, Y: Integer);
var
    left_side: Bool; { Records whether the mouse is on }
                     { the left of the window }
begin
    if Button = mbRight then
    begin
        left_side := X <= ClientWidth div 2;

        { Convert X and Y to screen coordinates }
        X := X + ClientOrigin.X;
        Y := Y + ClientOrigin.Y;

        if left_side then
           PopupMenu1.Popup (X, Y)
        else
           PopupMenu2.Popup (X, Y);
    end;
end;
```

In this particular case, the code is rather simple since we don't really have any drawing objects to click on - we've simply divided the application window into two halves. Clicking the right mouse button on the left half of the window brings up **PopupMenu1**, while clicking it on the right half of the window brings up **PopupMenu2** - in a real application, deducing which object has been clicked on would probably be a little trickier!

Whenever a pop-up menu is about to appear, Delphi generates a special **OnPopup** event. You can use this (for example) to make context-sensitive changes to a pop-up menu before it appears.

> **The above discussion only talks about adding pop-up menus to a form. However, you can also add pop-up menus to many other types of Delphi component since many components share the PopupMenu property. This can be particularly convenient in certain situations such as, for example, adding a Select All pop-up menu item to a Listbox component.**

Modifying Menus at Run-time

In most real applications, the appearance of menu items is continually changing to reflect the state of the system - to represent what can and can't be done at a particular moment. A classic example of this is the Cut, Copy and Paste facilities provided by many applications. If the Windows clipboard doesn't contain any data that's compatible with the application, then the Paste menu item should be disabled (and grayed out to indicate this). Similarly, if there is no current selection, then the Cut and Copy items should be disabled.

Luckily, Delphi makes it very easy to alter menus dynamically, as the program is running. (It's a lot simpler than using the conventional Windows SDK calls such as **CheckMenuItem** and **EnableMenuItem** - these calls require you to pass a menu handle, a menu item identifier and a flag to indicate whether you are specifying the item by position or by command number.)

Enabling Items

If you want to enable or disable a menu item, you simply assign **True** or **False** to its **Enabled** property, as follows:

```
Paste1.Enabled := False;
Cut1.Enabled := True;
```

Couldn't be much simpler, could it?

Checking Items

To check or uncheck a menu item, you use the item's **Checked** property in a similar fashion:

```
Speedbar1.Checked := True;
```

Hiding Items

Some people prefer to remove inappropriate menu items rather than graying them out. This approach should be used with some caution since your program's user may rightly start feeling insecure if menu options keep appearing and disappearing all the time!

There are at least two cases where this technique might be appropriate. Firstly, some complex applications provide a sort of 'novice' mode where advanced menu options are not available - once the user becomes familiar with the basics of the application, they can enable the full menus. Secondly, when a program has distinct modes, it can be a good idea to hide or remove an entire drop-down menu together with it's menu title (this is often applicable to MDI programs which deal with different types of documents.)

If you're removing an item or menu that you may want to put back at some later stage, then don't delete it - just make it invisible. You can hide a menu item as easily as this:

```
Item1.Visible := False;
```

Adding Items

It's often useful to be able to add one or more items to a menu. For example, you could envisage a large, sophisticated application which can come with a number of optional modules at extra cost. When the main program initializes, it could search for any optional modules and append the name of each one it found to a Tools menu.

The event handler below has been written to add items to a File menu - it's an **OnCreate** handler, so it will execute automatically when the form is loaded:

```
procedure TForm1.FormCreate(Sender: TObject);
var
    err: Integer;
    SearchRec: TSearchRec;
    Item: TMenuItem;
begin
    { Create an item for every matching file }

    err := FindFirst('C:\WINDOWS\SYSTEM\*.CPL', faAnyFile, SearchRec);
    while err = 0 do    { Give up when no more files }
    begin
        Item := TMenuItem.Create(Self);
        Item.Caption := SearchRec.Name;
        File1.Add(Item);
        err := FindNext(SearchRec);
    end;
end;
```

This procedure uses the routines **FindFirst** and **FindNext** to search the Windows system directory (**C:\WINDOWS\SYSTEM**) for any file whose name ends with **.CPL** (a Control Panel DLL). When such a file is found, a new **TMenuItem** is created, its **Caption** is initialized to the name of the file and then the **TMenuItem** is passed on to the menu title (**File1**) via its **Add** method. The **Add** method appends the menu item to the end of the menu.

Here's the result of running the code. (In a real-life application, you'd probably call your add-on modules something like ***.MOD** and make some sort of **GetName** call to each module to discover its plain English name for adding to the menu.)

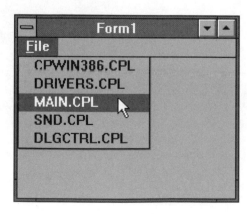

But, what if you want to insert an item *into* a menu rather than appending it to the end? To do this, you need to use the **Insert** method. This is similar to **Add**, but has an extra parameter - an integer index which specifies where the new item should be inserted (starting from 0). The following code adds the string 'Me First!' to the File menu each time the mouse is clicked in the form window. This becomes the first item in the menu, immediately below the menu title - any previous menu items are effectively pushed down. Again, remember that **File1** is the name of the menu title, not the name of the **MainMenu** component.

```
procedure TForm1.FormClick(Sender: TObject);
var
  NewItem: TMenuItem;
begin
  NewItem := TMenuItem.Create(Self);
  NewItem.Caption := 'Me First!';
  File1.Insert (0, NewItem);
end;
```

Deleting Items

To delete menu items, you can use the **Delete** method. This method takes only a single integer parameter which specifies the position of the item you wish to delete (starting from zero). For example, the following code will remove the first item from the File menu each time the user clicks on the form.

```
procedure TForm1.FormClick(Sender: TObject);
begin
  File1.Delete (0);
end;
```

> If you try to delete menu items from an already empty menu, an **EMenuError** exception will be raised. See Chapter 8 for more information on exception handling.

139

Menus: Implementation

We've now covered most of the fundamentals of menu handling in Delphi. It's time once more to roll up our sleeves and put that knowledge into practice.

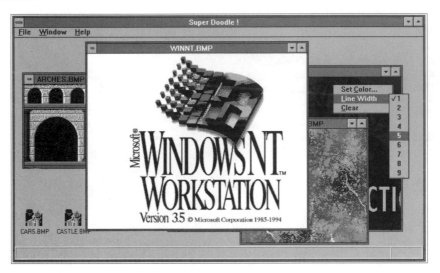

The Super Doodle Program

The sample application developed in this chapter is based on Chapter 3's Doodle application, but you'll find that there's a lot more to this one, particularly in respect of menu handling.

There are two major changes with Super Doodle. Firstly, it sports a presentable set of menus - there's a normal, application menu along the top of the screen that enables you to load and save bitmap images, and so on, there's also a pop-up menu which allows you to modify the behavior of each child window.

Secondly, Super Doodle is an MDI application. This means that you can load and work on several different bitmaps at the same time. In the screenshot shown, four different bitmaps are loaded, one of which (**CARS.BMP**) is iconised. The Window menu provides the functionality you'd expect to see in an MDI application, allowing you to Tile and Cascade the windows or arrange the iconised ones.

The aim of this tutorial is to show you not only how easy it is to incorporate menus into a real application, but also to demonstrate the ease with which you can build an MDI application (such as the Windows Program Manager itself).

Introducing the Delphi Gallery

Even with Delphi, creating an MDI application can involve quite a number of steps. In order to speed things up, we're going to get Delphi to create the 'skeleton' of the application automatically. To do that, we need to use a feature that we haven't encountered before - the Gallery.

The Gallery is essentially a collection of ready-built forms and projects. When enabled, the Gallery will invite you to choose a project type each time you select New Project from the File menu. To enable the Gallery, select the Environment Options dialog from the Options menu, click the Preferences 'tab' at the bottom of the dialog and then check the option marked Use on New Project. Click OK to end the dialog. From now on, each time you start a new project, Delphi will ask you what type of project you want to create, like this:

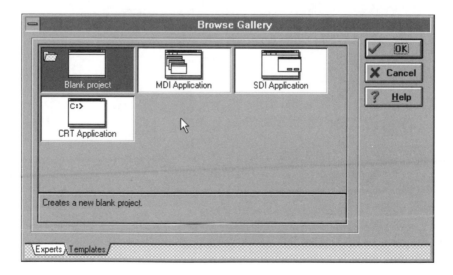

> Note that the Delphi Gallery is discussed more fully in Chapter 11.

Creating the Project

Let's begin by doing just that. Create a new project and, when prompted by the Gallery dialog, select MDI Application and click the OK button. Delphi will ask you for a directory in which to place the project. Choose a directory name and click OK again. Delphi will create the project in the directory you specified.

Even without any more work, we've now got a surprisingly developed MDI application. If you compile and run the application now, you'll see something like this:

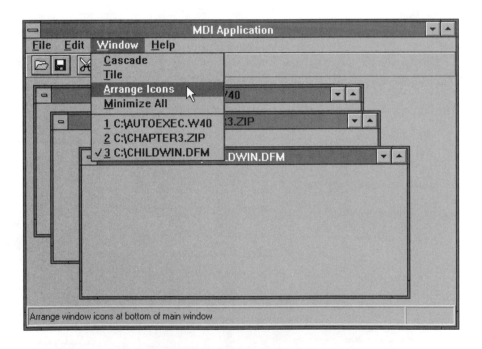

Not only have we got File, Edit, Window and Help menus and a fancy button bar, but Delphi has also given us a cute status bar which changes to reflect the current menu selection. Not bad considering that we haven't added any code so far!

> In actual fact, we could easily devote the rest of this book to an implementation of the facilities offered by this menu! For the sake of brevity, we've removed the button bar and it's associated speed buttons. The Edit menu has also been removed. Once done, you'll find that you get a few compilation errors resulting from references to non-existent components. Just keep removing the offending lines of source code until you get a clean compile.

If you click the Select form from list button on the SpeedBar, you'll notice that there are actually two different types of forms in the project - take care to work on the right one at the right time! The first, called MainForm, corresponds to the main application window or **frame window**. The second, MDIChild, corresponds to the individual document windows contained within the frame. Within one particular running instance of the program, there may be many child windows but only one frame window.

Setting up Properties

Change the Caption property of the main form to Super Doodle! or whatever else you want to call it. Then, resize the main form so that you can see the **MainMenu** and **OpenDialog** components. Select the **OpenDialog** and alter the **Filter** property so that it looks like this:

```
Bitmap Files (*.bmp) | *.bmp | All Files (*.*) | *.*
```

This string tells the **OpenDialog** to load **.BMP** (bitmap) files by default, but also allows the user to specify a different extension in traditional Windows fashion - the strings **Bitmap Files (*.bmp)** and **All Files (*.*)** will automatically be placed in the List Files of Type: combo box, while the strings ***.bmp** and ***.*** will appear in the File Name: combo box. While you have the **OpenDialog** component selected, open up the **Options** property and set the **ofHideReadOnly** sub-property to **True**. This will remove the optional Read-Only checkbox from the dialog.

Setting up the Child Window

Creating the Pop-up Menu

Let's continue by creating the child window's pop-up menu. Make sure that you have the child window selected and then add a PopupMenu component. Double-click the PopupMenu and set up the menu structure as shown in the original illustration. Set the **Checked** property of the first item of the line width sub-menu to **True**. This is because the program will default to an initial line width of 1 for each new window opened. Set the child form's **PopupMenu** property to **PopupMenu1**. If you re-run the program now, you should find that the pop-up menu works as advertised for each document window.

Adding the Image Component

Go to the **Additional** page of the Component Palette and add an **Image** control to the child form. Set the **Left** and **Top** properties of the new component to zero and stretch the **Image** component to a useful size for drawing. Alternatively, you may find it convenient to set the **Align** property of the **Image** to **alClient** - this will set the size of the **Image** to the initial client area of the child window. The important point here is that *you won't be able to grow your document bitmap at run-time so choose something now* that you'll be happy with.

> This is a serious shortcoming of the Windows API, not of Delphi. If you run the GRAPHEX demo program which comes with Delphi, you'll find that you're limited to a small drawing area which you can't resize. When you try to create a new bitmap with the **Bitmap Editor** (accessible via Delphi's **Tools** menu), you'll be prompted for the required size of the bitmap. Similarly, if you create a new bitmap with Borland's **Resource Workshop**, you'll once again be asked for the wanted bitmap size. This obsession with getting the image size now rather than later is simply because you can't easily resize a bitmap on-the-fly while preserving the original bitmap contents. It's a pain, but there you are ...

Go to the definition of the **TMDIChild** form in the **MDIChild** unit and add the following fields to the class definition - we'll be using the **FileName** field to store the current filename associated with the document.

```
public
    { Public declarations }
    Filename: String;
    fDrawing: Boolean;
  end;
```

Now modify the **TMainForm.FileNewItemClick** routine (in the **Main** unit) so that it looks like this:

```
procedure TMainForm.FileNewItemClick(Sender: TObject);
begin
    CreateMDIChild ('');
end;
```

Effectively, we're passing an empty, zero-length string to the **CreateMDIChild** routine if the window was created in response to a New menu selection. While you're at it, alter the **CreateMDIChild** routine itself so that it appears as below:

```
procedure TMainForm.CreateMDIChild(const Name: string);
var
  Child: TMDIChild;
begin
  { create a new MDI child window }
  Child := TMDIChild.Create(Application);
  Child.Color := clWindow;
  Child.FileName := Name;

  if Name = '' then
     { If new window, set up 'Untitled' caption }
     Child.Caption := 'Untitled - ' + IntToStr (MDIChildCount)
  else
  begin
     { Set caption to name of actual bitmap file }
     Child.Caption := ExtractFileName (Name);
     { And load the image }
     Child.Image1.Picture.LoadFromFile (Name);
  end;
  end;
```

With these changes, you'll find that you can now open (and display) existing bitmaps and that new document windows get sensible captions. Incidentally, we've used the handy **ExtractFromFile** function (found in the **SysUtils** unit) to extract the filename only, stripping the path information from the displayed caption.

Drawing on the Form

The drawing code is much like the original Doodle program in the last chapter. The biggest difference is that the three event handles (mouse down, mouse move and mouse up) are handlers for the **Image** component and not for the form itself. Take care to make this distinction when adding the three handlers shown below:

```
procedure TMDIChild.Image1MouseDown (Sender: TObject; Button: TMouseButton;
                         Shift: TShiftState; X, Y: Integer);
begin
    if Button = mbLeft then
    begin
        Image1.Canvas.MoveTo(X, Y);
        fDrawing := True;
    end;
end;
```

```
procedure TMDIChild.Image1MouseMove(Sender: TObject; Shift: TShiftState;
                         X, Y: Integer);
begin
    if fDrawing then Image1.Canvas.LineTo (X, Y);
end;
```

```
procedure TMDIChild.Image1MouseUp (Sender: TObject; Button: TMouseButton;
                         Shift: TShiftState; X, Y: Integer);
begin
    if Button = mbLeft then fDrawing := False;
end;
```

You should now be able to scribble all over new document windows, not to mention loading up pristine bitmap files and scribbling graffiti all over them too!

Event Handlers for the Menus

Right, finished scribbling? Let's move on. We need to implement event handlers for the various pop-up menu items. The event handler shown here allows us to set up the pen width.

```
procedure TMDIChild.N11Click(Sender: TObject);

    function MenuItem (width: Integer): TMenuItem;
    var
        CompName: String [10];
    begin
        { Build wanted component name }
        CompName := 'NX1';
        CompName [2] := Chr (width + Ord ('0'));
        MenuItem := TMenuItem (FindComponent (CompName));
    end;

begin
    { Uncheck current menu item }
    MenuItem(Image1.Canvas.Pen.Width).Checked := False;
    { Set new pen width }
    Image1.Canvas.Pen.Width := StrToInt ((Sender As TMenuItem).Caption);
    { Check current menu item }
    MenuItem(Image1.Canvas.Pen.Width).Checked := True;
end;
```

When you add this event handler to the child form, bear in mind that it's a shared event handler. Be sure to set all nine menu items in the pen width sub-menu to point to this handler.

The code assumes that it's dealing with menu items with certain, fixed names - the first item is called **N11** and the last is called **N91**. The **MenuItem** function builds the wanted menu item name and then calls the **FindComponent** routine to get a pointer to the actual item. We can then access the **Checked** property of the item in the usual way.

> Incidentally, the **FindComponent** routine is defined in the **SysUtils** unit so you'll need to add this unit name to the **Uses** clause at the top of the file.

The handler for setting the pen color is similar to the **FormKeyPress** handler in the last chapter, but this time it's responding to the selection of the **SetColor1** menu item:

```
procedure TMDIChild.SetColor1Click(Sender: TObject);
begin
    ColorDialog1.Color := Image1.Canvas.Pen.Color;
    ColorDialog1.Execute;
    Image1.Canvas.Pen.Color := ColorDialog1.Color;
end;
```

Before you try out this code, be sure to add a **ColorDialog** component to the child form! You may also wish to set the **Ctl3D** property of the dialog component to **True**.

Finally, the handler for clearing an edit form's canvas is similar to the action taken in response to a right-button click in the **FormMouseDown** handler of the last chapter - but this time it's responding to the selection of the **Clear1** menu item:

```
procedure TMDIChild.Clear1Click(Sender: TObject);
var
    Rect: TRect;
begin
    SetRect (Rect, 0, 0, ClientWidth, ClientHeight);
    Image1.Canvas.Brush.Color := Color;
    Image1.Canvas.FillRect (Rect);
end;
```

Saving Our Work

Our last job is to implement the Save and Save As... menu items so that we can save our work. Start by adding a **SaveDialog** component to the main form - make sure it's the main form, not the child form. Change the **Filter** property of the dialog to the same setting that you used for the **OpenDialog**. If it helps, you can Copy and Paste from one to the other.

The two menu item event handlers are shown here. Despite the amount of code involved, they're both very straightforward. Both event handlers use the **ActiveMDIChild** variable. This corresponds to the currently active child window. This variable is type-cast into **TMDIChild** so that we can access the application-specific fields and methods we've added to the child window.

If the window being saved is a new document, it's guaranteed to have a **FileName** field which is an empty string - that's the way we set it up when the window was created. In this case, the **FileSaveItemClick** routine will automatically call the **FileSavoAsItemClick** routine to prompt the user for a filename with which to save the bitmap. On the other hand, if we've already got a valid filename, then we just call the **CreateBackup** local routine to save the current file with an extension of **.BAK**. The bitmap is then saved with a simple call to the **SaveToFile** method.

```
procedure TMainForm.FileSaveItemClick(Sender: TObject);
var
    Child: TMDIChild;

    procedure CreateBackup(const FName: string);
    var
        BackupName: string;
    begin
        { Create backup file name }
        BackupName := ChangeFileExt(FName, '.BAK');
        { Ensure it doesn't exist }
        DeleteFile(BackupName);
        { Rename existing filename to backup name }
        RenameFile(FName, BackupName);
    end;

begin
    Child := TMDIChild (ActiveMDIChild);

    if Child.FileName = '' then FileSaveAsItemClick(Sender)
    else
    begin
        CreateBackup(Child.FileName);
        Child.Image1.Picture.SaveToFile(Child.FileName);
    end;
end;

procedure TMainForm.FileSaveAsItemClick(Sender: TObject);
var
    Child: TMDIChild;
begin
    Child := TMDIChild (ActiveMDIChild);

    { set initial filename for save dialog }
    SaveDialog1.Filename := Child.Filename;

    { Execute the dialog }
    if SaveDialog1.Execute then
    begin
        { Set up filename and caption }
        Child.FileName := SaveDialog1.Filename;
        Child.Caption := ExtractFileName(SaveDialog1.FileName);

        { Now do a regular save }
        FileSaveItemClick (Sender);
    end;
end;
```

The `FileSaveAsItemClick` routine is even simpler. It calls the `Execute` method of the `SaveDialog` to get a new filename from the user. This is then used to update the `FileName` and `Caption` fields of the child window before calling `FileSaveItemClick` to do a regular save. This is one of those relatively rare (but very useful) cases where two routines can each call the other.

Summary

In this chapter, we've explored regular application menus and pop-up menus. In both cases, we've seen how easy it is to incorporate menu processing into your application and the remarkably intuitive Menu Designer system which enables you to build useful menu structures quickly. Finally, we finished up by putting together a handy little MDI-based bitmap editing program - Super Doodle. This utility wouldn't win any prizes as a state of the art bitmap editor, but it does show the extraordinary productivity benefits that are to be had from programming with Delphi and how much work can be saved by using the Gallery facility.

Super Doodle was the first project we've encountered that had more than one form. This would therefore seem to be an appropriate time to discuss Delphi projects in more detail. That's the subject of our next chapter.

Exercises

1   Take a look at the **TEXTEDIT** sample program that Borland supply with Delphi. You'll see that it's very similar to Super Doodle. In fact, you can get much of the information on how to put together a Delphi MDI application by studying this code. See if you can figure out how to incorporate both bitmap documents and text files into the same MDI application.

2   As another exercise, how would you modify the Super Doodle program so as to prompt the user before closing a bitmap window which has been modified? Ideally, you want to display a message along the lines of File has been modified - save changes?. Where would you store a file-changed flag (remember, you need one for every open window) and what would be the simplest way of deciding whether or not this flag needs to be set?

3 How would you go about adding printer support to Super Doodle? **Hint: Again, take a look at the** TEXTEDIT **sample code.**

4 Based on your experiences with Super Doodle, do you think that displaying a pop-up menu of numbers is a good way of setting some quantity such as pen width? Can you think of a better way of doing it, using a standard Windows control?

Managing Delphi Projects

Up until now, most of the Delphi projects we've built have used only a single form. The only exception to this has been the Super Doodle program that we developed at the end of the last chapter. Although it's perfectly possible to develop a large number of genuinely useful, single-form programs, you're bound to need something more than this sooner or later. Remember, forms aren't just application windows. For example, dialog boxes are also forms - as soon as you add an About box to your program, you have more than one form!

Here are some of the topics that we'll cover in this chapter:

- What exactly is a Delphi project?
- The Project Manager.
- Managing a complex project with many forms.

The chapter ends with a demonstration of how to build an attractive About box which can be reused in other projects. In this way, you'll get a feel for how easy it is to create reusable forms.

Project Files: Concepts

So, what does a Delphi project consist of? Put simply, a project comprises all the files that are needed to build a particular Delphi application. The most important file in a project is the project file itself - it's this file which ties all the other files together, allowing Delphi to find all the various parts of a project. Other files contain form code, general facilities, and so on.

The Project File

A Delphi **project file** always has an extension of **.DPR**. For example, if you had a project called Doodle, the project file would be called **DOODLE.DPR**. Although a project file doesn't have the usual **.PAS** extension for Pascal source files, don't let this fool you - a project file is just another source file. Shown below is a listing of the project file that was used to build the Super Doodle program from the previous chapter:

```
program Sdoodle;

uses
  Forms,
  Mdiframe in 'MDIFRAME.PAS' {FrameForm},
  Mdiedit in 'MDIEDIT.PAS' {EditForm};

{$R *.RES}

begin
  Application.CreateForm(TFrameForm, FrameForm);
  Application.CreateForm(TEditForm, EditForm);
  Application.Run;
end.
```

As you can see, the project file starts off with the keyword **program**, which sets it apart as the main module of the application. There then follows a **uses** clause which lists the various units required by the project file itself.

The **Forms** unit is required by all Delphi programs, so the reference to it is always present. However, the next two entries in the **uses** clause require more explanation - they are not references to ordinary Pascal units but to

form units. In the **uses** clause of a program, a reference to a form unit looks somewhat different to the normal unit references that you will be used to seeing. Each reference to a form unit is made up of three parts:

1   The name of the form unit

2   The name of the source file in which that unit can be found

3   The name of the form variable defined in the unit.

So, in the second reference above, the project file is indicating that the form unit named **MDIFrame** will be needed by the application that it's located in the file **MDIFRAME.PAS** and that it contains a form variable called **FrameForm**.

> Note that although **FrameForm** is defined in the **MDIFrame** unit, it's actually created ('instantiated' in object-oriented terms) in the initialization part of the project file.

You should be able to relate this discussion to the code below, which is extracted from the **MDIFRAME.PAS** source file:

```
unit Mdiframe;

interface

uses
  SysUtils, WinTypes, WinProcs, Messages, Classes, Graphics, Controls,
  Forms, Dialogs, Menus, MDIEdit;

type
  TFrameForm = class(TForm)
    MainMenu1: TMainMenu;
    ...

var
  FrameForm: TFrameForm;

implementation

{$R *.DFM}

end.
```

The last part of a project file invokes the **Run** method of the **Application** object - an instance of **TApplication** which has been created automatically by the inclusion of the **Forms** unit.

Form Files

We've already discussed how form units are referenced by the project file, but what about **form files** - those with the extension **.DFM**. Where do they come into the picture? A form file is a binary file which contains information on all the properties you've set up for a particular form. It also includes information on each of the components you've placed on the form **and** the property settings for each of those components. For example, if you've added a **MainMenu** or a **PopupMenu** to a form, the text of all the menu items is stored in the form file too, along with all the properties for each of those menu items.

> Notice we said that a form file is a binary file - it's not a text file that you can just load into an editor like a project file. It uses a special format that's understood only by Delphi. Each time you make a change to a form, the corresponding form file is updated when you next save the project.

Actually, it **is** possible to open Delphi form files and edit them directly as if they were text. To do this, select Open File... from the File menu, choose Form file from the file type filter in the bottom, left corner and you can then load a form file directly. Delphi will translate the form file into human-readable form, 'on the fly' as the form is loaded into the Code Editor.

You might be wondering where form files are mentioned in the project file. Well, Delphi assumes that a form file will exist with the same base name as the corresponding source file. So, for example, if you save a form unit in a file called **MYFORM.PAS**, Delphi will also look for **MYFORM.DFM** when loading the project.

> Every form unit has exactly one associated form file and vice versa - they only ever exist in pairs! However, regular units - **Forms**, **SysUtils** and so on - have no corresponding form file.

Other Files

In addition to project files, form units and form files, you can refer to other file types such as **.RES** (compiled resource files) and **.OBJ** (object files created with another development system such as a C++ compiler or an assembler). However, these files are referenced indirectly through compiler directives which you add to your project's source code. For example, if you want to load the resources in **WOMBAT.RES**, it's up to you to add the appropriate **$R** compiler directive; if you want to include the fast assembler routines from **FASTCODE.OBJ** into a particular unit, you must put an appropriate **$L** directive in the source code for that unit.

> **These compiler directives have not changed from previous versions of Borland Pascal.**

The diagram below shows the most common types of file contained within a Dephi project, and how they all relate to the project file itself.

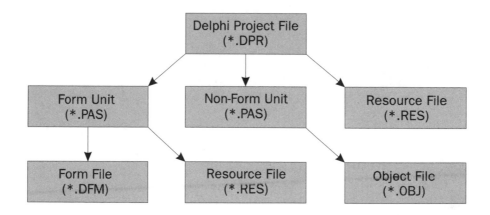

RES files can be referenced from the Project file, or from any form or non-form unit. OBJ files are used when you want a Delphi project to include code written in another language such as C or Pascal.

Delphi will also allow you to specify the help and icon files associated with your project, as we shall see when we come to the section entitled *Project Options*.

The Delphi Project Manager

Delphi comes with a powerful tool to help you manage your application files: the **Project Manager**. To start the Project Manager, select Project Manager from the View menu. You should then see a window something like the one below:

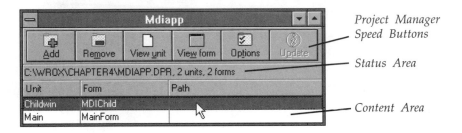

The project that you can see open here is the Super Doodle application from the previous chapter, complete with its two form definitions and their associated form units. The list at the bottom of the Project Manager window shows all the project's form units and the names of the forms defined therein. Also, any regular (non-form) units that you've explicitly added to the project using the Project Manager will show up here too.

The row of SpeedButtons along the top of the Project Manager can be used to perform a number of useful project-management functions. From left to right, the function of each of these buttons is given below:

Add a unit to a project. If it's a form unit, then the form is also added.

Remove the selected unit (and form if it's a form unit) from the project.

View the highlighted unit in the Code Editor window. Double-clicking on a unit name in the Project Manager window has the same effect.

- View the highlighted form. Again, double-clicking on a form name will cause that form to be displayed.

- Invoke the Project Options dialog.

- Update the Project file.

> **Note that when you remove a unit or form, the files are not actually deleted from your disk - all reference to them is merely deleted from the project.**

Yet another way of managing your project is to use the Project Manager **SpeedMenu**. Press the right-hand mouse button anywhere in the Project Manager and you'll see the **SpeedMenu** below:

```
Save Project
Save As Template...

New Unit
New Form
Add File...              Ins
Remove File              Del

View Unit                Enter
View Form                Shift+Enter
View Project Source

Options...
Update
```

The Save Project, New Unit, New Form, Add File..., Remove File, View Unit and View Form items are self-explanatory or have already been discussed. The others are outlined below:

- The Save As Template... option allows you to save the current project as a template. This means that you can easily use the project (including all the forms and code which it contains) as a 'starting point' for new projects. For more information on templates, see the section *Using Templates* in Chapter 11.

159

● The View Project Source item invokes the Code Editor but, rather than loading a unit into the editor, it loads the actual project (.DPR) file. This is useful on those occasions when you want to edit the project file yourself, although it's best to let Delphi do this for you if at all possible.

● The Options... item invokes the Project Options dialog box (see below).

● Finally, the Update item is used to save any changes that you have made to the project (.DPR) file. This option will be grayed out unless you have made modifications to the project file itself.

The Project Options Dialog

We've referred to the Project Options dialog several times so far, so now is a good time to investigate it. There are a number of ways of invoking this dialog:

● Select Project... from the Options menu.

● Click the Options **SpeedButton** in the Project Manager.

● Select the Options... item from the Project Manager's **SpeedMenu**.

Whichever route you choose, here's the dialog that you'll see.

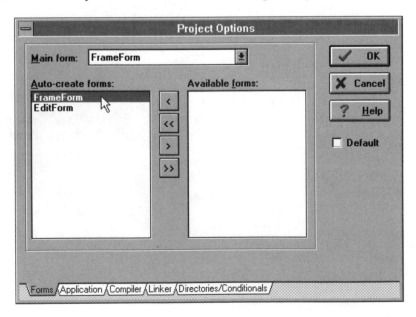

The Project Options dialog can be used to control all aspects of a project, as we'll see in the following sections. A series of tabs along the bottom of the dialog allow you to view and edit related sets of options on each dialog page. We'll work through each page in the order that they appear.

Form Options

The Forms page of the Options dialog is used to tell Delphi which of the forms in your project is the main form. It's also used to determine which forms will automatically be created when your program starts running and in what order they'll be created.

The Main form combo box contains a list of all forms used by your project. You can use it to set up the name of the project's main form - this is the form that users will first see when they start up the program. The main form is always created first and becomes the first form in the Auto-create forms list box.

> **If your application contains only a single form, then you won't need to specify it as the main form - this will happen automatically. If you create an MDI application, you won't need to set up the frame form as the main form, providing that you create the main form before creating the child document form.**

The Auto-create forms list box contains a list of all forms that you want to be created when your application starts. For example, Delphi itself automatically creates the main application window, the Object Inspector, an initial form window and a Code Editor window when the development environment is started. You can drag and drop forms between this listbox and the Available forms listbox or you can use the 'move' buttons provided. To select multiple forms, hold down the *Shift* key while clicking individual items.

Within the Auto-create forms list box, you can drag individual forms around to change their creation order - this can sometimes be important when one form relies on the existence of another. The double arrow buttons move **all** forms from one list box to another while the single arrow buttons move only the selected form(s).

Application Options

Various application options are grouped onto the next page of the Project Options dialog:

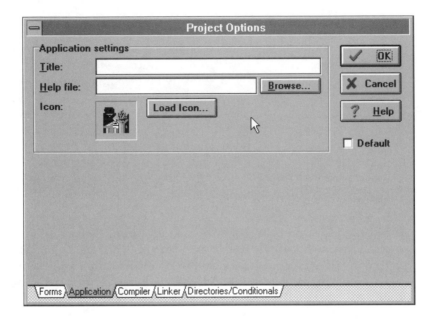

The Title edit box is used to enter a program title up to 255 characters in length. This program title is what appears under an application's icon when the application is minimized.

The Help file edit box is used to associate a Windows Help file (.HLP) with your application. Whenever your program requests help, this is the name of the file which will automatically be used. You can click the Browse... button to determine the path to the help file.

The Icon box displays the name of the currently selected icon. This is the icon which will appear on the Windows desktop when your program is minimized. If you don't choose an icon, then Delphi will use the default application icon shown above. To change this, click the Load Icon... button and select a new icon file (.ICO) by browsing around on your disk.

Compiler Options

If you're familiar with Borland Pascal, or indeed, any Windows compiler, then you should recognize many of the options on this page. The options are divided by category into Debugging, Code Generation, and so on. We'll briefly discuss each of these categories in turn, pointing out those that are particularly important as well as the ones that you can ignore most of the time.

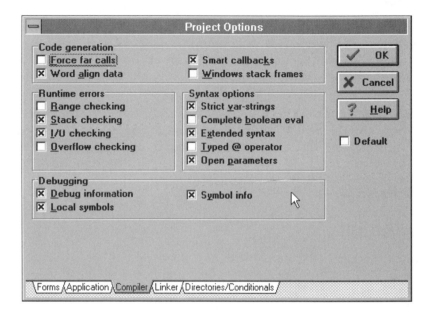

Code Generation

In most cases, you should leave these options set to their default values.

Only the routines exported by the **interface** part of a Pascal unit are 'far' by default - this improves the efficiency of the code that's produced. If you need a non-interface routine to be far, then it's better to use the **far** keyword rather than checking the Force far calls check-box which would affect **all** non-interface routines. A good example is the **ExitProc** facility - an **ExitProc** routine **must** be far so that it can be called from outside the unit.

Runtime Errors

Again, you can leave these options set to their default values most of the time. If you need as much help as possible from the run-time system while debugging a program, then turn all the Runtime errors options on. Turning all options off before shipping your debugged application will minimize the size of the executable (**.EXE**) file.

Debugging

By default, Delphi creates executable files (and **DLL**s) which contain full debugging information. This is appropriate during the development of an application, but you should be sure to turn all these options off before building the release version of your software. Doing so will drastically reduce the size of the executable file.

> **You should also bear in mind that if you leave debugging information turned on, you're giving the unscrupulous and the curious a big head-start when it comes to disassembling your software. You have been warned!**

Syntax Options

It's unlikely that you'll need to modify these project options - they affect the syntax of Pascal that's accepted by the compiler. You might wish to change these options if you're using a lot of Pascal source code from an older development system.

The Default Check-Box

Looking back at the screenshot, you should see a small check-box marked Default beneath the Help button. Contrary to what you might think, this checkbox doesn't reset all the dialog box options to their original default values. Rather, **clicking this box turns the current** Compiler **settings into the new default**. In other words, all new projects you create will automatically inherit this particular set of project options. 'Save as Default' might have been a better label for this check-box!

> This also applies to the **Default** check-box when it appears on other **Project Options** pages.

Linker Options

Turning now to the Linker page of the Project Options dialog, you'll be relieved to see that it's a great deal simpler:

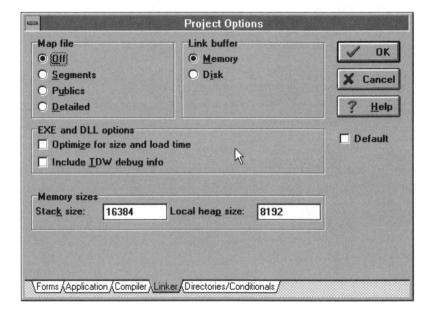

As before, we'll look at each group of options in turn.

Map File

This option determines whether or not the linker produces a map file (for debugging purposes) when an application is linked together. By default, it does not.

If you do want to produce a map file, the best setting to use is Publics, since this will produce a map file which is recognized by industry-standard tools such as MAPSYM. Nowadays, you won't often need a map file since development systems such as Delphi can embed the debugging information directly into the executable file itself (see below).

Here's what the start of a typical map file looks like:

```
Start           Length  Name                Class

0001:0002       0061H   Project1            CODE
0001:0063       0100H   Unit1               CODE
0001:0163       0922H   Printers            CODE
0001:0A85       0005H   Dates               CODE
0001:0A8A       0564H   TypInfo             CODE
0001:0FEE       0967H   Strings             CODE
0001:1955       0075H   WinProcs            CODE
0002:0002       59F1H   Graphics            CODE
0003:0002       1F2CH   Menus               CODE
0004:0002       5A6AH   Controls            CODE
0005:0002       532DH   Forms               CODE
0006:0002       47E5H   Classes             CODE
0007:0002       0974H   Excepts             CODE
0007:0976       1163H   System              CODE
0008:0000       0942H   DATA                DATA
```

This map file shows the names of all the Pascal units that have been included in the executable file. With this information (and the more detailed information that follows it) it's possible to narrow down bugs to specific routines. This can be preferable to a bug report from a user complaining about a '`GPF at offset $0C86 in segment 4`'!

Link Buffer

This option determines how the linker uses memory when building the executable file. By default, the linker uses RAM where possible. This means that your program will be linked much more quickly but, for very large programs, there's a danger that you could run out of memory during the linking process. If this happens, then change this option to Disk - it will take longer to create the executable file, but much more space will be available to the linker.

EXE and DLL Options

Turn on the Include TDW Debug Info option if you want to embed debugging information in your program's executable file. (After debugging a program, a quick way of stripping out debugging information is to use the **TDSTRIP**

utility that's provided as part of the Delphi package.)   You must select this
option when using Turbo Debugger for Windows.

The Optimize for Size and Load Time option compresses the executable file
and arranges the code segments in such a way as to minimise loading time
when an application is executed. You'll probably want to enable this option
when creating the shipping version of your application.

Memory Sizes

The two final options on the Linker page are concerned with the amount of
memory available to your application for the stack and the heap. You may
wish to increase these if your application does a lot of recursion or builds
large dynamic data structures, respectively.

Directories/Conditionals

As its name suggests, the Directories/Conditionals page is concerned with
directory information and conditional compilation. Here's what it looks like:

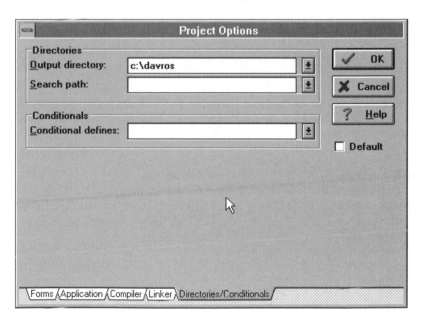

Directories

The Output directory: box tells Delphi where to place compiled units (.**DCU** files) and the final executable file - if you don't specify an output directory, then Delphi will put these items in the same directory as the project file.

The Search path: box contains the path names of the directories which Delphi will examine when searching for units - adjacent path names being separated by semi-colons. For example, you might set the Search path to **C:\MYUNITS;D:\EXTRA\WINCODE**. Delphi searches the directories in the order given, stopping when a matching unit is found. Delphi also looks in the current directory (the place where your project file is located) and in the **\DELPHI\LIB** directory.

Conditionals

The Conditional defines: box is used to define one or more compilation symbols. For example, you might have a customer who wants some non-standard features in their version of your software. You can achieve this - while maintaining only one copy of the source code - by using conditional compilation, like this:

```
{$IFDEF ExtraBits }
       ---- additional code goes here ----
{$ENDIF }
```

To enable this extra code, all you need to do is define the **ExtraBits** symbol by including it in the Conditonal defines: box. Multiple symbols can be defined by separating them with semi-colons.

> Note that if you're writing code that you want to be portable between the 16-bit and 32-bit versions of Windows, you can use the **$IFDEF** statement to check if the **WIN32** symbol is defined. If so, Delphi is building a 32-bit application, otherwise it's building 16-bit code.

Dialog Boxes: Implementation

Take a look at the slightly tongue-in-cheek dialog box in the picture above - looks nice doesn't it? After a thorough discussion of Delphi projects, a rather dry topic, you're probably thinking that a little liquid refreshment would go down very well!

We're going to round off this chapter by creating a simple, but attractive, dialog box that you can incorporate in any of your future projects. Along the way, we'll show you how to make the dialog box completely reusable and how you'd go about adding it to another project. This is one of the most exciting things about Delphi - forms can be just as reusable as components!

Creating the Application

To start with, create a new project and rename the default form as **Main**. Add a **MainMenu** to the default form and double-click on it to bring up the Menu Designer. Add the following menu items:

If you think this menu looks familiar, you'd be right - we've used Delphi's own Help menu as a model. When designing the user interface of your application, always take a look at other programs to see how they do the job. We're not suggesting that your applications should be a mish-mash of other people's interfaces. Rather, if you see a good idea, don't be afraid to copy it - especially if it's something that Windows users are already familiar with.

> In days of old, the About... menu item was often the last item on the first drop-down menu. Nowadays, the 'standard' place to put it is at the end of the Help menu. This rule is almost never broken (the Microsoft Clock application is an exception but, since it doesn't have a Help menu anyway, we can probably turn a blind eye to it!).

That's almost it as far as the application is concerned - it isn't going to do anything other than invoke the dialog box when the appropriate menu item is selected.

Save the project as **ABOUTBOX.DPR**, calling the form unit **MAINFRM.PAS** (you could, of course, pick your own names if you prefer - it makes no difference to how the application runs!).

Adding the About Box

Now, click the New form button on the **SpeedBar** to create the About box form:

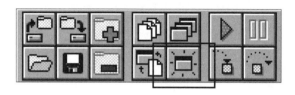

Change the **BorderStyle** property of the form to **bsDialog** (so that it looks like any other dialog), and change the **Position** property to **poScreenCenter** (so that it's centered on the screen). Next, name the form **About** and save the project again, putting the new form unit in **ABOUTFRM.PAS**.

Add an OK button to the dialog, name it as OK and set up an **OnClick** event handler for it, as shown below (this will cause the dialog to disappear when the OK button is clicked):

```
procedure TAbout.OKClick(Sender: TObject);
begin
    Close;
end;
```

Now, go back to the main application's form and add the following event handler for the About... menu item (you'll need to add **AboutFrm** to the **uses** clause, so that **About** is available):

```
procedure TMain.About1Click(Sender: TObject);
begin
    About.Show;
end;
```

If you run the program now, selecting the About... option will bring up the dialog box as advertised.

171

You may find that Delphi has mysteriously made the **About...** box into the main form. If this happens, just invoke the **Project Options** dialog as described earlier, select the **Forms** page and alter the **Main** form setting.

Decorating Your Dialog

Of course, at this point, the dialog box looks pretty uninteresting. Now is the time to go to town on our **About...** box and come up with something that will knock the users' socks off! We chose to hunt around on our hard disk for a nice-looking graphics file and came up with the wine and cheese picture that you saw earlier. You might wish to generate a picture yourself using your favorite editor, or you might already have some graphic that's suited to your application, or you might even have a company logo that you want to use.

Whichever option you choose, to add a graphic to the dialog box, go over to the Additional page of the Component Palette and double-click on the **Image** component:

Size the image component as required on the dialog box and then double-click on its **Picture** property in the Object Inspector - this will bring up the Picture Editor. By clicking on the Load... button of the Picture Editor, you can select which picture you want the image control to display - bitmaps (***.BMP**), icons (***.ICO**) and Windows metafiles (***.WMF**) are all supported:

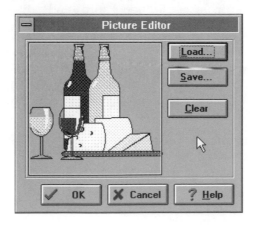

Note that if your chosen image is available in a number of different formats, then go for metafiles. They can easily be scaled and will continue to look good at different sizes. On top of that, they take up a lot less room in your program's executable file than the corresponding bitmap would. On the negative side, complex metafiles take a little longer to draw than bitmaps.

After adding a picture to your About box, you can modify the **Caption** of the box itself so that the title bar reflects the product name, as in our screenshot above. You can also add label components for the product name, a serial number and licensee information to the main part of the box. By varying the font size used for the labels - a large font for the product name and a smaller font for licensing information - you should easily be able to achieve a striking effect.

Reusability

If you went ahead and did as we said in the last section, you just prevented your About box being reusable! By adding specific product name information to the About box, you tied it to a particular product. Worse, inserting the serial number and user strings ties it to a single user! This is obviously not the way to go.

Dynamic Captions

A powerful possibility with components which have a **Caption** property is to use them simply as place holders for text which will be added at run-time, the **Caption** property being set up before the form is made visible.

Note that this is a far better technique than using Windows API calls, such as **DrawText** or **TextOut**, to write directly onto the form. To begin with, the contents of the form will be redrawn automatically and secondly, you don't have to use hit-and-miss techniques to determine what x and y coordinates to pass to **DrawText** and **TextOut**.

To try this out, rename the various labels in your About box as follows:

Old Name	New
ProdName	This label's **Caption** will hold the application's product name.
Licensee	The application's user.
SerialNum	The application's serial number.

Having done that, you'll need to alter the captions of the three labels: give each one an initial **Caption** which reflects its purpose (so that we can easily identify it on the form at design time). product name, licensee and serial number would seem to be good choices!

Adding a Method

The question then becomes: how do we pass the product name and other information from the main program to the **AboutFrm** unit? The obvious way to do this is via a new interface routine. Remember, however, that the whole purpose of a form unit is to encapsulate the functionality of the form object and make its methods and properties available to the host program - after all, this **is** object-oriented programming! We really need to add an extra **method** to the form object. To do this, add a **SetDetails** method to the **TAbout** class definition, as below:

```
type
  TAbout = class(TForm)
    Button1: TButton;
    Image1: TImage;
    Label1: TLabel;
    ProdName: TLabel;
    Licensee: TLabel;
    SerialNum: TLabel;
    procedure SetDetails(const PName, User, Serial: String);
    procedure Button1Click(Sender: TObject);
  private
    { Private declarations }
  public
    { Public declarations }
  end;
```

This method takes three string parameters: the name of the product, the name of the licensed user and the serial number, respectively. Now, add the actual code for **SetDetails** to the **implementation** part of the unit:

```
procedure TAbout.SetDetails(const PName, User, Serial: String);
begin
    Caption := 'About '  + PName;
    ProdName.Caption := PName;
    Licensee.Caption := 'Licensee: ' + User;
    SerialNum.Caption := 'Serial Number: ' + Serial;
end;
```

> Notice that we've used the **const** keyword for the three string parameters. Whenever you write a procedure or function that takes string parameters, it's a good idea to use the **const** keyword unless you know that the routine is going to modify the strings (in which case you should declare them as **var** parameters). The **const** keyword is a relatively recent addition to Borland Pascal. In this case, it produces faster, more efficient code because the **TAbout.SetDetails** routine doesn't have to allocate internal copies of the passed strings.

With the new method set up, all we need to do is modify the main form's unit to pass on the local information for this application. Here are the new parts of our unit for the Wine Master product:

```
const
  ProdName = 'Wine Master';
  Licensee = 'Dave Jewell';
  SerialNum = '563-26632-GDX';

procedure TMain.About1Click(Sender: TObject);
begin
    About.SetDetails(ProdName, Licensee, SerialNum);
    About.Show;
end;
```

> In a commercial application, of course, we wouldn't hard-code the user name and serial number as constants. A real-world program would probably obtain this information by loading string resources from the executable file, the assumption being that the license information and serial number are set up by the install program when the user installs the software.

Reusable Forms

Having created our reusable form, all that remains is to verify that it really is reusable. To do this, create yourself a new project and then use the Project Manager window to add the **ABOUTFRM** unit to the project. You'll see that Delphi automatically adds the associated form as well. You'll have to add the **AboutFrm** unit name to the **uses** clause of **Form1** (the default form unit):

```
unit Unit1;

interface

uses
  SysUtils, WinTypes, WinProcs, Messages, Classes, Graphics, Controls,
  Forms, Dialogs, AboutFrm;
```

Finally, try invoking your reusable About box by adding the following **OnClick** event handler to **Form1**:

```
procedure TForm1.FormClick(Sender: TObject);
begin
    About.SetDetails('Tom', 'Dick', 'Harry');
    About.Show;
end;
```

If you now run the program and click on the form, you should see something like this (except that you're using a different picture, of course):

So remember, just as we've been using reusable components every time we create a form, Delphi will also allow us to reuse entire forms. It's not even necessary for the reusable form unit and form file to be located in the same directory as the current project. Here's the project file that we ended up with:

```
program Project1;

uses
  Forms,
  Unit1 in 'UNIT1.PAS' {Form1},
  Aboutfrm in 'C:\WROX\CH5\ABOUTFRM.PAS' {About};

{$R *.RES}

begin
  Application.CreateForm(TForm1, Form1);
  Application.CreateForm(TAbout, About);
  Application.Run;
end.
```

As you can see, the reference to the **ABOUTFRM.PAS** unit (and, by implication, its form file) is now an absolute pathname. This means that you can locate reusable forms anywhere you want on disk. Delphi allows you to build up a library of proprietary forms which you can just drop in to new applications or sell as a form library to other developers. And, unlike the simple dialog box that we've developed here, a reusable form can be as large and complex as you like - in fact it can even reuse and invoke other forms itself!

> You may have noticed that the Delphi **Form Gallery** already includes a pre-built **About** box and you may prefer to use this one for your application. We've been through this exercise to demonstrate how easy it is to create your own reusable forms and create custom methods for interfacing with the main program. Certainly, if you create your own reusable **About** box, you'll have something that's far more flexible than what's in the **Gallery**. For more details on the **Gallery**, see Chapter 11.

Summary

In this chapter, we've covered the essentials of Delphi project management, looking at what tools are available to help you keep track of complex, multi-form projects. We've also spent some time looking at all the available project options and finished off by developing a simple but attractive dialog box which illustrates how you can turn any form into a general, reusable software component.

Of course, even when programming in Delphi, things do sometimes go wrong and when that happens you need to be familiar with the debugging facilities that are available in your development system. That is the subject of the next chapter.

Exercises

1   There's one aspect of our reusable dialog that isn't very reusable: the picture itself. How would you go about modifying the **SetDetails** method to take an extra parameter specifying the picture?

Hint: one way would be to pass the name of a bitmap, metafile or icon file but this means that you'd have to store the picture separately from the executable file. A better technique would be to load the resource in the main program and then pass a reference to the picture, perhaps as a **TPicture** parameter to **ShowAbout**.

2   Another shortcoming of our dialog box concerns the caption strings used: all the text is in English and might need to be changed when running the program in non-English-speaking countries. Think of how you'd overcome this problem.

Hint: you could set all **Caption** properties to empty strings and pass all the necessary information to the **SetDetails** method; this would be unwieldy because of the large number of parameters involved. Can you think of a simpler solution?

3 How about using a little animation to blow your users' minds? Imagine a few little bubbles streaming up in the wine glass in our example, and maybe bouncing up a little above the surface of the wine. To do a trick like this, you need to use a **Timer** component, something that we haven't dealt with yet. Read up on **Timer**s, work through the graphical drawing code in Chapter 7 and you should then have a good idea of where to start.

Hint: by placing a couple of invisible label components at the top and bottom of the wine glass, you'll easily be able to calculate the necessary x and y coordinate values for the bubbles.

Debugging Your Applications

We're sure you appreciate by now that Delphi is a productive and easy-to-use development system. Its powerful features, however, would be useless if they weren't backed up by quality debugging facilities. Delphi provides two completely separate approaches to debugging and, in addition, has an excellent object browsing tool for navigating object hierarchies.

In this chapter, we'll be covering the debugging and browsing facilities offered by Delphi. Along the way, we'll learn about:

- What bugs are and why they occur.
- The different species of bug.
- The two Delphi debuggers.
- How to prepare your application for debugging.
- The Integrated Debugger in detail.
- The Object Browser.

Bugs, and Why They Occur

The story goes that the first ever bug was caused by a moth that got into the innards of an old valve computer. The unfortunate insect managed to position itself in such a way that its body provided a convenient current path for the high-voltage electricity used by valve-based apparatus. That was the end of the story as far as the moth was concerned, but the start of a headache for the computer's users, who found that their pride and joy had begun to malfunction. Eventually, the cause of the problem was identified and the charred remains of the moth were removed. Henceforth, all computer problems were referred to as 'bugs'.

Strictly speaking, that first bug wasn't really a bug at all - the moth had actually caused a hardware malfunction. Today, when we use the word bug, we're usually talking about a software problem - an error in an application's code. The truth is, software faults are a lot more common than hardware faults - try not to blame the hardware when your application doesn't work!

Cause and Effect

When talking about bugs, it's important to distinguish between the real **cause** of the problem and the apparent **effect**.

For example, the first release of the Windows 3.1 calculator had a notorious bug: if you type in a number such as 12.01 and then subtract 12, you might be surprised to find that the result appears to be 0.00, rather than 0.01! If you then add 12 to this (apparently) zero result, the missing 0.01 magically reappears!

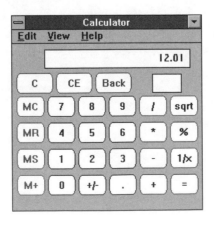

What's happening is this: the calculator is performing the floating point calculation **correctly**, but the routine responsible for **displaying** the result on the screen is broken. In this particular case, the bug isn't even in the source code for the calculator! It's actually in Microsoft's run-time library, with which the calculator was linked. (For your edification, the error is in the **ecvt** routine and has been fixed in later releases.)

This separation between cause and effect makes debugging tools even more important - they make it much easier to follow a detective trail from effect to cause.

Species of Bug

Like real-life bugs, software bugs come in all shapes and sizes! So that you're better prepared for Delphi development, we'll alert you to some of the more common ones now - they are listed below and described individually in the following sections:

- Range errors.
- I/O errors.
- Math errors.
- Running out of memory.
- Passing nonsense values to API calls.
- Overwriting buffers.
- Uninitialized variables.
- Run-time library errors.
- Windows API errors.

Range Errors

Object Pascal has particularly good support for range checking. As explained in the previous chapter, you can toggle range checking from the Compiler page of the Project Options dialog. With the option turned on, the compiler can generate code to perform range checking each time you do the following:

- Index into a string variable.
- Index into an array.
- Assign to a scalar type.

For example, suppose that you define a string variable like this:

```
var
    MyBuff: String[20];
```

With this declaration, **MyBuff** will actually occupy 21 bytes of storage: the first byte - **MyBuff[0]** - stores the current length of the string, while the remaining twenty bytes - **MyBuff[1]** through **MyBuff[20]** - store the consecutive characters. If you use an index which is less than zero, or greater than 20, you're accessing memory that doesn't belong to the string. With range checking on, the code will generate a range-check exception. (See Chapter 8).

The same applies to scalar types (such as integers, sub-ranges and enumerations). Here's a short program that illustrates the idea:

```
application DoNothing;

var
    scalar: 0..9;
    i: Integer;

begin
    scalar := 0;
    scalar := 9;
    scalar := i;
end.
```

You might expect that, with range-checking on, the compiler would generate range checking code for each of the three assignment statements above. In fact, it only does so for the last assignment. This illustrates the difference between **compile-time range checking** and **run-time range checking**. When the program is compiled, the value on the right-hand side of the assignment is examined - if it is a constant, the compiler can immediately determine whether the assignment is in range, generating a **compile-time error** if necessary. If the right-hand side uses a variable, however, the compiler has no easy way of knowing whether the value will be in range, so it must generate code to perform range-checking **at run-time**. Compile-time range checking cannot be disabled - it takes place irrespective of the range-checking option. Conversely, it is *your* responsibility to ensure that no out-of-range assignments take place at run time - the range-checking option is purely a development aid.

So, you should have range checking on while developing an application, but, once you've finished testing and debugging, you should turn it off before delivery to customers - for applications which perform extensive array subscripting (engineering applications which use matrices are a good example) the speed and size improvement can be very significant.

> **Languages such as C and C++ have no built-in support for range checking. When developing applications using these languages, you can buy tools from third parties to do some of the range-checking for you.**

I/O Errors

With the I/O error-checking option turned on, the Object Pascal run-time system will keep track of the success or failure of each I/O operation. If an error occurs, the application will generate an I/O exception. Without I/O error-checking, your application will be blissfully unaware that a particular I/O operation has failed unless you check for it yourself.

What exactly do we mean by an I/O operation? Not as much as you might think! Back in the days before Turbo Pascal became available for Windows, file operations were done with the built-in routines **Assign**, **Reset**, **Rewrite**, **BlockRead**, **BlockWrite** and **Close**. Object Pascal applications can use the same built-in routines and I/O error-checking works just the same as it did under DOS. However, under Windows, you can also use API routines (such as **_lopen**) for file I/O and, in this case, I/O error-checking is **not** performed. Let's illustrate this with a simple example:

```
var
    f: File;

begin
    Assign (f, 'MYFILE.DAT');
    Reset (f, 100);
    {---- etc ----}
```

This code fragment attempts to open a file called **MYFILE.DAT**. With I/O error-checking enabled, the application will terminate on the **Reset** statement if the file doesn't exist and a run-time error message will be displayed. Therefore, any code that follows the **Reset** statement can safely assume that the file is open. Now let's look at the situation when we use a Windows API routine instead:

```
var
    fd: Integer;

begin
    fd := _lopen ('MYFILE.DAT', 0);
    {---- etc ----}
```

The routine **_lopen** neither knows nor cares about the Object Pascal I/O error-checking. So, whether you turn I/O error-checking on or off, it is **your** responsibility to check Windows API calls (in this case, if **fd** is set to **-1**, the file doesn't exist).

> Note that Object Pascal's built-in file I/O routines will also set the value of the **IOResult** variable - a global variable defined in the **System** unit - which is used to determine the error code of the last I/O operation. **IOResult** is completely unaffected by Windows API calls.

Below is a table of the affected routines:

Built-in Object Pascal Routine	Equivalent Windows API Routine
Assign	no equivalent
Routine	_lopen, OpenFile
Rewrite	_lcreat, OpenFile
Close	_lclose
Seek	_llseek
Read, BlockRead	_lread, _hread
Write, BlockWrite	_lwrite, _hwrite

> Contrary to what Borland's on-line documentation might tell
> you, it's perfectly possible to use the `_hread` and `_hwrite`
> routines inside an Object Pascal application. They do *not* use
> C calling conventions, so they *can* be called just like any other
> Windows API routine. In fact, `_hread` and `_hwrite` are far
> more important to Object Pascal/Delphi developers than to C/
> C++ developers since Object Pascal has no concept of a huge
> pointer. We've reported this documentation error to Borland
> and it will hopefully be fixed in the final release of Delphi.

Math Errors

The classic way of generating a math error is to divide some number by
zero! That said, math errors can also result from underflows, overflows,
invalid opcodes and so on. Delphi provides an exception-handling
mechanism for math errors which is discussed fully in Chapter 8.

Out of Memory Errors

If you use the Windows API routines such as `GlobalAlloc` and
`GlobalFree`, or Delphi's `GetMem` and `FreeMem`, you really ought to check
whether the result is zero - indicating that the requested amount of memory
isn't available. OK, let's be honest here, we don't always do this ourselves -
if you look through this book, you'll probably find several examples! But, if
you're developing a complex application that makes extensive use of
memory, then you really ought to take memory management seriously.
Fortunately, Delphi's exception handling facilities make it very much easier
to write clean code that behaves in a sensible way whether or not you got
the memory you requested (see Chapter 8).

Passing Nonsense Values to API Routines

With the introduction of Windows 3.1, Microsoft added a special 'parameter
validation layer' to the core Windows system. This means that the majority
of API routines validate parameters passed from the calling application. If
any invalid parameters are detected, then the offending application is
terminated with a General Protection Fault (GPF).

There will certainly be times when you misunderstand or overlook some aspect of the Microsoft documentation and you accidentally pass a nonsense parameter to a Windows routine. Equally, this sort of scenario can result from one of the other types of problem mentioned earlier. You might, for example, use an invalid subscript to index an array of window handles, so that the array element you retrieve is actually a garbage value; passing this bogus element to an API routine will result in a GPF.

Passing a nonsense value to an API call is often the effect of a bug rather than a cause.

Overwriting Buffers

In a complex application, there are many opportunities for buffers to be overwritten with too much data. For example, you might copy the contents of an edit box representing a long pathname into a character buffer which is too small. If you use sensible sizes for your buffers, then you're unlikely to have problems, but nobody's perfect! Buffer overwriting can be difficult to spot, because the damage is often done a long time before the bug manifests itself.

Uninitialized Variables

Sometimes, you'll forget to initialize a variable to a usable value. Whereas, for example, the C/C++ run-time system guarantees to initialize all global variables to zero, no such guarantee is given for variables in Object Pascal.

Forgetting to initialize a variable (either global or local) can cause buffer overwriting, passing junk values to Windows API calls and pretty well all the effects mentioned above.

Run-time Library Errors

We've already mentioned one example of a run-time library error in the Windows calculator. If you're unlucky enough to encounter a bug in Delphi's run-time library, or in one of the supplied components, then you should report the problem to Borland so that it can be fixed in the next release. Borland have been good enough to supply the source code to the Visual Components Library so that, if you find a bug there, you should be able to fix it and recompile the affected component.

Windows API Errors

Though probably rarer than errors in the run-time library, it would be a brave developer who claimed that there are no bugs lurking in the Windows API. If you do find an error, or disagreement with the documentation, you should report it to Microsoft.

The Delphi Debuggers

Delphi comes with two different debuggers. Firstly, there's the **Integrated Debugger** which forms part of the Delphi development environment itself - the Integrated Debugger is the main focus of this chapter. Secondly, there's **Turbo Debugger for Windows** - or **TDW** for short - a tool which existed before Delphi and is available for use with, for example, Borland C++ for Windows.

It might seem strange to have two different debuggers, but in fact they each have their strengths and weaknesses and they each have a distinct role to play in the debugging process. The Integrated Debugger is a **soft-mode** debugger, whereas TDW is a **hard-mode** debugger, terms which are explained below.

Soft-Mode Debugging with the Integrated Debugger

When you're using the Integrated Debugger, you'll find that Delphi continues to work just like any other Windows application. For instance, you can launch a different application altogether, or temporarily minimize the application window to continue with some other work, or maybe use *Alt-Tab* to switch over to another active application. This is the essence of soft-mode debugging - during a debugging session, all other applications continue to execute alongside the application being debugged.

Hard-Mode Debugging with Turbo Debugger for Windows

Most of the time, there's no problem with soft-mode debugging since you're not interested in any of the other applications out there. However, there will be times when you need to freeze the Windows system so that, while the application being debugged is stopped, everything else stops too. This is called hard-mode debugging.

As an example of where you might need hard-mode debugging, suppose you're writing an application which uses DDE (Dynamic Data Exchange) to communicate with another application - installation programs do this all the time when communicating with the Program Manager, using special DDE commands to tell the Program Manager to add new application groups, add items to the groups, and so on. DDE is built on top of the Windows message system - it uses messages to pass information from one application to another. The DDE system uses time-outs to ensure that, for instance, if the application on one side of a DDE link crashes or is terminated, the application on the other end of the link doesn't hang, waiting for a response that never comes.

Now, imagine that you're trying to debug an installation program that communicates with the Program Manager. If you were to use the integrated Delphi debugger, the installation program would not be running for long periods of time while you stepped through the DDE code. While this was going on, the Program Manager would eventually assume that your application had crashed because of the time-outs, so it would abandon the DDE link. However, by using hard-mode debugging, the Program Manager, and every other executing application, goes into a 'suspended animation' - no time-out occurs and the DDE link is preserved.

In general, if you're debugging an application that needs to communicate in real time with another program, or which grabs some system resource for any length of time, then it's best to use TDW. When running TDW, you'll notice that the mouse cursor is confined to the TDW window - you can't move it out of the window and click on another application. Think of this as TDW giving you a gentle hint that you're debugging in hard mode!

We've chosen not to discuss TDW further for two reasons: firstly, we anticipate that most of the time, you'll be using the Integrated Debugger - you shouldn't need to use TDW except in specialized cases. Secondly, to be completely pragmatic, we couldn't figure out a way of including screenshots from TDW in this book - that's another reflection of the low level at which TDW operates!

Preparing Your Application for Debugging

Before you can debug your application with Delphi's special facilities, you need to turn on debugging information. This was covered in detail in the last chapter but, briefly, you need to open the Project Options dialog, select the Compiler page and ensure that all the debugging checkboxes are checked as shown below:

If you are going to use TDW, you also need to switch over to the Linker page of the Project Options dialog and check Include TDW debug info (you don't need to do this if you'll only be using the Integrated Debugger):

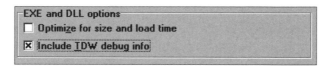

Selectively Generating Debugging Information

There may be times when you want to turn on debugging information for certain units, but not for others. This saves you having to rebuild your entire project each time you turn debugging information on or off. In order to do this, you can use Delphi's compiler directives which control the generation of debugging information:

Option	What it Does
`{$D}`	This option turns the generation of general debugging information on (`{$D+}`) or off (`{$D-}`). General debugging information enables the debugger to relate machine code instructions to lines of source code in your application.
`{$L}`	This option turns on the generation of local symbol information on (`{$L+}`) or off (`{$L-}`). Local symbol information enables the debugger to view and modify local variables within a procedure or function.
`{$Y}`	This option turns the generation of symbol reference information on (`{$Y+}`) or off (`{$Y-}`). Symbol reference information is used by Delphi's Object Browser, described later.

Having made the necessary changes to the Project Options, you can rebuild your project and start the debugging process.

Debugging: Implementation

In this section, we'll look at the facilities of the Integrated Debugger in detail: how to halt execution, how to continue execution, how to examine the values of variables, and so on.

Stopping Execution

When you start a debugging session, you need to decide where you want to start debugging from. It may be that your bug occurs almost as soon as your application starts. However, you should resist the temptation to try stepping all the way through from the very beginning until you get to the bug. Often, apart from wasting a lot of time, this approach just won't work. because Delphi uses an event-based, object-oriented approach, you can't just step through routines until you get to the location of your bug.

Setting a Breakpoint

Instead of stepping through your application from the beginning, you can set a **breakpoint** in your source code so that execution stops near where you suspect the bug is. A breakpoint is a bit like a trip wire - as soon as your application reaches the breakpoint, it will stop running and return control to the Integrated Debugger so that you can resume your investigations.

Using the Code Editor window, locate the place in your source code where you wish to start debugging and double-click the mouse on the left-hand side of the source where you want execution to stop (you need to click the mouse well over to the left-hand side of the window, but inside the window's size border). If you got it right, you'll see a red bar appear that crosses the selected source line. To the left of the red bar is a small stop sign, indicating that you've set a breakpoint:

```
DUALLIST.PAS
  var
    I, LastPicked: Integer;
  begin
    with SrcList do
    begin
      I := 0;
      while I < Items.Count do
      begin
        if Selected[I] and (not InDestList(Items[I])) then
        begin
          LastPicked := I;
          DstList.Items.Add(Items[I]);
          {comment out to Copy items instead of Move}
          Items.Delete(I);
        end
```

```
87: 1    Modified    Insert
Sdimain  DualList  About
```

> An alternative way of setting a breakpoint is to press the *F5* key when the text cursor is at the desired source code line.

Now run your application and perform whatever actions are necessary to get to your breakpoint. For example, if your breakpoint is in a menu item handler, select the appropriate menu item; if your breakpoint is in the **OnClick** event handler of a particular button, click on that button, and so on.

When your application hits a breakpoint, Delphi will switch over to the Code Editor window and place you at the breakpoint location. You'll see the mouse cursor change to a 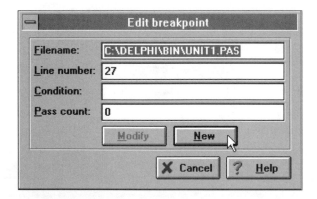 icon whenever it's over the application being debugged.

> **Remarkably, it's even possible to set up breakpoints *after* you've started the application running! Just switch to Delphi in the usual (Windows) manner and set up a breakpoint. This will take immediate effect, and when you return to your application, everything will stop if the new breakpoint is encountered.**

Using the Breakpoint Editor

You already know two ways of setting a breakpoint - using double-clicking or the *F5* key. A third approach is to select the Add Breakpoint... option from the Run menu. This will invoke the Edit breakpoint dialog shown here:

You can press the New key immediately to add a breakpoint at the current source line, or, alternatively, you can modify the Filename and Line number fields to set a breakpoint at a different location. The Condition and Pass count fields are described later.

Using Run to Cursor

Instead of setting a breakpoint, you can use the Code Editor SpeedMenu to halt execution at a certain point in your code. Just click on a source line to select it, and then right-click on the mouse to bring up the SpeedMenu. If you then select the Run to Cursor option, the application will automatically execute and stop on the selected source line (if you've modified the application since it was last executed, Delphi will recompile it first):

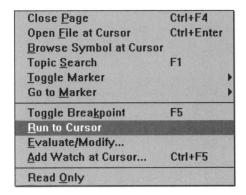

The big difference between this approach and setting a breakpoint is that breakpoints are 'sticky' in the sense that next time you run the application, the breakpoints will still be there. If you don't want a particular breakpoint, you must remove it - you can do this by double-clicking to the left of the source line again, or by pressing the *F5* key while the text cursor is within the line. On the other hand, the Run to Cursor option is strictly a one off - if you want to run to the same source line, you must make the SpeedMenu selection again.

Continuing Execution

Once you've stopped execution at a specific point, you're ready to track down your bug. You can use the Run, Step into and Step over buttons on the SpeedBar to control subsequent execution:

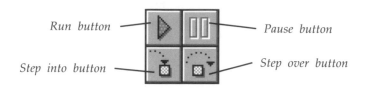

Run button — ▷ | ▯▯ — *Pause button*

Step into button — | *Step over button*

You'll notice that as you press the Step over or Step into buttons, a blue bar moves down the source code of your application. This bar indicates the current execution point - the next source statement that's about to be executed. In addition to its blue color, the bar also has a black arrow marker on its right side. You can see the execution point in the diagram below - it's over the call to the _llseek routine:

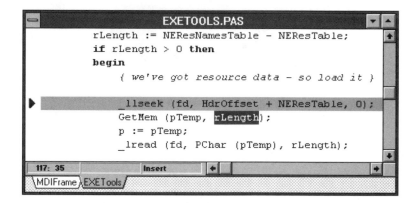

When the execution point is positioned over a routine call, you can step into the routine body by pressing the Step into button - this will take the execution point to the first source statement of the routine. Alternatively, if you press the Step over button, the execution point will move to the next statement in normal execution order - which may be in a different source file if, for example, the current statement is at the end of a routine.

> **On any particular debugging session, you will typically step over trusted routines and step into suspect ones.**

Note that if you press the Step into button and the called routine is not in a module for which debugging information is available, the execution point will step **over** the routine instead - the call isn't actually being bypassed, it's merely that Delphi isn't showing what's going on inside the call because it doesn't know! For example, in the screenshot above, the **_llseek** routine is actually part of the Windows API and, consequently, pressing the Step into button will simply step to the next line in the current source file.

> **If you want to step into a routine in Delphi's own run-time library, you will have to recompile the library with full debugging information. You will have to do this yourself because, by default, the library is compiled without debugging information (so as to reduce application size and link time).**

If the execution point is a statement that doesn't happen to involve any sort of routine call, the Step into and Step over buttons will both have the same effect - they will advance the execution point to the next statement.

At any time, you can press the Run button to resume normal execution of your application (subject to further breakpoints).

Managing Multiple Breakpoints

Delphi's Integrated Debugger will allow you to set up many different breakpoints within the same debugging session. This can be very useful if, for example, you are aware of more than one problem area inside your application, or if you've stepped into a large routine and now want to skip quickly to a point half way through it.

When debugging an application with a lot of breakpoints, it's easy to lose track of where your breakpoints are. However, if you select Breakpoints from the View menu, you'll see the useful Breakpoint list window shown here:

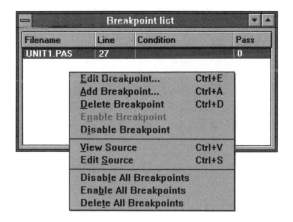

197

It should come as no surprise to learn that the Breakpoint list has its very own SpeedMenu (which is shown alongside it in the illustration above). The Edit Breakpoint... option allows you to edit the currently selected breakpoint via the dialog box shown previously, while Add Breakpoint... uses the same dialog to set up a new breakpoint. Delete Breakpoint deletes the currently selected breakpoint, while the next two items allow breakpoints to be enabled and disabled on a case-by-case basis - this is useful when you wish to ignore a particular breakpoint that you might need later in the debugging process. (A disabled breakpoint appears in gray in the source code, rather than red.) The View Source and Edit Source options take you back to the Code Editor with the cursor positioned on the source code line corresponding to the selected breakpoint.

The remaining options allow you to disable or enable all breakpoints, or to remove all breakpoints in a single operation.

Setting Up Conditional Breakpoints

From the above discussion, you'll gather that Delphi provides many facilities for interrupting and resuming the execution of your code. However, this isn't enough by itself. Suppose you have an application which routinely crashes on the hundredth iteration through a particular loop. Do you really want to have to step through that loop 100 times before finding out why the code isn't working? Of course not. It's for this reason that the Integrated Debugger includes the concept of a **conditional** breakpoint.

The Breakpoint Editor, which we introduced above, contains two fields which we didn't explain earlier: Condition and Pass Count. These are used as follows. Suppose you want a particular breakpoint to be passed 100 times before it actually halts execution. You can do this by setting the Pass Count field to 100. Each time the application gets to this breakpoint, the Pass Count is decreased by 1, and when it reaches zero, the breakpoint is activated. If you leave the Pass Count field set to its default value, the breakpoint is triggered immediately execution reaches that point.

The Condition field is even more powerful - it allows you to establish particular conditions which will be tested each time the breakpoint is reached. If the condition isn't true, the breakpoint isn't activated. For example, if you type the expression memLeft < 1000 into the Condition field, the breakpoint will only be activated if the `memLeft` variable happens to be less than 1000 when the breakpoint is reached. You can type any Boolean expression into the Condition field, but, any variables referred to must be in scope at the breakpoint location and you can't include any function calls.

> You can combine the **Condition** and **Pass Count** fields for even more powerful conditional breakpoints. If you set up a **Condition**, then the **Pass Count** will *only* be decremented if the **Condition** is true. For example, setting **Pass Count** to 50 and **Condition** to `Retries > 10` will trigger the breakpoint only when `Retries` has exceeded the specified value fifty times.

Setting up Watches

Watches are another excellent facility built into the Integrated Debugger. With a watch (no, nothing to do with telling the time!) you can set up a small window which continually displays the value of one or more application variables.

The Watch Properties Dialog

The simplest way of setting up a watch is to double-click on the name of the variable in the Code Editor window. This will highlight the variable name and you can then bring up the Code Editor SpeedMenu to select Add Watch at Cursor. Alternatively, select Add Watch... from the Run menu. Either way, you'll be presented with the Watch Properties dialog box below:

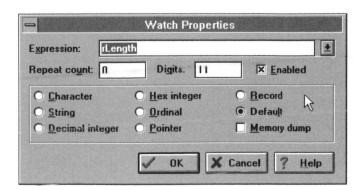

Normally, Delphi displays the variable in a format that matches the data type of the expression. However, this isn't always what you want - for example, you might want to display an integer as a hexadecimal expression. You can use the various radio buttons to select the wanted display format. The Digits field is specific to the floating-point display format - it specifies the number of significant digits to display.

A nice touch is the Repeat count field. If you set this to a non-zero value, you'll see a number of variables, starting with the first one indicated by the Expression field. Suppose, for example, that the variable **aPtrs** is an array of pointers. If you type aPtrs into the Expression field and select the Pointer radio-button, you'll see the first pointer in the array. However, if you type 5 into the Repeat count field, you'll see the first five pointers, and so on. This is extremely useful for array handling.

When you want to view the contents of an entire record in detail, just enter the name of the record variable and click the Record button. The record view shows the name of each field of the record alongside its corresponding value.

The Memory dump check box allows you to view memory as a series of consecutive bytes - the other formatting options affect the way in which the memory is displayed.

Finally, you can enable or disable a particular watch by checking or unchecking the Enabled checkbox.

As its name implies, the Expression field doesn't have to hold the name of a variable, it can hold an arbitrary expression (subject to scope rules) - 10*size, for instance, or if you have a variable called **pRec** which is a pointer to a record, pRec^.

The Watch List

Any watches that you establish will appear in the Watch List window, as shown on the next page:

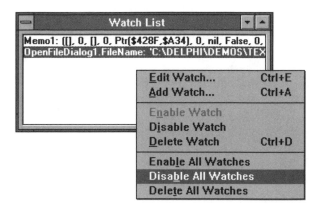

Of course, a particular watch won't always be valid - you may, for example, have set a watch on a local variable which is, therefore, only available while execution is suspended inside the associated routine. When a variable is out of scope, the message **Unknown Identifier** will be displayed alongside it in the **Watch List**.

Also, bear in mind that strange things will happen if you use variable names that are the same as built-in Object Pascal operators. For example, if you're watching a variable called **Ofs**, everything will be fine as long as you're in the routine where **Ofs** is defined. However, as soon as you exit this routine, the display in the watch window will start complaining that it's expecting a left parenthesis: "(" **expected**. If you think about it, this is perfectly reasonable. When the **Ofs** variable goes out of scope, the debugger will assume that **Ofs** is the built-in offset operator and expect you to supply a variable as a parameter to it. (This doesn't mean, by the way, that you can specify function calls as watch expressions - built-in operators such as **Ofs**, **Seg** and **Addr** aren't really functions at all.)

The Watch List also contains its own SpeedMenu - but I bet you were expecting that! The SpeedMenu is very straightforward, being similar to the Breakpoint Editor SpeedMenu: it allows you to add, delete and edit watches. You can also selectively enable and disable them, or enable/disable them all in one go.

> Incidentally, an even faster way of deleting an existing watch is to select it in the **Watch List** and then hit the *Del* key - Delphi will request confirmation before deleting the watch. Another short-cut is to double-click on a watch in the **Watch List** to bring up the **Watch Properties** dialog for it.

Using Command-Line Parameters

Although most Windows applications ignore command-line parameters, it's possible that you will occasionally want to write an application that does use them. The command line is a straightforward, and often-overlooked, mechanism for passing information from one application to another. As an example, the Windows Task Manager actually checks for a couple of numbers on its command line and, if present, they are used to set the initial location of the Task Manager on the screen. Similarly, the Windows Control Panel uses command line parameters when communicating with the currently configured screen saver.

An application can retrieve its command-line parameters with the **ParamStr** and **ParamCount** (from the **System** unit). If you prefer, you can use the **CmdLine** variable instead (**CmdLine** is also defined in the **System** unit), but this is less convenient since all the parameters are concatenated as one long string which you have to break apart yourself.

To set command-line parameters for an application which you're debugging, just pull down the Run menu and select the Parameters... option. The following dialog box will appear for you to fill in (remember that **ParamStr** requires you to separate distinct parameters with *Space* or *Tab* characters):

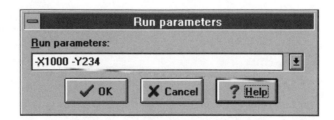

This is relevant to debugging for two reasons: firstly, you may sometimes need to write a program which - like the Task Manager described above - expects to receive extra information by way of its command line. Setting up command line parameters allows you to pass command line information to the program being debugged, just as if it were being called from the 'host' application.

Secondly, this is a useful debugging technique. By passing the appropriate command line parameter (for example, -DEBUG), you can tell your application to go into a special mode whereby it generates verbose fault-finding information. By enabling debugging code from the command line, you have the possibility of providing better telephone support to your customers when they encounter a problem.

Pausing and Restarting Your Application

Sometimes (particularly when you don't have appropriate breakpoints or watches set) it's useful to be able to halt an application temporarily, rather like pressing the pause button on your video: the application isn't terminated, it's simply frozen. You can do this by selecting Program Pause from the Run menu.

While an application is paused, the mouse cursor will change to a stop icon while it's over any application window. You can examine the application's global variables to get some clue as to the nature of a particular bug. Pressing the Run button on the SpeedBar (or hitting the *F9* key) will restart your application from where it left off.

> **In general, a paused application will not stop anywhere inside your source code. It actually stops within the internal message-handling code in the VCL library. What this means is that you can't examine the local variables of any particular function, but you do have access to the application's global variables, and you can even change them if you wish.**

There will be times when you want to discard the current debugging session and go back to square one. To do this, you can select Program Reset (again, from the Run menu). This option will release any memory allocated by the application, close any files that it may have opened and put Delphi in a state where it's ready to start debugging the application again. All of your watches and breakpoints will be retained, ready for having another crack at tracking down those pernicious bugs.

A few words of warning though: the **Program Reset** option will not deallocate any system resources (icons, brushes, bitmaps, and so on) that the application has grabbed, so, if you repeatedly use **Program Reset**, you'll eventually exhaust the system resources and Windows itself will grind to a halt. Consequently, you should try to terminate the application in the normal way if you can. This isn't a bug in Delphi - it's a reflection of the way 16-bit Windows works. System resources must be explicitly released by the owning application - if you pull the plug on the application, those resources won't be magically deallocated for you!

Using the Call Stack

As the name suggests, the Call stack window is used for viewing the Call stack - a list of routines in the order in which they have been called. If you want to know where a particular routine was called, and why, the best way to do this is via the Call stack. To make the Call stack visible, just select Call Stack from the View menu.

You'll see a list of routines in the Call stack, with the current (most recently called) routine at the top of the window. In the example below, the **LoadResources** procedure is the currently executing procedure - it has been called from the **EXEFileOpen** routine which, in turn, was called by the **TFrameForm.OpenChild** method:

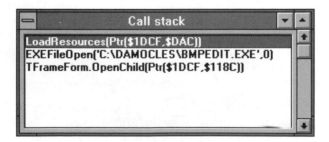

A nice touch here is the display of parameters - as you can see, each routine is listed alongside the parameters that were passed to it when it was invoked.

Even the Call stack has its own little SpeedMenu - clicking the right mouse button brings up a pop-up menu that will take you to the source code of the selected routine. An even faster way of doing this is to double-click on the routine item itself. For example, here's what the Code Editor looks like after double-clicking on the **EXEFileOpen** item:

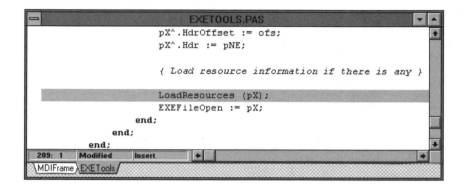

As you can see, the call to **LoadResources** is highlighted, indicating that it is from here that **LoadResources** was called within the current Call stack. Bear in mind that a particular routine may potentially be called from several points in the 'caller', so it's important to highlight the exact location from where the call took place.

> The Call stack is very useful in those situations where you accidentally step into a complex procedure that you'd intended to step over. In the above example, let's say that you've inadvertently entered the **LoadResources** code. By using the Call stack to bring up the source code of the *caller*, it's easy to select the next statement and then use Run To **C**ursor.

Evaluating and Modifying Application Variables

Setting a watch on a variable allows you to keep track of its value, but doesn't allow you to modify it. To do that, you need to use the Evaluate/Modify dialog box. You can access this from the Code Editor's SpeedMenu while the debugger is running, or from the E**v**aluate/Modify... item on the **R**un menu. You'll see something like this:

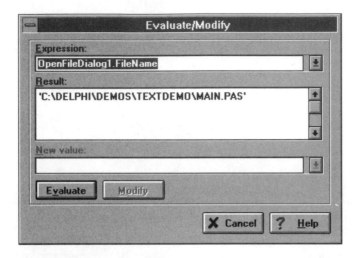

You can type the name of a variable, structure field or array element into the Expression field. Pressing the Evaluate button will display the current value of that variable in the Result box. You can then type in a new value and press the Modify button to change the value of the variable. As with the Watch Editor, you can type any valid Object Pascal expression into the Expression field, but you won't always be able to modify it (for example, it wouldn't be sensible to be able to modify the value of the expression x/3.4!).

You need to exercise some caution when using the Evaluate/Modify dialog. If, say, you accidentally set array subscripts or pointers to some invalid value, you can end up crashing your application. But, handled with care, the Evaluate/Modify dialog is invaluable - it can be used to test out your ideas about possible bugs, without going to the trouble, say, of adding code to print diagnostics and then recompiling.

The Object Browser

The Object Browser can be used to browse through the items used by your application in a convenient, graphical fashion. It's badly named really - it can be used to get information on almost **anything** that a Delphi application can refer to (directly or indirectly). So, you can browse global routines, units, objects, methods, and so on - it should really be called the *Thing* Browser! It's very useful for invoking a new page in the Code Editor, making it easy to track things down quickly. Here's what it looks like:

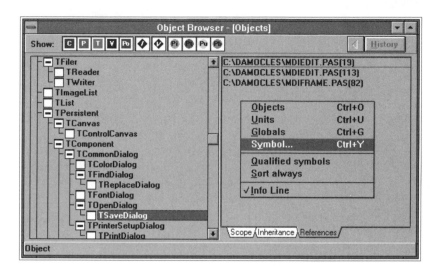

Using the Object Browser is one of those things that, like swimming or driving a car, would take a very long time to explain in detail, but is easy to understand when you're actually doing it. Take the time to play with the Object Browser - as you become more familiar with it, you'll find that it's a great way to explore the rich library of items available to a Delphi application. It's also an invaluable tool when familiarizing yourself with a Delphi project developed by somebody else.

To enable the Object Browser, you need to compile your application with Debug information, Local symbols and Symbol info all selected in the Compiler page of the Project Options dialog (otherwise, the Browser item will be grayed-out on the View menu).

The Object Browser comprises three distinct parts. On the left is the Inspector pane, on the right is the Details pane and along the top of the window is the Filter Options SpeedBar. By positioning the cursor between the Inspector pane and the Details pane, you can vary their relative width.

The Details Pane and the Inspector Pane

By default, the Object Browser shows the object hierarchy (from **TObject** downwards) in the Inspector pane. As you select different objects, the contents of the Details pane change to provide more information on the selected object. To get even more information on a particular object, you can double-click the object in the Inspector pane and the browser will move down a level in the hierarchy, shifting the previous contents of the Details pane to the Inspector pane and showing another level of detail in the Details pane.

The Inspector pane and the Details pane also have a shared SpeedMenu which can be used to select the category of information to be displayed in the Inspector pane - you can choose from objects (the default), units (Pascal source code), symbols (essentially, any Pascal identifier!) and globals (globally-visible routines, variables, types, and so on).

At any time, to step back to the previous display, just click the Rewind button in the top right corner of the Browser window (the left-pointing arrow in the screenshot below). If you want to review the items you've recently browsed, you can click the History button and a list of recent destinations will be displayed. Double-clicking on one of them will return you to the corresponding browser view (this is analogous to the History button used by the Windows Help engine):

Rewind button   Show Browser History

The Details pane contains a tab control, which can be used to select different pages of information for the item selected in the Inspector pane, labeled Scope, Inheritance and References:

- The Scope page can be used to list all symbols declared in a unit, object, or global (as currently selected in the Inspector pane).

- The Inheritance page displays a collapsible inheritance tree (as shown in the screenshot earlier). You can collapse branches of the tree by clicking on the - signs in the Inspector pane, or, you can expand branches by clicking on the + signs.

- The References page shows in which files a particular symbol, unit, object or global is referenced. This is done by displaying a list of filenames and line numbers. If you double-click on one of the listed locations, the Code Editor will be opened at that location (if the associated source code has been compiled with full debugging information).

Whether a particular page in the Details pane is meaningful depends on the context since, for example, units don't inherit from anything!

Using the Browser Filters

Using the small filter buttons above the Inspector pane, you have finer control over the information displayed, filtering out whatever you're not interested in. These buttons look a little cryptic, but fortunately, you'll find that each filter button has an associated fly-by hint. Experiment with the filter buttons and the SpeedMenu until you feel familiar with the various facilities.

Summary

In this chapter, we've reviewed the different types of bug you're likely to encounter when developing Delphi applications.

We then described Delphi's Integrated Debugger. Many of the techniques that we showed you apply equally well to TDW (Turbo Debugger for Windows), but the Integrated Debugger should be sufficient for your needs most of the time. Accordingly, we've placed the major emphasis on the Integrated Debugger.

Finally, we looked at the Object Browser which can be used to navigate your way, graphically, around inside Delphi's object hierarchy.

INSTANT

Where Are We Now?

This concludes the first part of this book. At this stage, you should have a solid grounding in Delphi and be able to put together both large and small applications with a minimum of time and fuss.

Much of the real power of Delphi, however, lies in its ability to dramatically simplify the whole business of Windows development. In particular, the comprehensive set of reusable components mean that you can build stunning user interfaces for your applications, with your own stamp.

At the same time, Delphi's graphics library enables you to create custom effects much more easily than if you were writing directly in the Windows API.

These are among the exciting topics covered in Part II of the book: *Advanced Programming Techniques*.

Chapter

Using Graphics in Delphi

If you've done much graphics work in Windows, you'll know that at times it can be pretty tedious. Delphi makes graphics programming a far more straightforward experience by placing an object-oriented skin on top of the bare-bones Windows API. This skin takes care of much of the housekeeping work associated with Windows. You don't, for example, have to keep pulling old brushes, pens and fonts back into a device context - Delphi does all this for you.

In this chapter, we're going to focus on the graphics capabilities of Delphi. Graphics programming is a pretty exciting topic. Have you ever run a new application and heard yourself exclaiming 'wow!' when you see the slick user interface? This chapter is all about getting this kind of reaction from your own users. Also, we'll take a look at the **TabSet** control, which can be used to provide tabbed dialogs and tab selections for your own applications. We conclude with the development of a practical drawing application.

In this chapter we cover:

- Painting forms
- The **Canvas** property
- Pen styles and modes
- Designing and using a user interface

Graphics: Concepts

When artists paint, they usually only hold one brush in their hand at a time - or at any rate, they only actually paint with one brush at a time! Changing over to a new brush usually involves putting down the current brush and picking up another.

As any Windows programmer will tell you, this is pretty much how Windows works, but we have to substitute the term 'device context' for 'hand'. Whenever an application wants to draw in a window, it must always use a device context - a handle to a stored set of drawing tools and assorted other information.

A device context can never hold more than one brush at the same time. It can simultaneously hold a brush, a pen, and a font but never more than one of each. Changing to a new pen font or brush can be tedious, since it means that you have to store a device context handle somewhere and restore it afterwards.

An example should serve to make this clear. In the code below, the procedure selects a gray brush for a device context, fills a rectangle with gray and then restores the status quo.

```
procedure GrayRect(dc: hDC; r: TRect);
var
    Old: HBrush;
begin
    Old := SelectObject(dc, GetStockObject(Gray_Brush));
    Rectangle(dc, r.left, r.top, r.right, r.bottom);
    SelectObject(dc, Old);
end;
```

There are three lines of code in the body of this routine. Of the three, only the middle one (the call to **Rectangle**) is actually doing anything useful. The other two lines of code are simply moving brushes in and out of the device context. In a real-life application, the situation is often more complex than this: the **Rectangle** call fills a rectangle using the gray brush, but draws an outline of it with the current pen. If we wanted to draw a gray rectangle with a blue border, we'd need more lines of code to select a blue pen and then to restore the previous pen.

You can see, then, that with traditional programming approaches, it's possible to spend a lot of your time writing housekeeping code, while relatively few program statements do the real work.

Painting a Form's Background

To illustrate graphics programming in Delphi, let's look at how you might implement a graduated blue window such as the one illustrated below - this effect is often used by installation applications:

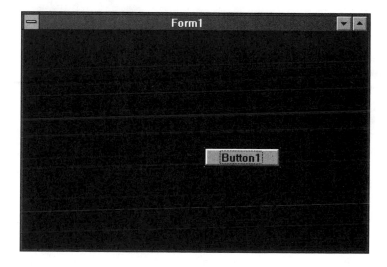

At first sight, this looks like a pretty sophisticated effect - it's easy to imagine that we might have to start manipulating the Windows palette in order to achieve the graduated effect, but in reality it's pretty straightforward. Here's the code to do it:

```
procedure TForm1.FormPaint(Sender: TObject);
var
  Row, Height: Integer;
begin
  Height := (ClientHeight + 255) div 256;
  for Row := 0 to 255 do
  begin
    Canvas.Brush.Color := RGB(0, 0, row);
    Canvas.FillRect(Rect(0, Row * Height,
                    ClientWidth, (Row + 1) * Height));
  end;
end;
```

This procedure handles the **OnPaint** event, which occurs whenever the form needs to be repainted (corresponding to the **WM_PAINT** message in the Windows API). This event will occur when it first appears, or when some part of the form is uncovered. The code works by dividing the form's client area into 256 horizontal strips, one on top of the other. First, the height of each strip is calculated and stored in the variable **Height** (the **ClientHeight** property gives the height of the window minus its border). Then, each strip is drawn in a slightly different shade of blue so as to create the graduated effect (using the **RGB** function from the Windows API to calculate the color value each time).

Notice the way we calculated the value of **Height**. Think what would happen if we were to code this as follows:

```
Height := ClientHeight div 256;
```

If **ClientHeight** happened to be 400, we'd get a value for **Height** of 1 since, of course, **div** performs integer division. After drawing 256 rows on the screen, each row being 1 pixel high, we would have covered only 256 pixels vertically, leaving 144 pixels unaccounted for. This would leave an unpleasant, blank area at the bottom of the window. By adding 255 before performing the divide, we get a row height of 2 meaning that we end up covering 512 pixels vertically. Of course, in this situation, since the **ClientHeight** is only 400, we'll end up overshooting, but this isn't a problem because Delphi's graphics routines clip everything to the form's canvas area.

On the subject of graduated form backgrounds (or indeed, any sort of custom form background) remember that if you want to use code like this in a real-world application, you'll also have to arrange for the form to be repainted when the user changes its size. The easiest way to do this is to make the `FormPaint` routine into a shared event handler, by pointing the `OnResize` event at it and you'll find that everything will work as expected.

Look - No Device Context!

You'll notice that the procedure above doesn't actually do any device-context manipulation at all. We simply set the `Color` property of the `Brush` object, which is itself a property of the form's `Canvas` and we're ready to roll. (Don't worry about the `Canvas` for now - it's explained fully later on.) We haven't had to create a new brush, nor add one to a device context, nor salt away the handle of the brush that was originally there. It should be emphasized that these things *are* still happening - but everything is done behind the scenes by Delphi - we don't have to worry about it.

When is a FillRect not a FillRect?

If you've had much exposure to the Windows API, you may be confused by the look of `FillRect`. The `FillRect` that you know and love takes a device context as its first parameter and it takes a brush handle, too. The point is that we're not calling the Windows API `FillRect` routine, we're actually calling a **method** of the `Canvas` which happens to have the same name.

This is an important point for Windows programmers, crucial to the understanding of graphics programming with Delphi. Many of the `Canvas` methods have identical names to the Windows API functions that they replace. Most of the time, however, they're easier to use and take fewer parameters. Examples include `FillRect`, `LineTo`, `MoveTo` and `PolyLine`. Whenever you see a familiar routine name somewhere, with an unfamiliar set of parameters, suspect that it's a method of the `Canvas` rather than a call to the Windows API.

The **FillRect** method doesn't need a device context because it obtains this information from its associated **Canvas**. Similarly, you don't need to specify a brush handle because the **Canvas** gets the brush information from its own **Brush** property. In this way, the API routines are often drastically simplified.

By default, when a **Canvas** property is in scope, Delphi will assume that you're trying to use one of the **Canvas** methods. If you particularly want to use one of the API routines for some reason, then you must say so! The easiest way to do this is to prefix the routine name with the unit name in which it is found. For example:

```
with Canvas do
begin
  MoveTo(5, 5);                { MoveTo method on Canvas }
  WinProcs.MoveTo(dc, 5, 5); { MoveTo API call }
end;
```

Obviously, if no **Canvas** object is in scope, this distinction doesn't need to be made - the compiler will assume you're issuing an API call.

Some people prefer not to use the **with** statement for this reason - without it, you could rewrite the above code fragment like this:

```
Canvas.MoveTo(5, 5); { MoveTo method on Canvas }
MoveTo(dc, 5, 5);          { MoveTo API call }
```

This is certainly clearer for a beginning Delphi developer, but Delphi has a very layered architecture with several levels of 'nesting' of one object inside another. Without the **with** keyword, you might occasionally be forced to write something like this:

```
{ Cycle the three primaries }
Canvas.Brush := CreateSolidBrush (RGB (
                            GetGValue (Canvas.Font.Color),
                            GetBValue (Canvas.Font.Color),
                            GetRValue (Canvas.Font.Color)));
```

It goes without saying that this would look a lot simpler using a **with** statement. At the end of the day, it's a matter of personal taste - using the **with** statement, you'll have cleaner, more concise code but you run a slight risk of confusing API calls with **Canvas** methods. If you're not that familiar with the Windows API, this is less likely to be a problem and - anyway - the compiler will soon tell you if you've got it wrong since the methods always have a different number of parameters to the API equivalents.

Look - No TRect Either!

Another interesting oddity (from the viewpoint of a seasoned Windows programmer) is the fact that the **FillRect** method doesn't take a **TRect** record as a parameter. Or, at least, the rectangle seems to get created within the call to **FillRect** itself.

Rect is actually the name of a predefined Delphi function which takes four parameters and returns a **TRect** record directly. Here's the definition for **Rect**:

```
function Rect(ALeft, ATop, ARight, ABottom: Integer): TRect;
```

Again, this sort of facility makes for more compact source code. Without **Rect**, we'd have had to write the **FormPaint** routine something like this:

```
procedure TForm1.FormPaint(Sender: TObject);
var
  R: Trect;
  Row, Height: Integer;
begin
  Height := (ClientHeight + 255) div 256;
  for Row := 0 to 255 do
  begin
    Canvas.Brush.Color := RGB (0, 0, Row);
    SetRect(R, 0, Row * Height, ClientWidth, (Row + 1) * Height);
    Canvas.FillRect(R);
  end;
end;
```

This variation works just as well as our original, but includes a couple of extra lines of code. Why write code when you don't need to and why declare local variables (**R** in this case) when they're not necessary? Object Pascal has a lot of neat features like this - track them down and use them!

> This idea of creating data structures on-the-fly has been extended to arrays as well. See Appendix A which, amongst other things, explains Object Pascal's new open array language facilities.

The Canvas Property

You'll have realized by now that the key to Delphi graphics programming is the **Canvas** property, therefore, we're going to look at it in some detail. It's not just forms that have a **Canvas** - many other types of Delphi component also have a **Canvas** property. However, for now, we'll restrict ourselves to discussing the form's **Canvas**.

As the name suggests, you can think of a canvas as the actual painting surface of a form. Microsoft's documentation tells you to think of a device context in this way. However, a canvas is much more than a device context. Because it's object-oriented, a canvas encapsulates not only the most useful characteristics of a painting surface (the current pen, brush, pen position, font, and so on), but also methods for painting on that surface. We've already come across the **MoveTo**, **LineTo** and **FillRect** methods and there are a lot more. A form's **Canvas** property is actually an object of type **TCanvas**. Here's the full class definition for the **TCanvas** object:

```
TCanvas = class(TPersistent)
private
  FHandle: HDC;
  State: TCanvasState;
  FFont: TFont;
  FPen: TPen;
  FBrush: TBrush;
  FPenPos: TPoint;
  FCopyMode: TCopyMode;
  FOnChange: TNotifyEvent;
  FOnChanging: TNotifyEvent;
  procedure CreateBrush;
  procedure CreateFont;
  procedure CreatePen;
  procedure BrushChanged(ABrush: TObject);
  procedure DeselectHandles;
  function GetClipRect: TRect;
  function GetHandle: HDC;
  function GetPenPos: TPoint;
  function GetPixel(X, Y: Integer): TColor;
  procedure FontChanged(AFont: TObject);
  procedure PenChanged(APen: TObject);
  procedure SetBrush(Value: TBrush);
  procedure SetFont(Value: TFont);
  procedure SetHandle(Value: HDC);
  procedure SetPen(Value: TPen);
  procedure SetPenPos(Value: TPoint);
  procedure SetPixel(X, Y: Integer; Value: TColor);
```

```
     procedure RequiredState(ReqState: TCanvasState);
  protected
     procedure Changed; virtual;
     procedure Changing; virtual;
     procedure CreateHandle; virtual;
  public
     constructor Create;
     destructor Destroy; override;
     procedure Arc(X1, Y1, X2, Y2, X3, Y3, X4, Y4: Integer);
     procedure BrushCopy(const Dest: TRect; Bitmap: TBitmap;
       const Source: TRect; Color: TColor);
     procedure Chord(X1, Y1, X2, Y2, X3, Y3, X4, Y4: Integer);
     procedure CopyRect(const Dest: TRect; Canvas: TCanvas;
       const Source: TRect);
     procedure Draw(X, Y: Integer; Graphic: TGraphic);
     procedure DrawFocusRect(const Rect: TRect);
     procedure Ellipse(X1, Y1, X2, Y2: Integer);
     procedure FillRect(const Rect: TRect);
     procedure FloodFill(X, Y: Integer; Color: TColor;
                         FillStyle: TFillStyle);
     procedure FrameRect(const Rect: TRect);
     procedure LineTo(X, Y: Integer);
     procedure MoveTo(X, Y: Integer);
     procedure Pie(X1, Y1, X2, Y2, X3, Y3, X4, Y4: Integer);
     procedure Polygon(const Points: array of TPoint);
     procedure Polyline(const Points: array of TPoint);
     procedure Rectangle(X1, Y1, X2, Y2: Integer);
     procedure Refresh;
     procedure RoundRect(X1, Y1, X2, Y2, X3, Y3: Integer);
     procedure StretchDraw(const Rect: TRect; Graphic: TGraphic);
     function TextHeight(const Text: string): Integer;
     procedure TextOut(X, Y: Integer; const Text: string);
     procedure TextRect(Rect: TRect; X, Y: Integer; const Text: string);
     function TextWidth(const Text: string): Integer;
     property ClipRect: TRect read GetClipRect;
     property Handle: HDC read GetHandle write SetHandle;
     property PenPos: TPoint read GetPenPos write SetPenPos;
     property Pixels[X, Y: Integer]: TColor read GetPixel write SetPixel;
     property OnChange: TNotifyEvent read FOnChange write FOnChange;
     property OnChanging: TNotifyEvent read FOnChanging write FOnChanging;
  published
     property Brush: TBrush read FBrush write SetBrush;
     property CopyMode: TCopyMode read FCopyMode
                               write FCopyMode default cmSrcCopy;
     property Font: TFont read FFont write SetFont;
     property Pen: TPen read FPen write SetPen;
  end;
```

As you can see, there's a quite a lot to it.

> Incidentally, if you're not familiar with the Object Pascal class definition, then you can get more information from Appendix A at the back of this book.

What's significant here is the **public** section and the **published** section of the class definition.

Let's examine some of the most important facilities provided by the **Canvas** property.

The Brush

Under Windows, brushes are used as filling tools. You use them to fill in areas, especially the interior of shapes such as rectangles, ellipses and so on. Just as a device context can only have one brush selected for it at any one time, so the **Canvas** has only one **Brush** property. Here's the Object Pascal class definition for the brush:

```
TBrush = class(TGraphicsObject)
private
  procedure GetData(var BrushData: TBrushData);
  procedure SetData(const BrushData: TBrushData);
protected
  function GetBitmap: TBitmap;
  procedure SetBitmap(Value: TBitmap);
  function GetColor: TColor;
  procedure SetColor(Value: TColor);
  function GetHandle: HBrush;
  procedure SetHandle(Value: HBrush);
  function GetStyle: TBrushStyle;
  procedure SetStyle(Value: TBrushStyle);
public
  constructor Create;
  destructor Destroy; override;
  procedure Assign(Source: TPersistent); override;
  property Handle: HBrush read GetHandle write SetHandle;
published
  property Bitmap: TBitmap read GetBitmap write SetBitmap;
  property Color: TColor read GetColor write SetColor default clWhite;
  property Style: TBrushStyle read GetStyle
                            write SetStyle default bsSolid;
end;
```

For our purposes, the most important fields in this data structure are the last three - the **published** properties of the class: the **Color** property can be set up using global constants such as **clRed**, or using the **RGB** function, as we saw earlier; the **Bitmap** property allows you to specify the handle of a bitmap which is used as an 8-pixel-squared fill pattern (analogous to using the Windows API **CreatePatternBrush** call). The **Style** property can be used to set the brush style to various patterns:

```
TBrushStyle = (bsSolid, bsClear, bsHorizontal, bsVertical,
          bsFDiagonal, bsBDiagonal, bsCross, bsDiagCross);
```

Brush Style

To get a feel for the different brush styles that are available, try opening a new project and type in the following code as the form's **OnPaint**/**OnResize** handler:

```pascal
procedure TForm1.FormPaint(Sender: TObject);
const
  Gap = 10;     { Gap between boxes }
var
    r: TRect;
    BoxNum, xBox, yBox: Integer;
begin
    { Paint the form silver }
    Canvas.Brush.Color := clSilver;
    Canvas.FillRect(Rect(0, 0, ClientWidth, ClientHeight));

    { Calculate the dimensions of a box }
    xBox := (ClientWidth - (Gap * 5)) div 4;
    yBox := (ClientHeight - (Gap * 3)) div 2;

    { Set R to the position of the first box }
    r := Rect(Gap, Gap, Gap + xBox, Gap + yBox);

    { Use a white, solid brush }
    Canvas.Brush.Color := clWhite;
    Canvas.Brush.Style := bsSolid;

    { Draw eight boxes in alternating styles }
    for BoxNum := 0 to 7 do
    begin
        Canvas.Rectangle (r.left, r.top, r.right, r.bottom);
        if BoxNum <> 3 then
            OffsetRect (r, Gap + xBox, 0)
        else
            OffsetRect (r, -3 * (Gap + xBox), Gap + yBox);
        if BoxNum < 7 then
            Canvas.Brush.Style := Succ (Canvas.Brush.Style);
    end;
end;
```

223

This code divides the form up into eight rectangles arranged on two rows. The constant **Gap** is used to specify a gap between adjacent rectangles and between the edges of the form. We've used the Windows API routine **OffsetRect** to shift the position of the rectangle each time for each of the eight values of **BoxNum**. The **xBox** and **yBox** variables correspond to the width and height of each of the eight rectangles, calculated from the **ClientWidth** and **ClientHeight** properties. Because we've **calculated** rectangle sizes and positions, the handler will continue to work correctly if the form is resized. After displaying each rectangle, using the canvas's **Rectangle** method, the **Style** property is advanced using the **Succ** procedure (unless we're at the last one).

Here's the result:

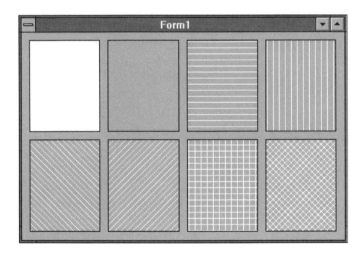

> You'll see that the code initially sets the brush's **Color** to **clSilver** and fills the entire form. This is important: you need to realize that by defining an **OnPaint** handler, you take on *all* responsibility for painting the form's canvas - try removing the **FillRect** call and you'll see what we mean. We didn't need to do this with the graduated fill example because the entire form was painted each time.

If you want to make the application look even cuter, add the following constant definition (alongside **Gap**):

```
StyleNames: Array [TBrushStyle] of PChar = (
  'bsSolid',
  'bsClear',
  'bsHorizontal',
  'bsVertical',
  'bsFDiagonal',
  'bsBDiagonal',
  'bsCross',
  'bsDiagCross'
);
```

Also, add the following code immediately after the call to the **Rectangle** method:

```
Inc (r.top);
SetBkMode(Canvas.Handle, Transparent);
DrawText(Canvas.Handle, StyleNames[Canvas.Brush.Style],
         -1, r, dt_Center);
Dec (r.top);
```

The **SetBkMode** call determines whether or not the background 'shows through' when we draw text, while the **DrawText** routine is responsible for drawing the text itself. Both these routines require a Windows device context which is accessible as the canvas' **Handle** field. Run the application again and you should see a big improvement!

The Pen

The other important canvas drawing tool is the pen. The brush is used to fill the inside of shapes, while the pen is used to draw the outside boundary of shapes. You can draw arbitrary straight lines between two points, or you can use the pen to outline a shape at the same time as drawing it. Here's the Object Pascal definition for the **TPen** object:

```
TPen = class(TGraphicsObject)
private
  FMode: TPenMode;
  procedure GetData(var PenData: TPenData);
  procedure SetData(const PenData: TPenData);
protected
  function GetColor: TColor;
  procedure SetColor(Value: TColor);
  function GetHandle: HPen;
  procedure SetHandle(Value: HPen);
```

```
     procedure SetMode(Value: TPenMode);
     function GetStyle: TPenStyle;
     procedure SetStyle(Value: TPenStyle);
     function GetWidth: Integer;
     procedure SetWidth(Value: Integer);
  public
     constructor Create;
     destructor Destroy; override;
     procedure Assign(Source: TPersistent); override;
     property Handle: HPen read GetHandle write SetHandle;
  published
     property Color: TColor read GetColor write SetColor default clBlack;
     property Mode: TPenMode read FMode write SetMode default pmCopy;
     property Style: TPenStyle read GetStyle write SetStyle default psSolid;
     property Width: Integer read GetWidth write SetWidth default 1;
  end;
```

As with the brush, the most important fields here are the published properties at the end of the class definition, but in passing, you should take note of the **Handle** property that's used to obtain a Windows-API-compatible handle for the pen.

The meaning of the **Color** property is easy - you just set this field to the desired color for drawing. The **Width** property can be used to set the pen width in pixels - by default, pens are one pixel wide. We've encountered the pen width before, while developing the Doodle application.

Pen Style

The **Style** property is used to specify the type of line drawn by the pen. The following different styles are available:

```
TPenStyle = (psSolid, psDash, psDot, psDashDot,
    psDashDotDot, psClear, psInsideFrame);
```

Each style is described in the table below:

Pen Style	Resulting line type
psSolid	A solid, unbroken line.
psDash	A line made up of dashes.
psDot	A line made up of dots.
psDashDot	A line made up of alternating dashes and dots.

Continued

Pen Style	Resulting line type
psDashDotDot	A line made from a repeating dash–dot–dot pattern.
psClear	This style specifies an invisible pen.
psInsideFrame	Draws lines inside the frame of closed shapes (such as those drawn with the **Rectangle** and **Pie** methods).

Pen Modes

Pens also have a **Mode** property. Sixteen different modes are available, as is evident from the definition of **TPenMode**:

```
TPenMode = (   pmBlack, pmWhite, pmNop, pmNot, pmCopy,
               pmNotCopy, pmMergePenNot, pmMaskPenNot,
               pmMergeNotPen, pmMaskNotPen, pmMerge,
               pmNotMerge, pmMask, pmNotMask, pmXor,
               pmNotXor);
```

Exploring Pen Styles and Modes

There are a lot of different pen styles and modes, so you can be forgiven for feeling stumped at this point! In order to make things easier to visualize, we'll develop a simple Instant Pen Explorer which can be used to examine the effects of each different pen mode and style. Here's how it will look:

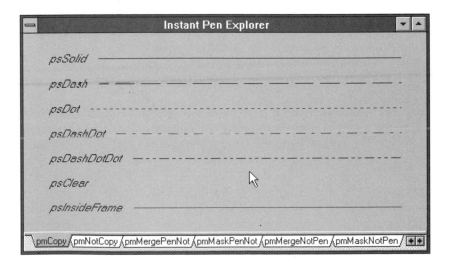

As you can see, the seven different pen styles are illustrated in the window, with a tab control to allow you to select different pen modes. We haven't used the TabSet component before - this application is a thinly veiled pretext for introducing it to you!

Using the TabSet Component

The easiest way to use a TabSet component is to place it inside a Panel. You can add other components to the Panel and, by moving the Panel around, you can treat all the components as a single group. This is, in fact, what Borland have done in their design of Delphi itself: look at the bottom of the Code Editor in the screenshot below:

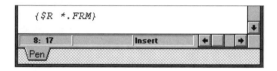

Here, the TabSet component, the three small Panel components (which together make up the status bar) and the horizontal ScrollBar are actually all contained within a larger Panel component.

To try this out for yourself, create a new project. Now, add a Panel component to the form and set its **Caption** property to an empty string. Set the panel's **Align** property to **alBottom** to force the panel to hug the bottom of the form - at run time, as the form is resized by the user, the panel will continue to sit at the bottom of the form and will automatically change its width to match any width changes in the form. (This all happens without any programming effort - to get the same effect with the Windows SDK, we'd have to start fooling around with **WM_SIZE** messages.)

Now, with the Panel component selected, double-click on the TabSet component in the Additional Component Palette to add one to the panel. Set the **Align** property of the TabSet component to **alBottom**, too - this aligns the TabSet component to the bottom of the panel (**not** at the bottom of the form - important if you ever decide to move the panel). By putting the TabSet component at the bottom of the panel and increasing the size of the panel, you could make room for one or more subsidiary panels, scroll bars or whatever.

Double click on the right-hand side of the TabSet component's **Tabs** property in the Object Inspector. Alternatively, click the small button containing the ellipsis symbol. This will invoke the String list editor.

In the String list editor window, you can enter the various strings that you want to appear as tab names on your TabSet control. Add the sixteen pen mode names (see definition of **TPenMode** earlier). You can see the first thirteen of them in the String list editor shown here. When you've got the string list as you want it, click the OK button and you'll find that the TabSet control will immediately change to display the new tab names.

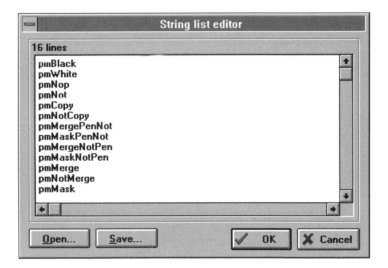

It's unlikely that you'll be able to widen the form so as to display all the tab names at the same time unless, that is, you're using a very high-resolution screen! The TabSet component gets around this problem by displaying a small pair of scroll arrows to its right. As you click these arrows, you can bring any tab into view:

Tabset scroll arrows

When entering tab names into the String list editor, be careful not to type any control characters accidentally, as these will appear as garbage in the tab names. Also, be careful not to add any blank lines between items, or at the top or bottom of the string list: if you inadvertently do this, you'll see one or more unnamed tabs, like this:

Writing the Code

Give the TabSet component a **Name** of **ModeList**. Double-click on it and you'll find yourself in the Code Editor at the start of a new **OnChange** event handler - this is the procedure that gets called each time that the user selects a tab. Add the following code:

```
procedure TForm1.ModeListChange (Sender: TObject;
                                 NewTab: Integer;
                        var AllowChange: Boolean);
begin
    Canvas.Pen.Mode := TPenMode(NewTab);
    Refresh;
end;
```

As you can see, using a **TabSet** control is straightforward - when a new tab is selected, the **OnChange** handler is called, passing the tab number as the **NewTab** parameter. Tabs are ordered from zero so, for example, the pmBlack tab corresponds to 0, pmWhite to 1, and so on. This is exactly the same as the value assigned to these constants by the **TPenMode** definition, so we can just use the **NewTab** parameter as the new value for the pen's **Mode** property (after first type-casting it to keep the compiler happy). Finally, the form's **Refresh** method is called to redraw the form and show the changes.

Now add the code below to the form's **OnCreate** handler

```
procedure TForm1.FormCreate(Sender: TObject);
begin
    Canvas.Pen.Color := clRed;
    ModeList.TabIndex := Ord(Canvas.Pen.Mode);
end;
```

Firstly, this procedure sets the pen's color to red (you'll get more interesting effects with a colored pen than with a plain black one). Then, the procedure sets the default tab in the TabSet component to agree with the default pen mode (**pmCopy**).

Finally, define the **OnPaint** event handler shown below:

```
procedure TForm1.FormPaint(Sender: TObject);
const
  StyleNames: array [TPenStyle] of String = (
    'psSolid',
    'psDash',
    'psDot',
    'psDashDot',
    'psDashDotDot',
    'psClear',
    'psInsideFrame'
  );

var
    style: TPenStyle;
    gap, th2: Integer;
begin
  { Calculate the line spacing }
  th2 := Canvas.TextHeight('pP') div 2;

  { Clear the window }
  Canvas.Brush.Color := Color;
  Canvas.FillRect(Rect (0, 0, ClientWidth, ClientHeight));

  { Calculate the gap between lines }
  gap := Panel1.Top div 8;

  { Draw a label and line for each pen style }
  for style := psSolid to psInsideFrame do
  begin

  { Move to the label position }
   Canvas.MoveTo(gap, (Ord(style) + 1) * gap);

  { Draw the label }
  Canvas.TextOut (Canvas.PenPos.x, Canvas.PenPos.y - th2,
           StyleNames[style]);

  { Move to the line position }
  Canvas.MoveTo (Canvas.PenPos.x + 10, Canvas.PenPos.y + th2);

  { Draw the line }
   Canvas.Pen.Style := style;
   Canvas.LineTo (ClientWidth - gap, (Ord (style) + 1) * gap);
  end;
end;
```

While you're at it, use the same event handler as the target for **OnResize** messages so that the form display will be updated each time the user changes the size of the form - just as we've done before.

The **OnPaint/OnResize** handler uses the **TextHeight** function, which we haven't come across before. **TextHeight** takes a text string and returns the height of that string in pixels. In this case, we pass a string that contains both descenders and ascenders to **TextHeight** so as to get the maximum possible vertical extent for characters in the current font. The resulting height is divided by two and used to center the various style labels vertically, next to the corresponding pen lines.

> Another **Canvas** method, **TextWidth**, can be used to return the pixel width of a given text string. These two methods are more convenient than the Windows API routine **GetTextExtent**, which returns width and height together in one 32-bit **LongInt**. Also, the **Canvas** methods are portable to 32-bit Delphi.

You'll also notice that, when calculating the total available area in which to display information, we used **Panel1.Top** rather than **ClientHeight**. This is because Delphi doesn't subtract the vertical height of the panel component from the available **ClientHeight** - we have to do this ourselves.

Finally, look at the **PenPos** property of the canvas. This is a run-time-only property which returns the current pen position. (It is equivalent to the Windows API call **GetCurrentPosition**, but, again, no device context needs to be specified.)

The illustration below summarizes what we've learnt so far. This isn't an object-oriented inheritance diagram - it's more of a 'property ownership' diagram. Fonts, pens and brushes all have **Color**, **Handle** and **Style**, while properties such as **Height**, **Mode** and **Bitmap** are specific to one or other of the drawing tools.

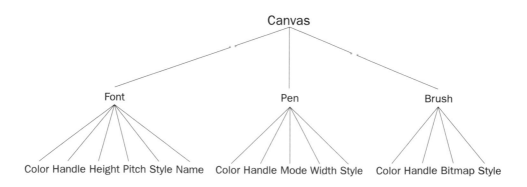

Modifying Canvas Pixels

Canvasses also have a pseudo-array property called **Pixels**, which can be used to read and write individual pixels on the surface of a form. We use the term pseudo-array because it isn't a normal Pascal array at all. Although it can be accessed just like an array, **Pixel**s maps onto a couple of private methods, **GetPixel** and **SetPixel**. Here's the definition of the **Pixel**s array taken from the VCL library:

```
property Pixels[X, Y: Integer]: TColor read GetPixel write SetPixel;
```

As you can see, reading the color of a pixel from the array results in a call to **GetPixel** (with appropriate actual parameters), while writing a color into the array corresponds to a call to **SetPixel**.

> **This illustrates the power of one of Delphi's object-oriented extensions to the Pascal language: it's very easy to build a convenient, array-like interface to any *n*-dimensional set of data which is implemented as private methods operating on the data. In this way, you can control and validate access to the data, in a way that wouldn't be possible if the caller really did have access to the raw pixel information. More on this in Appendix A.**

To try this out, create a new project and add a Timer control to the form (from the System page of the Component Palette). Set the **Interval** property of the Timer to 1 (millisecond), so that the **OnTimer** handler will be called 1000 times per second (or, as frequently as your machine can handle!). Now add the following **OnTimer** handler:

```
procedure TForm1.Timer1Timer(Sender: TObject);
var
  x, y: Integer;
  col: TColor;
begin
  x := Random(ClientWidth);
  y := Random(ClientHeight);
  col := RGB(Random(256), Random(256), Random(256));
  Canvas.Pixels[x,y] := col;
end;
```

This handler code uses the **Random** function (in the **System** unit) to determine random locations and colors for drawing dots, writing the resulting information into the canvas's **Pixel**s array.

233

Add an OK button to the form which, with the help of the following event handler, halts the drawing activity when the user clicks on it (setting the timer's interval to 0 effectively disables it):

```
procedure TForm1.OKClick(Sender: TObject);
begin
  Timer1.Interval := 0;
end;
```

When you run the application, nothing will appear to happen for a moment or so, but as you watch closely, you'll see that the form gradually fills up with random dots:

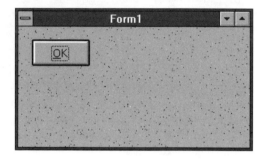

Incidentally, you'll notice that the button control doesn't get covered with dots - that's because any child controls of the form are automatically excluded from the form's drawing region. (If you're familiar with the Windows API, you'll appreciate that this corresponds to assigning a window style of **WS_CLIPCHILDREN** when the form is created.)

> In practice, using the **Pixels** array is not very efficient - typically, you'll use it sparingly and often only to retrieve the color of a particular pixel (in an arcade game application, for example).

Painting Shapes on the Canvas

If you want to create custom effects in your form, a much better approach is to make use of Delphi's built-in shape-drawing routines. The available routines are:

Routine	What it Does
Arc	Draws an arc (a sub-section of an ellipse).
Chord	Draws a chord (a shape defined by the intersection of an ellipse and a straight line).
Ellipse	Draws an ellipse (if the width and height are the same, a circle is produced).
Rectangle	Draws a rectangle.
FrameRect	Draws a border around a rectangle.
Pie	Draws a wedge-shaped section of an ellipse - like a slice of pie.
Polygon	Draws a closed shape made up of a series of lines between an array of arbitrary points.
PolyLine	Same as for **Polygon**, except that the shape is not closed.
RoundRect	Draws a rectangle with rounded-corners.

All of these routines are methods of the **Canvas** and correspond to Windows API calls of the same name. Take care, therefore, not to confuse the two - you won't be able to access these graphics drawing methods unless you explicitly reference the **Canvas** property (or use '**with Canvas do**') inside your source code. Without doing this, Delphi will assume that you're referencing the Windows API.

To show how simple these routines are to use, here's the same form that you saw last time. Instead of lots of little spots, it now sports a host of multi-colored circles.

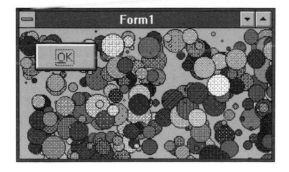

The changes required to do this are very simple. As you can see, the code to access the **Pixel**s array has been replaced with a call to the **Canvas'** **Ellipse** routine - because the **size** variable is used for both the width and height of the ellipse, a circle is actually painted. If you wanted, you could use different random values for each, resulting in an even jazzier display.

```
procedure TForm1.Timer1Timer(Sender: TObject);
var
  x, y, size: Integer;
begin
  x := Random(ClientWidth);
  y := Random(ClientHeight);
  Canvas.Brush.Color := RGB(
    Random(256),
    Random (256),
    Random (256)
  );
  size := Random(30);
  Canvas.Ellipse (x, y, x + size, y + size)
end;
```

Drawing Graphics: Implementation

In the remainder of this chapter, we're going to show you the development of the graphics drawing application illustrated below:

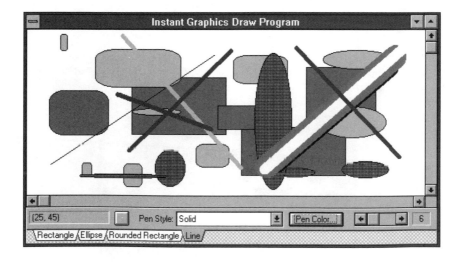

This application (which is based on one of Borland's demonstration programs) doesn't claim to be a full-featured, commercial-quality drawing package, but it does have an attractive user interface and it represents a great opportunity to consolidate everything we've learned about graphics programming in Delphi.

The Design of the User Interface

Before getting down to the development issues, let's look briefly at the user interface. Right at the bottom of the window is the now-familiar TabSet component which is used to select the current drawing tool - Rectangle, Ellipse, Rounded Rectangle or Line.

Above the tabs is what we've chosen to refer to as a **style panel**, a compact panel which can be used to select various attributes for the drawing tools. The small display on the left hand side of the style panel is for information only - you can't modify it - it displays the current cursor location within the window as an x/y coordinate pair. While you're drawing, this display changes to show two coordinate pairs - the upper-left and lower-right corners of the shape as you draw.

Immediately to the right of the coordinate display is a mode button. Pressing this button toggles the style panel between one of two modes. In the pen mode (shown above) you can choose pen style, pen color and pen width (the scrollbar on the right-hand side of the style panel is used to select the pen width in pixels, with the current setting displayed on the extreme right). The other mode - brush mode - is shown below:

In brush mode, no width information is displayed, since there's no such thing as a width for brushes - only pens have width.

Whether in pen or brush mode, pressing the Color... button gives access to a standard ColorDialog. A brush or pen style can be selected using the ComboBox component in the center of the style panel.

Building the User Interface

As ever, let's begin by putting together the user interface of our drawing application.

Firstly, open a new project, set the default form's **Font** to 8-point-MS-Sans-Serif, or whatever you prefer. Set the **Caption** to Instant Graphics Draw Program, or whatever you wish to call it.

Add a Panel component: give it an empty **Caption**, a **Name** of **StylePanel** and an **Align** property of **alBottom**.

Now *with the panel selected,* add a TabSet component and set its **Align** property to **alBottom** too. Use the String list editor to add the four tab names in the illustration above. Adjust the height of the TabSet component so that its tabs are just above the bottom of the window. Adjust the height of the Panel so that it's high enough to accommodate the other controls. Now, again *with the panel selected each time,* add the following components working from left to right: a Panel, a Button, a Label, a ComboBox, a Button, a ScrollBar and another Panel. Phew!

For each of these new components set their properties as follows, again working from left to right.

Component	Properties
Panel	**Name = SizePanel**
	Alignment = taLeftJustify
	BevelOuter = bvLowered
Button	**Name = ModeSelect**
	Caption = ''
Label	**Name = StyleLabel**
	Caption = 'Brush Style:'
ComboBox	**Name = StyleCombo**
	Style = csDropDownList
	Text = ''

Continued

Component	Properties
Button	**Name = ColorButton**
	Caption = 'Brush Color...'
ScrollBar	**Visible = False**
	LargeChange = 10
Panel	**Visible = False**
	Caption = 1
	BevelOuter = bvLowered
	Name = WidthPanel

You might be wondering why the width scroll bar and width display panel are initially invisible. The reason is that the application starts up in brush mode - you have to press the mode button before the other components will appear.

Obviously, in addition to the above, you'll need to position the various components as shown in the illustration. we suggest that you take your time over this. It can be quite fiddly, but it's worth getting it right.

> At this point, it's easy to feel that you're fighting against the snap-to-grid system. You could turn this off, but, experience has shown that one of the easiest ways round this problem is to edit the **Top**, **Left**, **Width** and **Height** properties for each component directly - this ensures pin-point accuracy. Also, don't forget about the time-saving **Size** and **Alignment** facilities described in Chapter 1.

Once you've got the style panel looking right, it's time to add the other components to the main part of the form. Firstly, add a ColorDialog - you don't need to change any of its properties except, perhaps, to set the **Ctl3D** property to **True**.

> The reason that `ColorDialogs` have `Ctl3D` `False` by default is simple - there's a bug in Microsoft's implementation of `COMMDLG.DLL`! If you turn `Ctl3D` on and then watch closely as you select one color after another, you'll see faint white lines left around the previously-selected color boxes. The `ColorDialog` is (wrongly) assuming that it will always have a white background!

Now, add an Image component to the form and give it the **Name Image**. Set the **Left** and **Top** properties of the Image component to zero and set its **Align** property to **alClient** - this will cause it to occupy all the remaining space above the style panel.

Adding the Code

That's it, as far as the user interface design goes. Now, it's time to glue it all together with the code.

A Few New Fields and Globals

Let's begin by adding some fields to the form's class definition:

```
public
  { Public declarations }
  fBrush: Boolean;
  Drawing: Boolean;
  Origin, MovePt: TPoint;
  DrawingTool: TDrawingTool;
```

As shown, these fields go into the **public** part of the class definition. The **fBrush** variable determines whether the style panel is in brush mode (when its value is **True**) or pen mode (when its value is **False**). The **Drawing** variable indicates whether a drawing operation is currently taking place. The **Origin** and **MovePt** variables are used to keep track of the mouse location as a shape is being drawn. **DrawingTool** determines the currently selected drawing tool - line, ellipse, and so on. Here's the definition for the **TDrawingTool** type, which you'll need to add immediately before the class definition, after the **type** keyword:

```
TDrawingTool = (dtRectangle, dtEllipse, dtRoundRect, dtLine);
```

You'll notice that the various drawing tools occur in the same order that they do in the **TabSet** control. This allows us to simplify the code, as we'll see later.

Along with these new fields, you'll also need to add the following method declaration to the public part of the class definition:

```
procedure DrawShape (TopLeft, BottomRight: TPoint;
                     AMode: TPenMode); virtual;
```

Now add a couple of constant definitions, before the **type** part of the unit's implementation:

```
const
  BrushStyles: array [TBrushStyle] of String = (
    'Solid',
    'Clear',
    'Horizontal',
    'Vertical',
    'ForwardDiagonal',
    'BackDiagonal',
    'Cross',
    'DiagCross'
  );

  PenStyles: array [TPenStyle] of String = (
    'Solid',
    'Dash',
    'Dot',
    'DashDot',
    'DashDotDot',
    'Clear',
    'InsideFrame'
  );
```

These string arrays contain plain-English names for all the possible brush and pen styles. Notice that, again, the various strings occur in the same order as in the **TBrushStyle** and **TPenStyle** types, thus greatly simplifying the resulting code.

Drawing the Shape

Since we've forward-referenced the **DrawShape** routine, we may as well write the code for it first (in the **implementation** part of the form's unit):

```
procedure TForm1.DrawShape(TopLeft, BottomRight: TPoint;
        AMode: TPenMode);
begin

    { Set the pen mode of the image's canvas  as requested }
    Image.Canvas.Pen.Mode := Amode;

    { Draw a shape according to the current tool setting }
    case DrawingTool of
        dtLine:
        begin
            Image.Canvas.MoveTo (TopLeft.X, TopLeft.Y);
            Image.Canvas.LineTo (BottomRight.X, BottomRight.Y);
        end;

        dtRectangle:
        Image.Canvas.Rectangle (TopLeft.X, TopLeft.Y,
                BottomRight.X, BottomRight.Y);

        dtEllipse:
        Image.Canvas.Ellipse (TopLeft.X, TopLeft.Y,
                BottomRight.X, BottomRight.Y);

        dtRoundRect:
        Image.Canvas.RoundRect (TopLeft.X, TopLeft.Y,
                BottomRight.X, BottomRight.Y,
                    (TopLeft.X - BottomRight.X) div 2,
                    (TopLeft.Y - BottomRight.Y) div 2);
    end;
end;
```

Although this procedure looks complicated, it's actually quite straightforward. The code simply draws the currently selected shape (stored in the **DrawingTool** variable) on the canvas of the **Image** component. The shape is drawn from the top-left to bottom-right coordinates specified as parameters to the call. The code for calling **RoundRect** looks particularly complicated - this is because the **RoundRect** method needs an extra couple of parameters to specify the roundness of the corners (we've chosen a curvature related to size of the rectangle itself).

The **OnMouseDown** event handler is straightforward:

```
procedure TForm1.ImageMouseDown(Sender: TObject; Button: TMouseButton;
                    Shift: TShiftState; X, Y: Integer);
begin
    Drawing := True;
    Image.Canvas.MoveTo (X, Y);
    Origin := Point (X, Y);
    MovePt := Origin;
    SizePanel.Caption := Format (' (%d, %d)', [X, Y]);
end;
```

Notice that we don't try to draw a shape at this point - since we've only just pressed the mouse, any shape would have zero width and zero height! Instead, we record the fact that a drawing has started and move to the current mouse location; next, the **Origin** and **MovePt** fields are initialized for the benefit of the **OnMouseMove** handler (defined later); finally, the **SizePanel**'s **Caption** is over-written with the mouse location.

Another thing to notice is this: because we're responding to mouse activity on the **Image** component rather than the form, it's the **Image** control for which we need to set up event handlers - **TForm1.ImageMouseDown** is the **OnMouseDown** handler for the **Image** component, not for the form. The same is true of the **OnMouseUp** and **OnMouseMove** handlers which we'll look at in a moment.

> If you're used to ordinary Turbo Pascal programming, you'll probably be floored by those odd-looking **Format** function calls in the above code. The **Format** function (in the **SysUtils** unit) is extremely useful. It gives Object Pascal developers the same flexibility that C programmers get with **sprintf**, namely, the ability to pass a variable number of parameters to a string-formatting routine. In using **Format**, we've also exploited Object Pascal's ability to create arrays on-the-fly, a new language feature that's discussed fully in Appendix A.

Here's the code for the **OnMouseUp** event handler:

```
procedure TForm1.ImageMouseUp(Sender: TObject; Button: TMouseButton;
                    Shift: TShiftState; X, Y: Integer);
begin
    DrawShape (Origin, Point(X, Y), pmCopy);
    Drawing := False;
    SizePanel.Caption := '';
end;
```

This code just cleans up at the end of the drawing operation. The **DrawShape** routine is called, using a pen mode of **pmCopy**, to draw the new shape. The **Drawing** variable is set to **False** and the **SizePanel**'s **Caption** is cleared.

The **OnMouseMove** handler below is responsible for tracking mouse movements on the form:

```
procedure TForm1.ImageMouseMove(Sender: TObject; Shift: TShiftState;
                                 X, Y: Integer);
begin
    if Drawing then
    begin
        { Erase old shape }
        DrawShape(Origin, MovePt, pmNotXor);

        { Draw new shape }
        DrawShape(Origin, Point(X, Y), pmNotXor);

        { Update size panel caption }
        SizePanel.Caption := Format(' (%d, %d)-(%d, %d)',
                                    [Origin.X, Origin.Y, X, Y]);
    end
    else    { Just update size panel caption }
    SizePanel.Caption := Format(' (%d, %d)', [X, Y]);

    { Store the current point }
    MovePt := Point(X, Y);

    { Reset the pen mode }
    Image.Canvas.Pen.Mode := pmCopy;
end;
```

You'll see that, if the **Drawing** field is **False**, this procedure does little more than update the **Caption** property of the **SizePanel** to display the current mouse coordinates; otherwise, a new shape is drawn. An important point here is the way in which the **DrawShape** routine is called: once to draw the shape at the old position (this is the purpose of the **MovePt** variable) and then again to draw it at the new position (specified by the new **X** and **Y** parameters). In both cases, the **Origin** (the top-left corner of the shape) doesn't change - it's the bottom-right corner of the shape that's changing as the mouse is dragged around.

> **You can drag the mouse above and to the left of the starting point, so terms like top-left and bottom-right aren't strictly accurate. But, let's not get too picky here - the basic argument still applies!**

Why should we want to draw the shape twice? The key to this is the special pen mode that we're using: **pmNotXor**. If you draw a shape with this pen mode, the shape will appear on the screen. If you then draw the shape again at the same location and with the same pen color, the shape will disappear. What the **OnMouseMove** routine is doing then, is **erasing** the old shape on the first call and drawing the **new** shape (with different bottom-right coordinates) on the second call. In this way, a smooth rubber-banding effect is achieved.

Managing the User Interface

Now, we need to turn our attention to the code that handles the user interface. Firstly, let's deal with the matter of initialization. Obviously, it's important that the application starts up in a usable state, so to begin with, here's the form's **OnCreate** handler:

```
procedure TForm1.FormCreate(Sender: TObject);
var
    Bitmap: TBitmap;
begin
    fBrush := True;
    Bitmap := TBitmap.Create;
    Bitmap.Width := ClientWidth;
    Bitmap.Height := StylePanel.Top;
    Image.Picture.Graphic := Bitmap;
    UpdateStyleCombo;
end;
```

The code here sets **fBrush** to **True** (so that the application starts up in brush mode) and adjusts the Image component's **Picture** property (a bitmap) to fill the entire client area of the form (excluding the style panel). Finally, a call is made to the **UpdateStyleCombo** routine (defined later) to ensure the following pertain:

- The style **ComboBox** has the appropriate string list for the current mode (pen styles aren't the same as brush styles).

- The current pen or brush style is displayed in the style **ComboBox**.

Incidentally, the **UpdateStyleCombo** routine is a method of the form, so be sure to add its declaration to the **public** section of the class definition, before you add the following body:

245

```
procedure TForm1.UpdateStyleCombo;
var
    i: TBrushStyle;
    j: TPenStyle;
begin
    StyleCombo.Items.Clear;
    if fBrush then
    begin
        for i := bsSolid to bsDiagCross do
            StyleCombo.Items.Add(BrushStyles[i]);
        StyleCombo.ItemIndex := Ord(Image.Canvas.Brush.Style);
    end
    else
    begin
        for j := psSolid to psInsideFrame do
            StyleCombo.Items.Add(PenStyles[j]);
        StyleCombo.ItemIndex := Ord(Image.Canvas.Pen.Style);
    end;
end;
```

Once again, the code here is pretty straightforward. It begins by clearing out the current contents of the **ComboBox** and then adds the contents of either the **BrushStyle**s or **PenStyle**s string array, according to the setting of the **fBrush** field. Finally, the **ItemIndex** property of the **ComboBox** is set to reflect the current brush or pen style.

> When this code was being written, a frustrating **EInvalidOp** exception was triggered each time the application reached the line where the **ItemIndex** property was set. This was eventually found to be due to the fact that the **Image** component's **Picture** property wasn't set by this point. This job is done in the **OnCreate** initialization code, whereas the **UpdateStyleCombo** routine was originally being called as the first line of the **OnCreate** handler. Let this be a lesson to you: don't fiddle with an **Image** component's **Picture** property until a bitmap has been assigned to it!

The **ComboBox**'s **OnClick** event handler is simple, setting the **TImage**'s brush style or pen style (as appropriate) to the value of the **ComboBox**'s **ItemIndex**:

```
procedure TForm1.StyleComboClick(Sender: TObject);
begin
    if fBrush then
        Image.Canvas.Brush.Style := TBrushStyle(StyleCombo.ItemIndex)
    else
        Image.Canvas.Pen.Style := TPenStyle(StyleCombo.ItemIndex);
end;
```

Bear in mind here that this only works because the ComboBox isn't sorted - if you set the **Sorted** property to **True**, you'd lose control over the order of items, and have to compare the ComboBox's **Text** property (the string corresponding to the selected item) against each string in **PenStyles** or **BrushStyles** until a match was found. Again, type-safe, but certainly less convenient to program!

Below is the **OnChange** code for the TabSet control:

```
procedure TForm1.TabSet1Change (Sender: TObject; NewTab: Integer;
                       var AllowChange: Boolean);
begin
    DrawingTool := TDrawingTool(NewTab);
end;
```

Since we've arranged the various tab names to correspond with the definition of **TDrawingTool**, it's just a matter of copying the currently-selected tab number into the **DrawingTool** field.

This leaves us with three trivial routines needed to complete the application. Firstly, here's the **OnChange** event handler for the scrollbar in the style panel, updating the pen width display in the **WidthPanel** component and setting the pen width as required:

```
procedure TForm1.ScrollBar1Change(Sender: TObject);
begin
    WidthPanel.Caption := IntToStr(ScrollBar1.Position);
    Image.Canvas.Pen.Width := ScrollBar1.Position;
end;
```

Secondly, the **OnClick** handler for the ColorButton is responsible for invoking the **ColorDialog** and for setting the brush or pen color according to the user's wishes - before the dialog is invoked, its **Color** property is set to the current pen or brush color, for visual feedback on the current selection:

```
procedure TForm1.ColorButtonClick(Sender: TObject);
begin
    if fBrush then
    begin
        ColorDialog1.Color := Image.Canvas.Brush.Color;
        ColorDialog1.Execute;
        Image.Canvas.Brush.Color := ColorDialog1.Color;
    end
    else
    begin
        ColorDialog1.Color := Image.Canvas.Pen.Color;
        ColorDialog1.Execute;
        Image.Canvas.Pen.Color := ColorDialog1.Color;
    end;
end;
```

Thirdly, and finally, here's the **OnClick** event handler for the **ModeSelect** button:

```
procedure TForm1.ModeSelectClick(Sender: TObject);
begin
    fBrush := not fBrush;
    UpdateStyleCombo;
    if fBrush then
    begin
        StyleLabel.Caption := 'Brush Style:';
        ColorButton.Caption := 'Brush Color...';
        ScrollBar1.Visible := False;
        WidthPanel.Visible := False;
    end
    else
    begin
        StyleLabel.Caption := 'Pen Style:';
        ColorButton.Caption := 'Pen Color...';
        ScrollBar1.Visible := True;
        WidthPanel.Visible := True;
    end;
end;
```

This toggles the style panel between pen and brush modes as follows: the value of the **fBrush** field is flipped; the **UpdateStyleCombo** procedure is called, to reflect the mode change in the **ComboBox**; the **StyleLabel** and **ColorButton** captions are set appropriately; finally, the pen width components are hidden if switching into brush mode or revealed if going into pen mode.

Having typed in all the code, get yourself a cup of coffee and try running your new application. Happy drawing!

Summary

In this chapter, we've covered the graphical capabilities of Delphi. We've reviewed the way in which Delphi's methods make it easier to do graphics programming under Windows and we've developed a practical drawing application with a snazzy user interface in only a couple of hundred lines of code!

While discussing the **UpdateStyleCombo** code, mention was made of run-time exceptions. This is an important area of Delphi software development which we'll be looking at in the next chapter.

Exercises

1   A big shortcoming of the graphical drawing application is its inability to draw text. How would you go about adding text capabilities to it? One possibility would be to add a text mode to the style panel, allowing for selection of text color, font family, point size, and so on (the simplest way of setting up font attributes is to use a FontDialog component).

2   Another problem with our drawing application is the lack of support for loading, saving and printing the bitmap. Again, these capabilities are easy to add. For some ideas, take a look at the Super Doodle application we developed earlier in the book. Also, check out the **GRAPHEX** demonstration application, supplied with Delphi, for some sample code which demonstrates printing.

Chapter

8

Creating Bullet-Proof Applications

This chapter is concerned with Object Pascal's **exception-handling** facilities - namely, language extensions which help you to deal gracefully with run-time situations which might otherwise crash your application. Exception handling has received a lot of attention in recent years (exception-handling facilities are now a standard part of C++, for instance). Such facilities can make applications easier to write, easier to maintain and more robust to use.

This chapter looks in detail at exception handling - how, why and where you might use it - and discusses the advantages of exception handling over a more traditional error-handling approach. More specifically, we'll see:

- What constitutes an exception.
- Protecting code blocks.
- Different types of exception.
- Nesting exception handlers.
- Raising and re-raising exceptions.
- Declaring your own exceptions.
- Protecting resource allocations.

If you're an experienced Pascal programmer, you might like to read Appendix Λ to get a quick overview of the new exception-handling facilities in Object Pascal.

Exceptions: Concepts

Put simply, an exception is some sort of unusual, but predictable, error condition which occurs while your application is running. As any seasoned programmer knows, there are many different types of error that can occur - Delphi attempts to trap the most common ones. As an example, try typing in this small code fragment as the **OnCreate** handler of a form:

```
procedure TForm1.FormCreate(Sender: TObject);
var
    p: ^Integer;
begin
    p := Nil;
    if p^ > 0 then MessageBeep(0);
end;
```

When you run the application, the form's **OnCreate** handler will be called before the form appears on screen. In fact, the form won't appear at all - instead, you'll see:

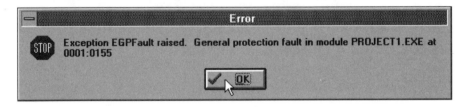

Delphi has detected that the application code tried to dereference a **Nil** pointer - never a good idea! A General Protection Fault (GPF) exception was generated and trapped by Delphi's integrated debugger, which in turn displayed the error dialog above. If the application had been running outside the Delphi environment, Windows would have displayed its own, all-too-familiar GPF error message.

> In this example, the exception was caused by a *programmer* error. In general, it's *Delphi's* job to trap programmer errors, not the programmer's job - programmers should do their best to ensure that finished applications have no such errors in them in the first place! In general, the kind of exceptions that programmers handle are databases crashing, files being in use by other applications, and so on - namely, circumstances which don't occur during normal operation of your application, but for which you should be prepared.

Protecting Code Blocks

In order to protect critical areas of your application - areas where problems might occur - you should use **exception handlers**. Any block of code that's protected by an exception handler is referred to as a **protected block**.

Before you protect a block of code, you need to understand what might go wrong in a particular area of your application. For example, an area of code that makes a lot of memory allocation calls might be protected with an exception handler that's called when no memory is available. A chunk of code that performs a lot of file access might be protected with an exception handler that detects file access problems, and so on. You also need to appreciate that an exception handler doesn't automatically fix the problem - it enables the application to regain control and take some action depending on the error that's occurred.

An exception handler frees the programmer from having to test for error conditions all over the application. As an example, suppose you design a form which has an **OnCreate** hander like this one:

```
procedure TForm1.FormCreate(Sender: TObject);
var
    f: File;
begin
    AssignFile(f, 'C:\WINDOWS\NOTTHERE.CFG');
    Reset(f);
end;
```

The routine tries to open a file called **NOTTHERE.CFG** in the **WINDOWS** directory (at least, we're assuming that you don't have such a file!). We're also assuming that the application expects this file to exist, because of installation requirements, for example. If you were to run this application inside Delphi, you'd see the following dialog:

If you were to run the application outside Delphi - by **compiling** it in Delphi and then launching it from, say, Program Manager or File Manager - you'd get the following dialog box:

The difference between these two dialogs is due to the presence of Delphi's integrated debugger. When you run an application inside Delphi itself, an unhandled exception (more precisely, an exception not handled by the application) causes an exception dialog to be displayed and a debugging session is started automatically. When you run the same application outside Delphi, it's Delphi's run-time library which provides an error indication to the user.

> **In order to keep things clean, from now on we'll assume that you're running your application outside Delphi because that is how your users will do it.**

In the above example, how would we go about protecting the block of code which opens the non-existent file? Try modifying the **OnCreate** handler so that it looks like this:

```
procedure TForm1.FormCreate(Sender: TObject);
var
    f: File;
begin
    try
        AssignFile(f, 'C:\WINDOWS\NOTTHERE.CFG');
        Reset(f);
    except
        MessageBox(0, 'Ooops!', '', mb_ok);
    end;
end;
```

If you compare this code with the previous listing, you'll see that we've placed new keywords either side of the **AssignFile** and **Reset** statements - **try** at the beginning and **except** at the end - which identifies the two statements as a protected block. Any exception that takes place after the **try** statement and before the **except** statement will cause control to be transferred to the statement immediately after the **except** keyword - in this case a call to **MessageBox**. If you execute this application - remembering to do it outside Delphi - you'll see the **MessageBox** below:

When you click on the OK button, the application continues executing in the normal way and the form appears.

> You might find it surprising that the application continues to execute. After all, when a GPF is encountered in a Windows application, that's normally the end of the story. The important thing about an exception handler is that it gives us a chance to get back into the driving seat - depending on the type of error, we can get the exception handler to terminate the application, retry or maybe ask the user for new information (such as a different directory). It's our choice.

A protected block of code can be as large as you like, subject to the obvious restriction that it's all got to fit into one procedure or function - you can't put the **try** keyword in one routine and the **except** keyword in another! However, any other routines that you call within the protected block will themselves become protected - any exception that occurs in a called routine will cause control to return to the first statement after the **except** keyword. As we'll see later, it's possible to nest exception handlers: a called routine can have its own protected block - when an exception occurs, the most-recently-entered protected-block gets to handle it.

Different Types of Exception

In the last example, **any** exception occurring in the protected block will cause the **MessageBox** to appear, but this won't always be appropriate. Suppose we want the application to behave differently depending on the type of exception that occurs. To do this, we can use an **on** statement as shown below:

```
on EInOutError do MessageBox(0, 'Ooops!', '', mb_ok);
```

Try putting this statement after the **except** keyword, replacing the simple **MessageBox** call that we saw earlier. Now the exception will only be triggered for a file I/O error. If, for instance, you replace the **AssignFile** and **Reset** statements with the **Nil**-pointer-dereferencing code that we saw earlier (see below), an **EGPFault** exception will be generated and the exception handler will be ignored:

```
procedure TForm1.FormCreate(Sender: TObject);
var
    p: ^Integer;
begin
    try
          p := Nil;
          if p^ > 0 then MessageBeep(0);
    except
          on EInOutError do
              MessageBox(0, 'EInOutError', '', mb_ok);
    end;
end;
```

Go, and Don't Come Back!

Consider the following snippet of code:

```
procedure TForm1.FormCreate(Sender: TObject);
var
    p: ^Integer;
    f: File;
begin
    try
          p := Nil;
          if p^ > 0 then MessageBeep(0);
          AssignFile(f, 'C:\WINDOWS\NOTTHERE.CFG');
          Reset(f);
```

```
    except
        on EGPFault do
            MessageBox(0, 'EGPFault', '', mb_ok);
        on EInOutError do
            MessageBox(0, 'EInOutError', '', mb_ok);
    end;
end;
```

What will be the result of running this? You might be forgiven for expecting that the first line of erroneous code will cause an **EGPFault** exception *and* that the **Reset** statement will then cause an **EInOutError** exception. However, this isn't what happens at all. Once the first exception occurs, control is transferred to the exception handling part of the procedure and control never returns to the place where the exception occurred. Therefore, the **AssignFile** and **Reset** statements never get executed. In this respect, an exception handler is like a **goto** statement and definitely *not* a routine call! This needs to be stressed so that you're clear on how exception handling works. (If you have a Visual Basic background, just remember that an exception is like **ON ERR GOTO**, *not* **ON ERR GOSUB**!)

Trying Again

So, how do you retry an operation which fails? Take a look at the following code fragment:

```
procedure TForm1.FormCreate(Sender: TObject);
const
    Names: array [0..3] of String = (    'C:\FILE1.DAT',
                                         'C:\FILE2.DAT',
                                         'C:\AUTOEXEC.BAT',
                                         'C:\CONFIG.SYS' );
var
    f: File;
    i: Integer;
begin
    for i := 0 to 3 do
        try
            AssignFile(f, Names[i]);
            Reset(f);
            Caption := Names[i];
            Exit;
        except
            on EInOutError do MessageBeep(0);
        end;
end;
```

In this **OnCreate** handler, we're trying to set the form's **Caption** to the name of the first file we find in a list of four: when the **OnCreate** event occurs, the procedure searches through the root directory of drive **C:**, looking for a file that matches one of the names in the **Names** array. If a matching file is found, the procedure sets the **Caption** property to that filename and the procedure exits. If no matching file is found, **Caption** will still be empty on exit.

There are a couple of important points to make here. Firstly, you can see that it's perfectly okay to put a complete **try/except/end** block inside a **for** statement. You can also include exception handlers inside **while** statements or pretty well anywhere that you'd expect to put a normal Object Pascal statement. What we're trying to emphasis here is that there's nothing magic about exception handlers - initially, they may seem strange and mysterious, but if you remember that it's no more than a controlled **goto** statement that's triggered by an error condition then you won't go far wrong.

The second point concerns the assignment to the **Caption** property in the above code. Bear in mind that if the **Reset** statement fails, the assignment won't take place - as soon as the **Reset** statement causes the exception to occur, control will be transferred to the **on EInOutError** ... clause.

This is the essence of exception handling - when we use exceptions in an application, we can program the main part of a routine without worrying too much about any run-time errors that might crop up. The error handling code can then be located in a separate set of **except/end** statements. By doing things in this way, you don't have to check that things are OK after each and every statement that might possibly go wrong. The end result is cleaner, more readable code.

Accessing an Exception Object

Up until now, we've talked about exceptions in a very abstract way. However, Delphi is an object-oriented system, and it should come as no surprise to discover that exceptions are actually a specialized type of object - just the same as push buttons, forms and so on. When an exception occurs, Delphi creates an **exception object**. Different types of Delphi exception correspond to different classes of exception object, but every exception is ultimately derived from the **Exception** class. When an exception handler terminates, the exception object is automatically destroyed - there's no need for you to do this yourself.

By using a specialized form of the **on** statement, you can get access to the exception object and access any other information which it contains. To see how this works, try the following **OnCreate** handler:

```
procedure TForm1.FormCreate(Sender: TObject);
var
    f: File;
begin
    try
        AssignFile(f, 'C:\WINDOWS\NOTTHERE.CFG');
        Reset(f);
    except
        on E: Exception do
            MessageDlg('Oops: ' + E.Message, mtError, [mbOK], 0);
    end;
end;
```

If you recompile and rerun the application, you'll see this dialog appear:

You can see that the string File not found has been retrieved from the **Message** field of the exception object. This is very useful if you want to handle several different types of error within the same exception handler - the **Message** field will provide a plain-English indication of what went wrong.

It's possible to use the **on** statement to type-cast an exception object to a more specific type if you know that it's safe to do so (that is, if it's the only possible type of exception at this point in the code). For example:

```
on MErr: EMathError do HandleMyMathException(MErr);
```

Here, **HandleMyMathException** is assumed to be a procedure, written by you, which takes appropriate action when a math exception occurs.

When you use this form of the **on** statement, it's important to be clear about what it is you're looking at. In our example, the variable **MErr** (we could have called it anything we liked) is actually a special exception object created just for us; it contains the same information that's to be found in the real exception object (which we're not allowed to access directly). Although **MErr** is a temporary variable, only visible within its exception handler, you shouldn't try to destroy it: it will be destroyed by Delphi at the appropriate time.

Internationalization

At this point, you might well be wondering where the string File not found came from. Any sort of string constant is a potential problem if you want to customize your application for the international marketplace. Any user-visible text needs to be stored as a string resource so that it can be selected dynamically, without the need to recompile the application.

Fortunately, it turns out that the exception-handling mechanism *does* use string resources to store exception messages. If you make use of message strings, you must make sure that you modify the appropriate resource strings when customizing your application for a foreign country.

ID Source	ID Value	String
65408	65408	'%s' is not a valid integer value
65409	65409	'%s' is not a valid floating point value
65410	65410	'%s' is not a valid date
65411	65411	'%s' is not a valid time
65412	65412	'%s' is not a valid date and time
65413	65413	Invalid argument to time encode
65414	65414	Invalid argument to date encode
65415	65415	Out of memory
65416	65416	I/O error %d
65417	65417	File not found
65418	65418	Invalid filename
65419	65419	Too many open files
65420	65420	File access denied
65421	65421	Read beyond end of file
65422	65422	Disk full
65423	65423	Invalid numeric input

STRINGTABLE : 65408

The screenshot shown on the previous page was produced with Borland's Resource Workshop. It shows some of the exception message strings inside a compiled executable file. If you want more information on exactly which string resources are involved, then look in the **SYSUTILS.PAS** file - you'll find it in your **\DELPHI\SOURCE\RTL\SYS** directory. If you look at the **CreateRes** method of the **Exception** class, and the places where it's called, you should get the idea. To modify the strings themselves, just edit the file **\DELPHI\SOURCE\RTL\SYS\SYSUTILS.RC**.

> **This really only applies to the run-time library exceptions. However, Delphi has a lot of other exceptions which relate to problems with components. The message strings relating to these exceptions are stored in the following files:**
>
> **\DELPHI\SOURCE\VCL\CONSTS.RC**
>
> **\DELPHI\SOURCE\VCL\DBCONSTS.RC**
>
> **\DELPHI\SOURCE\VCL\MCIMSG.RC**
>
> **\DELPHI\SOURCE\VCL\VBXMSG.RC**

Nesting Exception Handlers

Delphi makes it easy to nest one exception handler within another. By default, when an exception is raised (in other words, when an exception instance is created), Delphi's run-time library code will try to find an exception handler within the current block which handles that type of exception. If none is found, Delphi widens the search to the next higher block and so on, until a compatible exception handler is found.

> **Bear in mind here that - in the context of a Pascal application - the term 'block' doesn't just relate to nested begin ... end statements within a particular routine. Every procedure and function is a block which may be contained within another procedure or function, or within the outermost scope of the application.**

261

Why might you want to nest exception handlers anyway? Well, nesting exception handlers allows you to apply error checking to a range of operations, while augmenting that error checking where necessary. For example, suppose that you wanted to write something like Program Manager using Delphi. One of Program Manager's first jobs is to look for the file **PROGMAN.INI** in the **WINDOWS** directory. This file, in turn, contains the names of the various group files which Program Manager uses to store group information. A few lines of a typical **PROGMAN.INI** file are shown below:

```
[Groups]
Group1=C:\WINDOWS\MAIN.GRP
Group2=C:\WINDOWS\ACCESSOR.GRP
Group4=C:\WINDOWS\STARTUP.GRP
Group5=C:\WINDOWS\AMEOL.GRP
Group6=C:\WINDOWS\MICROSOF.GRP
Group8=C:\WINDOWS\PAINTSHO.GRP
Group9=C:\WINDOWS\TABPRO11.GRP
```

When it starts up, Program Manager goes through all the nominated group files, loading each one and processing its contents. If one of these group files is missing, you get a warning dialog. However, if the **PROGMAN.INI** file can't be found, things are more serious - or at least they should be! In practice, Program Manager will obligingly start up without a murmur, creating an empty **PROGMAN.INI** file in the background and display a window that's conspicuously lacking in groups!

If we were implementing a Program Manager look-alike, we might choose to check for and load all required files within one routine. Inside that routine, we could install an exception handler which checks for an **EInOutError** and displays a warning message. The check for **PROGMAN.INI** would involve an additional, nested block, which would have its own exception handler. This handler would abort the application if **PROGMAN.INI** wasn't found.

A rough sketch of the code might look something like this:

```
try
    open \WINDOWS\PROGMAN.INI file
    for each group file in PROGMAN.INI
    begin
        try
            open specified group file
            process the group file
        except
            on EInOutError: Tell user couldn't open group file
        end;
```

```
    end;
except
    on EInOutError: Tell user PROGMAN.INI isn't there...
    ...and exit gracefully....
end;
```

> In the case of our hypothetical **Program Manager**, it might be
> better to nest another procedure within the main procedure.
> This nested procedure would be exclusively responsible for
> loading and parsing PROGMAN.INI, but by making it into a
> separate procedure, it would have a more clearly-defined role
> and the exception handling mechanism would be neater. It's
> all a matter of personal taste. But, it's recommended that you
> don't have too many levels of nested exception handlers
> within the same routine. After all, part of the purpose of
> exception handling is to simplify code, not to make it more
> complicated and hard to understand.

Default Exception Handlers

As has already been explained, there are several different forms of the **on**
statement that you can use. There's yet another form which we haven't seen
yet; here it is below:

```
try
    { ...statements... }
except
    on EMathError do
        { specific math error handler }
    else
        { default exception handler }
    end;
```

In this case, the exception handling code will provide specific error-handling
for math errors, while all other exception types will be handled by whatever
statements you add to the **else** part.

Often, this is not a good way of doing things. If there's a lot of code in the
try/**except** part, then you may well get exceptions thrown at you which
you don't really know how to handle. It's better to code for specific
exceptions where possible - any exception you're not prepared for will then
be passed up to a more suitable handler.

OnException - The Global Exception Handler

By default, a Delphi application which contains no exception-handling code will display a message box in response to an exception. We saw this message box in action right at the beginning of the chapter. This behavior is implemented through a procedure in the **SYSUTILS.PAS** unit called **ShowException**.

You can install your own application-wide exception-handler which overrides this default behavior. To do this, you need to modify the **OnException** property of the **Application** object (you must do this at run time, not design time). For further details on this, see *Handling Application Exceptions* in the Borland documentation.

Raising Exceptions Yourself

Normally, exceptions are detected automatically by Delphi, an exception object is created and the appropriate handler is called. However, there will be times when it's convenient to **raise** an exception yourself. This might seem like an odd thing to do, but there are good reasons. For example, you might want to debug or test the exception handling code you've built into your application; by temporarily adding code to raise an exception, you can check the operation of your exception handler. Another example is if you want to write your own device driver in Object Pascal - if the device crashes unexpectedly, you'll need to detect the fact and raise an appropriate exception.

You'll also need to raise an exception if you're implementing a new exception type (we'll see how to do this later). When you first encounter exceptions, it almost seems as if they're created by magic, but if you examine the **SYSUTILS.PAS** file (and the component sources in **\DELPHI\SOURCE\VCL**), you'll see that this isn't so. The built-in exceptions are all raised behind the scenes in the usual way.

Raising an exception is very simple, but it does involve you creating a new exception instance. Fortunately, you can do both jobs at the same time. The following function - one of the **TControl** methods - is taken from the Visual Components Library. It creates an **EInvalidOperation** exception if the **GetClientOrigin** method is called when the component has no parent:

```
function TControl.GetClientOrigin: TPoint;
begin
    if Parent = Nil then
        raise EInvalidOperation.Create(LoadStr(SParentRequired));
    Result := Parent.ClientOrigin;
    Inc(Result.X, FLeft);
    Inc(Result.Y, FTop);
end;
```

As you can see, the syntax is quite straightforward. Apart from the **raise** keyword, it's just the same syntax that you'd use to create any other object using Object Pascal: first the type name, then a period, then the **Create** method name and any parameters. In this particular case, the **LoadStr** function is called to load a string resource into memory. The string resource, defined in the **CONSTS.RC** file, contains the text **Control has no parent window**. (There are many types of **EInvalidException** that can occur - the message string discriminates between them.)

Re-Raising an Exception

If raising an exception under application control seems initially like an odd concept, then re-raising an exception must seem positively screwy! The key to this concept is an understanding of what normally happens at the end of an exception handler - the exception object is destroyed without trace. To extend the life of an exception object, you must **re-raise** it.

To re-raise an exception, you simply use the **Raise** keyword from *within* the exception handler, like this:

```
try
    { ...statements... }
except
    { ...statements... }
    Raise;
end;
```

No parameters are necessary because as we're operating in the context of an exception handler, it's assumed that we're referring to the exception that's currently being handled.

You're only likely to re-raise an exception if you want to perform some special processing for a particular exception, before the exception is handled by the regular exception handler in an outer block. For example, you might choose to implement an exception handler for a certain type of exception at an outer block of your application, so that the exception can be raised from a large number of places within the application. In order to provide clearer error handling, local handlers can then be used at certain key points in the application code. These local handlers might set a global string variable indicating the approximate location of the exception (for example, **Out of Memory in Input Parser**) before re-raising the exception. The exception will then be processed by the outer-level handler which can display the string variable along with other pertinent information.

Defining Your Own Exceptions

Since an exception is, fundamentally, just another object class, you can easily define your own exception types. Suppose, for example, that you were writing a compiler for some programming language. You might decide to implement the compiler's error-message handling using Delphi's exception facilities. You could define a special class of exception for handling syntax errors like this:

```
type
    ESyntaxError = class (Exception);
```

This definition is all you need. Now you can just go ahead and create exception handlers for this new exception type. At various places in your application, you'll need to raise your new custom exception. You do it in the normal way like this:

```
if token <> ';' then
    raise ESyntaxError.Create('Semicolon expected');
```

As you can see, adding your own types of exception couldn't be easier.

Protecting Resource Allocations

By now you should be realizing that exceptions represent a powerful way to keep all your error-handling logic under control without having it strewn all through your application code in an untidy way.

However, if this was all there was to say about exception handling, it would probably create almost as many problems as it solves. To see why this is the case, consider the following code fragment:

```
Procedure AllocateBuffers;
var
    Buff1, Buff2, Buff3: PBuffer;
begin
    GetMem(Buff1, sizeof (Buffer));
    GetMem(Buff2, sizeof (Buffer));
    GetMem(Buff3, sizeof (Buffer));

    {...…use the buffers.…}

    FreeMem(Buff1, sizeof (Buffer));
    FreeMem(Buff2, sizeof (Buffer));
    FreeMem(Buff3, sizeof (Buffer))
end;
```

This procedure assumes that it's being called from an outer block which has an exception handler capable of responding to **EOutOfMemory** exceptions. Consequently, it isn't necessary for this procedure to worry about out-of-memory conditions - or is it? Suppose that the first two buffers were successfully allocated and the third allocation failed, triggering an **EOutOfMemory** exception. Because the exception isn't handled inside the **AllocateBuffers** procedure itself, control would immediately be transferred to the outer exception handler, wherever that might be. All well and good…

But, cripes! What's going to happen to the two memory allocations that have already been made? The short answer is: nothing! Because the **AllocateBuffers** routine is no longer in scope, **Buff1** and **Buff2** disappear from view, but the memory reserved for each of them is still allocated. This is obviously bad news - we've allocated memory which we can't deallocate. In the same way, if another routine were to load a cursor, an icon or a bitmap and then trigger an exception, those resources could potentially get 'lost in memory'.

The solution to this seems obvious - add a local **EOutOfMemory** exception handler which deallocates any buffers that were successfully allocated. This local exception handler can re-raise the exception so as to pass it to the outer handler …

Hm ... does this mean that any routine which allocates memory, loads bitmaps or other resources, must have its own local exception handler? This sounds like a lot of hassle. Surely there must be a simpler way.

Introducing try ... finally Blocks

Fortunately, there is. In addition to the **try** ... **except** block which we've been looking at so far, Delphi provides another form of statement called the **try** ... **finally** block. Here's how we could recode the **AllocateBuffers** procedure to use a **try** ... **finally** block:

```
procedure AllocateBuffers;
var
    Buff1, Buff2, Buff3: PBuffer;
begin
    Buff1 := Nil;
    Buff2 := Nil;
    Buff3 := Nil;
    try
        GetMem(Buff1, sizeof(Buffer));
        GetMem(Buff2, sizeof(Buffer));
        GetMem(Buff3, sizeof(Buffer));

        {..…use the buffers.…}

        finally
        if Buff1 <> Nil then
    FreeMem(Buff1, sizeof(Buffer));
        if Buff2 <> Nil then
    FreeMem(Buff2, sizeof(Buffer));
        if Buff3 <> Nil then
    FreeMem(Buff3, sizeof(Buffer));
    end;
end;
```

Here, the variables **Buff1**, **Buff2** and **Buff3** are initialized with the value **Nil** on entry to the procedure, so that we can tell which ones are successfully allocated. The **GetMem** calls are then arranged as before. You'll notice the **finally** keyword part way through the procedure - this ensures that whenever the **AllocateBuffers** procedure is exited, control first passes to the **finally** clause of the block to deallocate buffers as necessary: each of the calls to **FreeMem** is preceded by a check to ensure that the corresponding buffer variable is not **Nil**.

You need to be very clear about how this works. Two different scenarios are possible. Let's suppose that all the memory allocations are successful. In this case, any other statements in **AllocateBuffers** will be executed and then control will pass to the final **end** statement of the procedure. At that point, just before the procedure terminates, control will be passed to the **finally** clause and the three buffers will be deallocated.

Now consider the situation if one of the allocations failed. In this case, an **EOutOfMemory** exception will be generated and the procedure will terminate. However, even though the routine exits by virtue of an exception, the **finally** code will *still* be executed. Thus, you can perform any necessary clean-up of allocated buffers and - most importantly - the programmer can guarantee that no matter what happens, this clean-up will always take place.

> To summarize: the **finally** clause is *always* executed, regardless of whether or not an exception occurs.

The order in which code is executed when an exception occurs is shown in the diagram below.

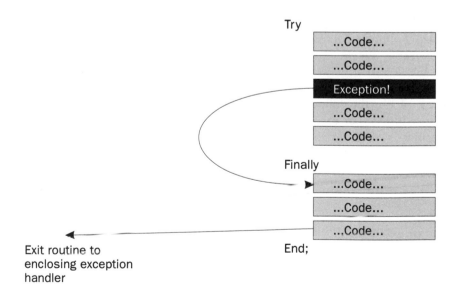

The Importance of Clean-Up Code

Reliable clean-up code is critically important in a multi-tasking environment such as Microsoft Windows. As you'll no doubt be aware, one of the great banes of the Windows developer's life is the so-called 'System Resources' limitation. The **USER** and **GDI** DLLs contain much of the core Windows code and they store a great deal of information on their local heaps - the **USER** library's heap, for instance, contains all the window records, menu structures and window class information for every running application.

A local heap is restricted to a maximum of 64 KBytes in size. With the advent of Windows 3.1, Microsoft went to some lengths to alleviate the problem by introducing multiple local heaps into the **USER** library. With Windows 95, the problem has been eased even further, but you need to move up to Windows NT if you want to get completely away from the System Resources constraint. It represents an Achilles heel in the design of the 16-bit Windows system.

Because of all this, an application needs to take special care when deallocating resources such as windows, dialogs, menus, bitmaps, cursors and icons. All these things take up room in the **USER** and **GDI** local heaps, so you must be very careful to deallocate them as soon as they're no longer required. Failure to do so can leave you with acres of global memory but an inoperable system due to 'RAM cram' in those all-important local heaps.

In order to illustrate how to protect resource allocations using the **try** … **finally** block, the following procedure demonstrates how to load and display a bitmap in response to a form's **OnPaint** event. (Normally, of course, you would do things like this using a **TImage** or **TPaintBox** component - this code is for illustrative purposes only.)

```
procedure TForm1.FormPaint(Sender: TObject);
var
    SrcDC: hDC;
    hbm: HBitmap;
    bm: WinTypes.TBitmap;
begin
    try
        SrcDC := 0;
        SrcDC := CreateCompatibleDC(Canvas.Handle);
        { Load the internal obm_CheckBoxes bitmap }
        hbm := LoadBitmap(0, PChar(obm_CheckBoxes));
        { Get the bitmap size information }
        GetObject(hbm, sizeof(bm), @bm);
        { Select the bitmap into the device context }
        hbm := SelectObject(SrcDC, hbm);
        { Blit it into top left corner of canvas }
        BitBlt (Canvas.Handle, 0, 0, bm.bmWidth, bm.bmHeight,
                SrcDC, 0, 0, SrcCopy);
    finally
        if SrcDC <> 0 then
        begin
            { Deselect and delete the bitmap }
            DeleteObject(SelectObject (SrcDC, hbm));
            { Delete the source device context }
            DeleteDC(SrcDC);
        end;
    end;
end;
```

As you can see, the **finally** clause takes care to remove the loaded bitmap from memory and deallocates the temporary device context.

Here's the effect of using this **OnPaint** handler (the weird-looking bitmap we've loaded is actually one of the internal bitmaps used by Windows to implement dialog boxes):

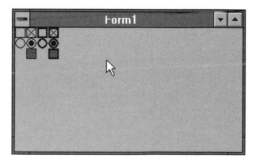

Summary

This chapter has looked at exception handling - a very useful technique for improving the robustness and error-handling capabilities of your applications. But, you should be careful not to litter your code with too *much* exception handling - this just makes things worse: remember that exceptions, as their name implies, are designed to handle **exceptional** circumstances, such as running out of memory.

Also, try not to use exception handling to surround parts of your application which you don't trust - it's better to test and debug your application properly!

We've also seen in this chapter the importance of protecting resource allocations, so that other applications aren't hampered by your exceptions.

If you need more examples of these techniques, you're encouraged to study the Visual Component library source code provided with Delphi.

Exercises

Take another look at the outline code which checks for the presence of the **PROGMAN.INI** file and then loops through each of the group files in turn. See if you can convert this outline into real working code. Obviously, we're not asking you to create a real Program Manager replacement, but see if you can write a simple project whose **OnCreate** handler loads **PROGMAN.INI** and then tries to read all the group files into memory. If **PROGMAN.INI** can't be found, the application should abort with a fatal error. If any of the group files can't be loaded, then you should display a non-fatal warning message and go on to the next one. Use exception handling throughout.

Chapter

A Tour of the
Visual Component Library

In the course of this book, we've touched on many of the common Delphi
components. However, there are a lot of other components that we haven't
been able to cram in yet. This chapter is devoted to a whirlwind tour of
the component library.

For the sake of space, we won't bother describing in detail the components
that we've seen already, except to highlight useful features that haven't been
mentioned before. For ease of reference, the various components are
grouped in the same categories as on the Component Palette.

You should bear in mind that this chapter is somewhat subjective - for
practical reasons, we've expanded on the features of each component which,
to us, seem most useful. Please take the time to examine the capabilities of
each component for yourself.

In summary, this chapter is a reference guide to the various pages of the
Component Palette and as such leaves the experimentation and
implementation to you.

Components: Concepts

To begin with, you should know that while the Object Inspector's Properties page is active, pressing the *F1* key will give you online help for the currently selected property. Similarly, when the Events page is active, *F1* will yield help relating to the currently selected event handler. This is a fast and convenient way of exploring an unfamiliar component.

The Standard Page

The Standard page of the Component Palette is shown below:

The MainMenu and PopupMenu Components

The MainMenu and PopupMenu components were described in detail in Chapter 4.

The Label Component

The Label component is used to annotate other items on a form.

FocusControl

Specifies the name of another component which should receive the focus rather than the Label component itself. This is useful when placing a Label next to some other component such as an Edit box. If you associate a hot key with the Label (*Alt-P* in the illustration below) and the Label's **FocusControl** is set to the name of the Edit box, pressing that hot key will set the focus to the Edit box.

Transparent

The **Transparent** property can be used to make a Label's background transparent. This is great when you want to put a Label on top of a bitmap. For example, your application's startup screen might display a fancy bitmap, on which you want to write variable data such as product version, serial number and so forth. This is easy when you set the **Transparent** property to **True**. You will, of course, need to set the font color of the component (a sub-property of the **Font** property) so that the color of the Label contrasts well with the underlying bitmap.

The Edit Component

The Edit box is used to display text and provide a standard method for user modification of the text. Where you need to handle multiple lines of text, use the Memo component.

AutoSelect

Setting this Boolean property to **True** will cause the entire text of the component to be selected each time the user tabs to it. Since this is standard Windows behavior, **AutoSelect** is **True** by default.

MaxLength

Specifies the maximum number of characters which can be typed into the component. This makes it easy, for example, to create Edit boxes that will only accept a maximum of two characters for USA state abbreviations. Zero, the default value of **MaxLength**, means that there is no limit to the number of characters which can be entered.

PassWordChar

Setting this property to a specific character means that Delphi will display the character for each key that the user types. This is handy for creating password boxes or for entering any sort of confidential data. Although the user can't see what's being typed in, your application can and it can be processed in the usual way.

ReadOnly

If this Boolean property is **True**, the user won't be able to change the data displayed in the Edit box. You might use this, for instance, when displaying read-only data in a database record.

The Memo Component

The Memo component is one we haven't used so far. A Memo is much like an Edit component, with one important difference: it can store multiple lines of text, whereas the Edit component can only store one. A typical use of the Memo component is shown below:

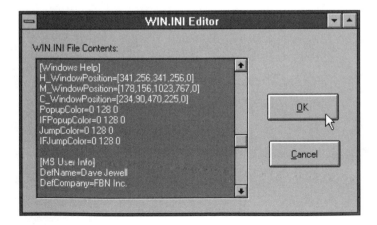

As you might expect, Memo components share many properties with Edit components. However, they do have a few unique properties as well.

Lines

At design-time, you can use this property to fill a Memo component with a large amount of data. In the illustration on the previous page, we used the String list editor's Open button to load the contents of **WIN.INI** into the component. You could enter text directly using the **Text** property, but this would be tedious and cumbersome for a large amount of text.

ScrollBars

You can give a Memo component scroll bars to help with displaying large pieces of text - just set the **Scrollbars** property to one of these values:

Property	Behavior
scNone	Component has no scroll bars.
scHorizontal	Horizontal scroll bar only.
scVertical	Vertical scroll bar only (see above illustration).
scBoth	Both horizontal and vertical scrollbars.

WantTabs

When this property is set to **False** (the default), pressing the *Tab* key will cause the focus to be transferred to the next component in the tab order. However, when **WantTabs** is **True**, pressing *Tab* will cause a tab to be inserted into the text of the Memo component at the current insertion point. Only use this facility if you want to give your users the ability to type tabs into the text being displayed.

The Button Component

The ubiquitous Button component!

ModalResult

The Button component has a property called **ModalResult**. If you start a form using the **ShowModal** method, setting **ModalResult** to a non-zero value will terminate the enclosing form, with **ModalResult** returned as the result of **ShowModal**.

This is useful when you want to return a variety of values according to which button was pressed on a modal form. You can minimize the amount of code involved by simply setting the **ModalResult** to the **Tag** property of whichever button was pressed, using a shared **OnClick** event handler for all the buttons involved.

If you have a limited number of common responses on a form (OK, Cancel, and so on), you can even avoid writing an **OnClick** handler altogether by setting the **ModalResult** property at design-time. For example, if you use the ComboBox in the Object Inspector to select **mrOK** for a particular button, clicking on that button at run-time will terminate the enclosing modal form with the result **mrOK**.

The ListBox Component

This is a (scrollable) list of items from which one or more can be selected.

Columns

The **Columns** property is used to set the number of columns.

IntegralHeight

If **True**, the bottom of the ListBox is adjusted on-the-fly so that an exact number of items fit into the ListBox. By default, this property is **False**, which means that the item at the bottom of the ListBox may only be partially visible. You can get a better-looking effect if you set this property to **True** but, if the ListBox **Style** property (see below) is set to **lbOwnerDrawVariable**, the value of **IntegralHeight** is ignored.

ItemHeight

This is the height of each item in the ListBox. This property is ignored unless the ListBox **Style** property is **lbOwnerDrawFixed**.

MultiSelect

This property allows more than one item in a ListBox to be selected at the same time.

Style

This property can have one of three values:

Property	Behavior
lbStandard	Every item in the ListBox is of the same height (20 pixels).
lbOwnerDrawFixed	Every item in the ListBox is of the height specified by **ItemHeight**.
lbOwnerDrawVariable	Each item can be a different height.

In the second two cases, the ListBox component generates **OnDrawItem** events. You need to provide an **OnDrawItem** event handler to draw the items in the ListBox. For the **lbOwnerDrawVariable** style, you also need to provide a **OnMeasureItem** event handler which returns the desired height of each item.

> For an example of a **lbOwnerDrawFixed** ListBox and the creation of a **OnDrawItem** handler, refer to the icon viewing application at the end of Chapter 1.

The ComboBox Component

The **ItemHeight** property also applies to the ListBox part of a ComboBox. However, there is no **IntegralHeight** property for a ComboBox and you can't enable multiple selections.

Style

The **Style** property of a ComboBox component can take on any of the values shown on the next page:

Property	Behavior
csDropDown	The Edit box has an associated drop-down list.
csSimple	The ListBox part of the component is always visible.
csDropDownList	The drop-down list has no associated Edit box.
csOwnerDrawFixed	Each item in the list has the height specified by ItemHeight.
csOwnerDrawVariable	Each item in the list can be of variable height.

Again, for the last two cases, the component generates **OnDrawItem** events for which you will need to provide an event handler. For the **csOwnerDrawVariable** style, you'll also need to provide an **OnMeasureItem** event handler.

The ScrollBar Component

The Scrollbar is used to scroll through information which - for reasons of size - can't all be displayed in one go. It can also be used to change the value of important program variables, as in the drawing program of Chapter 7.

Large and Small Change

This property determines the change of value in the scroll bar when the mouse is clicked between the scroll box and the end arrows.

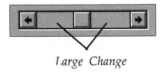

Large Change

This property determines the change of value in the scroll bar when the mouse is clicked on either of the end arrows, or the arrow keys are pressed while the scroll bar has the input focus.

Small Change

The GroupBox Component

The GroupBox component is used to enclose one or more related controls. You can see three different group boxes in the accompanying illustration.

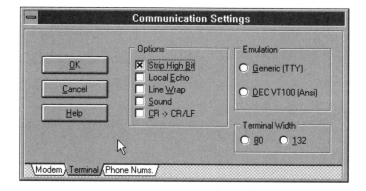

The GroupBox, Panel, ScrollBox and NoteBook components are all examples of container components - that is, they may be used to contain one or more other components. In the above example, you could grab the Options group and drag it to a different part of the form, treating it as a single unit. Obviously, this makes the process of user interface design much more convenient.

> When setting the `Caption` property of a **GroupBox**, leave a single space before and after the caption string. This stops the border colliding with the text and produces a more pleasing effect.

283

The RadioGroup Component

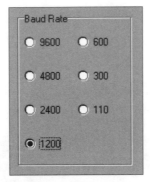

The RadioGroup component is a neat way of gathering together a number of related radio buttons into a single control. Rather than having to create each radio button individually, the RadioGroup is a single component where each radio button title corresponds to an entry in the RadioGroup's Items property.

ItemIndex

This is the index of the currently 'pushed' radio button. (Can be set at design-time)

Columns

This is the number of columns used to display the various radio buttons.

The Additional Page

The Additional page of the Component Palette is shown below:

The BitBtn Component

A BitBtn component works just like an ordinary push button, except that you can add a small bitmap (Borland refer to this as a **glyph**) to the button.

Kind

This property selects the bitmap that's displayed. Delphi has a number of built-in bitmaps corresponding to Yes, No, Cancel, OK and Help buttons. In addition, you can set the **Kind** property to **bkCustom**, in which case you're responsible for specifying the bitmap.

Glyph

Double-click this property in the Object Inspector to specify a custom bitmap. The built-in bitmaps are fairly small, but you can specify a bitmap of any reasonable size, providing, of course, that you make the button large enough to accommodate it. The illustration below shows two bitmaps - one of the built-in ones on the left and a custom bitmap (actually **ARGYLE.BMP** from the Windows system directory) on the right:

Layout

The **Layout** property controls the arrangement of the text and the bitmap within the button.

Property	Behavior
blGlyphLeft	The bitmap is to the left of the text (default).
blGlyphRight	The bitmap is to the right of the text.
blGlyphTop	The bitmap is above the text.
blGlyphBottom	The bitmap is below the text.

The SpeedButton Component

In addition to buttons, and BitBtns, Delphi also offers SpeedButtons. Why the need for all these different types of button? Here's a simple summary of their respective characteristics:

Component	Has Caption?	Has Bitmap?
Button	Yes	No
SpeedButton	No	Yes
BitBtn	Yes	Yes

As you can see, a SpeedButton is the opposite of a button - a bitmap only, with no caption. Why would you want a button with no caption? The answer is simple: for toolbars! (Actually, you *can* add a caption to a SpeedButton if you really want to, but this isn't normally done, since they're usually used in toolbars.)

Down

This property specifies whether the button is down (pushed in).

GroupIndex

If a SpeedButton has a **GroupIndex** of zero, it works independently of other SpeedButtons on the form. If, however, the **GroupIndex** is non-zero, the button will be associated with all the other **Speed**Buttons with the same **GroupIndex**.

Also, if a SpeedButton has a **GroupIndex** of zero, the button will go down when the user clicks on it, but it will pop back up again when the user releases the mouse button. In contrast, if a SpeedButton has a non-zero **GroupIndex**, it will stay down when the mouse button is released, but any other button in the group which was down already will pop back up - therefore, at most one button in the group will be down at any one time (a bit like the waveband selectors on a radio).

AllowAllUp

This property, if **True**, allows all SpeedButtons in a group to be up simultaneously. If **False**, at least one button will be pushed in (if no buttons are down when the application starts, the first one clicked will stay down).

Layout

This works just like the **Layout** property on a BitBtn.

NumGlyphs

A SpeedButton's bitmap can actually contain up to four images side-by-side, displayed separately according to the state of the button. The **NumGlyphs** property corresponds to the number of images in the assigned bitmap.

Button State	Image Number (Left to Right)	Notes
Up	1	The normal, unselected button state.
Disabled	2	The grayed-out, disabled button state.
Down	3	The state of the button while held down.
Stay Down	4	The state of a button that has stayed down.

The TabSet Component

The TabSet component, which we saw in Chapter 7, has a large number of properties for controlling its appearance and behavior - you're encouraged to familiarize yourself with them all. Perhaps the most interesting is the **Style** property.

Style

This property can take one of two values:

Property	Behavior
tsStandard	Each tab has the standard size and appearance.
tsOwnerDraw	When **Style** is set to **tsOwnerDraw**, all tabs have the height specified by the **TabHeight** property.

In the latter case, **OnMeasureTab** events are generated to request the width of each tab, while **OnDrawTab** events are generated to draw the contents of each tab. You must provide event handlers for both event types. This style means that you could, for example, display a small icon alongside each tab name.

The NoteBook Component

NoteBook components are often used with TabSet components to implement what are commonly called **tabbed dialogs**. You can think of a NoteBook as a container component which can contain more than one page. At design-time, you set up all the desired pages using the **Pages** property and then, subsequently, you choose which page you want to work with by setting the **ActivePage** property.

At run-time, you'd typically place a TabSet component at the bottom of a NoteBook component and use the **TabSet**'s **OnClick** event handler to change the displayed page, like this:

```
procedure TPrefsDlg.TabSetClick (Sender: TObject);
begin
    { set Page to selected tab }
    Notebook.PageIndex := TabSet.TabIndex;
end;
```

The TabbedNoteBook Component

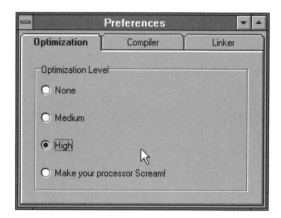

The TabbedNoteBook component gives you a simple, no-frills, tabbed dialog. Unlike the combination of TabSet and NoteBook components, you don't have the flexibility of where to position the tabs and so on. However, what you lose in flexibility, you gain in ease of use.

The MaskEdit Component

This component works very much like an Edit box except that it has the ability to restrict user input to a certain format. In a simple case, you might want to ensure that a user is only able to type a number into an input field. Alternatively, you might want to do something more complex such as ensuring that only a valid phone number, date or time is entered. You can do all this with the functionality built into the MaskEdit component.

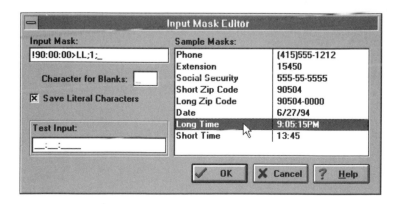

The Outline Component

The Outline component can be used to display hierarchical information in a convenient, tree-structured fashion. This is typically used to display disk directory information, but you can also set up custom bitmaps and the control provides a high degree of customization. If you want to design your own family tree viewer, an Outline component will probably save you a lot of effort!

The StringGrid Component

You can use a StringGrid component to display data in a tabular form such as you're used to seeing in a spreadsheet application. The StringGrid control provides an extraordinary degree of customization but you are limited, as the name suggests, to textual information. The StringGrid is a more specialized version of the DrawGrid component.

The DrawGrid Component

The DrawGrid component allows any information (graphical or textual) to be displayed in a tabular form. This might be useful if (for example) you were implementing something like a Program Manager group view. By displaying an icon in each cell, you wouldn't have to worry about lining up each icon, scrolling through the list of icons and so on - all this would come for free.

The Image Component

The Image component can be used to display icons, bitmaps and Windows metafiles on a form. These correspond to file extensions of .ICO, .BMP and .WMF respectively.

> Sometimes, device-independent Windows bitmap files are given the extension .DIB. You'll find that the Image component will also be able to display these files without any problems.

AutoStretch

If you want an image component to automatically adjust to the size of the bitmap, icon or metafile, set this property to **True** *before* associating an image file with the component.

Stretch

Set this to **True** if you want to stretch the image at design-time. Note that you can only stretch bitmaps and metafiles, not icons. If you want to stretch an image, it's better to work with metafiles - stretched bitmaps often look very poor.

The Shape Component

In Chapter 7, we discussed ways of adding graphical effects to your Delphi applications. An alternative approach is to make use of the Shape component. Using a Shape, you can add ellipses, rectangles (plain and round-cornered), squares and circles to your form's background.

Consider the following example. Not everybody likes the **Ctl3D** effect, so you could try creating an alternative 3D style by exploiting Shape components on your form. You can do this by adding a dark gray rectangle Shape to act as a shadow behind each component as shown below:

If you want to try this out, you should turn off the **Ctl3D** property for the form itself and by implication, the **Ctl3D** property of all the components on the form (assuming that they all have their **ParentCtl3D** property set to **True**).

> There are drawbacks with this approach. For example, when altering the font used by a component at design-time, components such as **Edit** boxes will resize according to the height of the current font (assuming that their **AutoSize** property is **True**). To get round this particular problem, you could add code to the form's **OnCreate** handler to resize the drop shadows accordingly - simply adjust the height of each drop shadow to match that of the component placed over it.

Brush

The **Brush** property of a Shape specifies the brush used to paint the interior of the shape.

Pen

The **Pen** property of a Shape specifies the pen used to draw the shape boundary (see Chapter 7 for a more detailed explanation of brushes and pens).

The Bevel Component

Bevels look a lot like Panel components, but they're purely decorative - they're not container components, so Delphi won't let you put other components inside them. The appearance of a Bevel is affected by two properties.

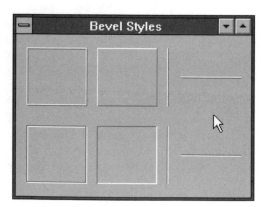

Style

This property can have one of two settings as given in the table below. In the accompanying picture, the four bevels in the top row have **Style** set to **bsRaised**, while those along the bottom row have it set to **bsLowered**.

Property	Behavior
bsLowered	The bevel has a sunken 3D appearance.
bsRaised	The bevel has a raised 3D appearance.

Shape

As you might expect, the **Shape** property controls the shape of the Bevel. There are six possible settings for this property, given in the table below:

Property	Behavior
bsBox	The bevel is a raised or sunken box.
bsFrame	The bevel is a hollow frame.
bsTopLine	The bevel is a line along the top of the component's bounding rectangle.
bsBottomLine	The bevel is a line along the bottom of the component's bounding rectangle.
bsLeftLine	The bevel is a line along the left of the component's bounding rectangle.
bsRightLine	The bevel is a line along the right of the component's bounding rectangle.

The last four settings will yield bevels comprising a single vertical or horizontal line. These lines make good separators between different groups of components in a dialog box. Note that Bevel components are constrained to use the button-shading colors set by the Windows Control Panel - you can't assign arbitrary colors to them.

The Header Component

A Header component, as the name suggests, is used to display headings for a list of tabular information, as shown in the sample window below. When the user moves the cursor over the header, it changes to a double-ended arrow at each title boundary, so that the relative widths of columns can be changed.

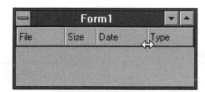

The ScrollBox Component

Again, the ScrollBox is another type of container. Use a ScrollBox when you want a part of your form to be scrollable. Using a ScrollBox, you can easily create scrollable dialog boxes - something that is by no means trivial when using C.

The Dialogs Page

The Dialogs page of the Component Palette looks like this:

The OpenDialog and SaveDialog Components

OpenDialog components have been discussed elsewhere in this book - we first encountered the OpenDialog in Chapter 4 when opening bitmap files. The OpenDialog and SaveDialog components are similar, both of them being object-oriented 'wrappers' around the Common Dialogs library provided by Microsoft. An interesting feature of both components is the ability to display a **history list**. For example, look at the dialog shown below:

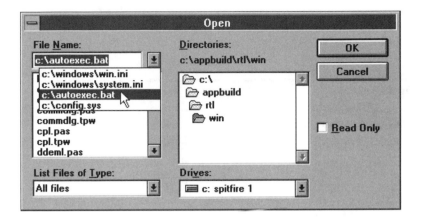

As you can see, the usual File Name Edit box has been replaced with a ComboBox, with a list of the most recently opened files in its drop-down list. In order to get this behavior, you need to modify the **FileEditStyle** and **HistoryList** properties.

FileEditStyle

This property defaults to **fsEdit**. Change it to **fsComboBox** to turn the File Name Edit box into a ComboBox.

HistoryList

The dialog's **List** should contain the previously opened or saved filenames, as appropriate.

You could initialize the list at design-time, but, bearing in mind the nature of the information, you wouldn't normally do so. Rather, you'd modify the list as new files were opened or saved at run-time. You could also store the history list in, say, your application's **.INI** file, so that it can be recalled the next time your application is started.

Options

The OpenDialog and SaveDialog components have a large number of options that can be set before the dialog is invoked, controlled by the **Options** property. **Options** is a nested property, whose sub-properties are all **False** by default. The effect of setting each sub-property to **True** is explained in the table below:

Option	Purpose
ofAllowMultiSelect	Allows the user to select multiple files in the File Name ListBox.
ofCreatePrompt	If the file doesn't exist, a dialog will be displayed inviting the user to create a new file.
ofExtensionDifferent	This option is returned from the dialog, rather than being passed in to it. If **True**, the filename selected by the user had a different extension to that specified in the **DefaultExt** property.
ofFileMustExist	Forces the user to enter the name of a file that exists - if the file doesn't exist, an error dialog will be displayed telling the user to try again.
ofHideReadOnly	Removes the Read Only check box from the dialog.
ofNoChangeDir	Prevents the user from changing directory inside the dialog.
ofNoReadOnlyReturn	Prevents the display of and selection of read-only files.
ofNoValidate	Allows the user to enter invalid filenames (rather than invoking an error dialog).
ofOverwritePrompt	Causes a confirmation dialog to appear before an existing file is overwritten.
ofReadOnly	Checks the Read Only box when the dialog first appears.

Continued

Option	Purpose
ofPathMustExist	Forces the user to type an existing path name - non-existent path names will result in an error dialog.
ofShareAware	Ignores sharing errors and violations.
ofShowHelp	Displays a <u>H</u>elp button in the dialog.

The FontDialog Component

This component is responsible for displaying the Font selection dialog (from **COMMDLG.DLL**). A typical example is shown below:

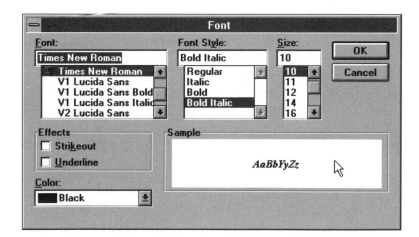

Options

Like the OpenDialog and SaveDialog components, the FontDialog has a large number of options (Boolean sub-properties of the **Options** property). All the options, with the exception of **fdEffects**, are **False** by default. Here are the options in detail:

Option	Purpose
fdAnsiOnly	Ensures that the user can only select fonts that use the Windows character set.
fdEffects	If **False**, the Effects and Color portions of the dialog don't appear.
fdFixedPitchOnly	Display only mono-spaced fonts.
fdForceFontExist	Causes an error dialog to be displayed if the user enters an invalid font name.
fdNoFaceSel	Don't display an initial font name.
fdNoVectorFonts	Display only non-vector fonts.
fdNoSimulations	Don't display GDI-simulation fonts.
fdNoSizeSel	Don't display an initial point size.
fdNoStyleSel	Don't display an initial style.
fdNoOEMFonts	Same as **fdNoVectorFonts**.
fdShowHelp	Display the dialog's Help button.
fdTrueTypeOnly	Display only **TrueType** fonts.
fdWysiwyg	Display only those fonts which are common to the screen and printer.

Font

Use this property to set the font that is selected when the FontDialog opens. (Don't confuse this with the font used by **COMMDLG.DLL** to display the font name itself - the latter cannot be changed.)

The ColorDialog Component

The ColorDialog component was first introduced in Chapter 3. When using ColorDialogs, be careful about the bug (in **COMMDLG.DLL**) that appears when the **Ctl3D** property is set to **True**: moving the current selection from one color to another will leave a white footprint round a previously selected color - see the lower-left color in the following illustration:

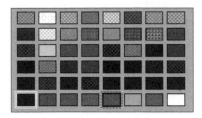

Options

The following **ColorDialog Options** are available (again, all false by default):

Property	Behavior
cdFullOpen	Open the dialog at full size, so that custom colors can be defined.
cdPreventFullOpen	Disable the Define Custom Colors... button.
cdShowHelp	Display a Help button.

The PrintDialog Component

The PrintDialog is responsible for displaying the standard print dialog shown below.

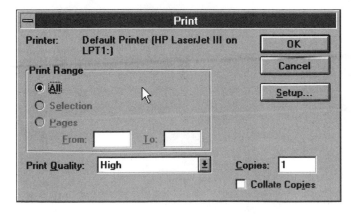

You can use this dialog to collect information on the user's print job.

Options

The following options are available, all **False** by default:

Property	Behavior
poHelp	Display a Help button.
poPageNums	Enable the Pages radio button, allowing the user to select a page range.
poPrintToFile	Give the user the option to print to a file instead of the printer.
poSelection	Enable the Selection radio button, giving the option to print the current text selection.
poWarning	If no printer is installed, causes a warning dialog to be displayed.

FromPage

This is to do with the starting page number for the print job. This information is returned by the dialog. However, if you set **poPageNums** to **True** (see above), the value of this property will be displayed when the dialog first appears.

ToPage

This provides the ending page number for the print job. Again, this is returned from the dialog, but may be displayed as an initial value by setting **poPageNums** to **True**. Typically, when printing a multi-page document, you'd set FromPage to 1 and ToPage to the number of pages in the document.

MaxPage

The maximum page number that may be specified. If the user exceeds this, an error message is displayed. You'd normally set this to the number of pages in the document but, in some cases, you may wish to disallow printing outside a certain page range.

MinPage

The minimum page number that may be specified. Normally, this will be 1.

The PrinterSetupDialog Component

This component displays the standard printer-set-up dialog shown below:

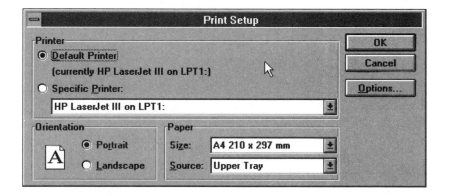

Using this dialog, the user can select different printers, change the paper size for printing and so on. This dialog can be invoked by pressing the Setup... button in the print dialog shown above. Although you don't have to have a PrinterSetupDialog component on your form if you already have a PrintDialog, it's customary to have one so that you can allow users to set up the printer via a menu item on the File menu.

The PrinterSetupDialog has almost no properties because it actually reads and modifies the **WIN.INI** file - you don't need to concern yourself with current printer information since this is all handled by the system. However, if the **ChangeDefault** property is **True** on leaving the PrinterSetupDialog, the setup has been changed. In these circumstances you may (depending on the type of your application) need to see if the page size has changed, and repaginate your document accordingly.

The FindDialog & ReplaceDialog Components

While we're on the subject of word-processing applications and the like, Delphi encapsulates a couple of other **COMMDLG.DLL** routines as the FindDialog and ReplaceDialog components. As for all the other dialogs implemented by **COMMDLG.DLL**, these components have a large number of options which determine which sub-components are visible as well as their properties.

In all cases, you'll find that setting up the **Options** property for one of these components and calling the **Execute** method is a far simpler proposition than making direct calls to **COMMDLG.DLL** (which involves the construction of complex data structures). Not only that, but, by doing things the Delphi way, you'll guarantee painless portability to the 32-bit version of the development system.

The System Page

We first saw the System components in Chapter 1, when developing the icon browser application. Although they're really meant to be used together in dialogs, they have other uses too. Here's what the System page looks like.

The Timer Component

The Timer component is used to generate **OnTimer** events at regular intervals. You can use this for controlling the timing of a graphical display, as a mechanism for causing the display to update itself periodically, and so on.

The PaintBox Component

The PaintBox component is primarily intended as a convenience when drawing on a form. If you want to confine custom drawing to a certain rectangular area of the form, then set up a PaintBox component and draw on its **Canvas** property. Unlike an Image component, the PaintBox doesn't have associated **LoadFromFile** and **SaveToFile** methods.

The FileListBox Component

The FileListBox component provides a scrolling, sorted display of the files in a directory:

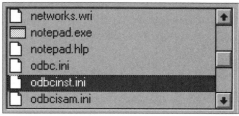

Directory

By assigning to the **Directory** property of the component, you can control which directory's contents are displayed.

FileType

This nested property controls which files are displayed in the ListBox. For example, you might wish to include system and hidden files such as **MSDOS.SYS** and **IO.SYS**. All of **FileType**'s sub-properties, except for **ftNormal**, are **False** by default - here they are in detail:

Property	Behavior
ftReadOnly	Display files with the read-only attribute.
ftHidden	Display files with the hidden attribute.
ftSystem	Display files with the system attribute.
ftVolumeID	Display the volume name.
ftDirectory	Display directories.
ftArchive	Display files with the archive attribute.
ftNormal	Display files with no attributes.

FileName

This affects the name of the currently-selected file. In the above illustration, **odbcinst.ini** would be the current value of this property.

Mask

This is used to select only those files which match the given pattern. For example, setting the mask to ***.dll** means that only dynamic link libraries will be displayed.

ShowGlyphs

Turning on this Boolean property causes mini-icons to be displayed alongside each filename. Currently, only two mini-icons are defined: a generic document icon, and a slightly wider application icon that's associated will all files having the **.EXE** extension. Both types of icon can be seen in the screenshot above.

The DirectoryListBox Component

Just as the FileListBox is in the business of showing files, so the DirectoryListBox is there to present the user with a list of directories:

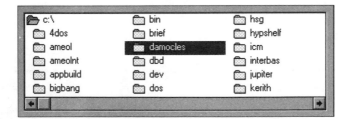

Columns

The FileListBox component is restricted to a single-column format, but you can use the **Columns** property of a DirectoryListBox to specify an arbitrary number of columns - three in the screenshot above, for example. When using a single-column format, the DirectoryListBoxes have a vertical scroll bar. However, when using multiple columns, they have a horizontal scroll bar too. The small directory glyphs are always present with this component.

The DriveComboBox Component

A DriveComboBox displays a list of available drives:

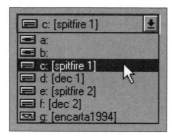

As you can see, Label information isn't displayed for floppy-disk drives. In fact, you're not even informed whether there are disks in the drives. This might seem rather sloppy, but it does speed things up, since the floppy-disk drives are not being continually accessed for Label information. A DriveComboBox also detects CD-ROM drives (look at the icon beside the last drive in the picture above) and shows their Labels too.

TextCase

You can use this property to decide whether the user sees drive Label information in upper or lower-case.

The FilterComboBox Component

This component displays a list of possible file masks, such as:

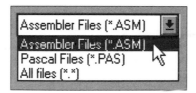

It's used in conjunction with the other File components to implement specialized directory-handling and file-handling dialogs. A FilterComboBox's only important property is the **Filter** string, which works just the same as for the OpenDialog component.

Although it's easy to put together an **Open** or **Save** dialog for files using Delphi, for consistency, you shouldn't do this unless you have a good reason for avoiding the `OpenDialog` and `SaveDialog` component. Occasionally, you might want more control than these components (via `COMMDLG.DLL`) can give you.

The MediaPlayer Component

For reasons of space, a detailed description of the MediaPlayer component is beyond the scope of this chapter. Suffice it to say that it is a sophisticated, high-level component designed to control MCI (Media Control Interface) devices such as MIDI sequencers, sound cards and CD-ROM drives - it's far more than just a collection of VCR-style buttons.

Using this component's **DeviceType** property, you can specify which type of MCI device you wish to control - when the MediaPlayer is opened via the **Open** method, the various buttons give the user control over the device. All buttons can be re-colored, hidden or disabled on an individual basis.

The OLEContainer Component

Traditionally, OLE (Object Linking and Embedding) programming has been something of a nightmare for Windows application developers. It's been regarded as a black art, guaranteed to reduce a grown developer to floods of tears! Be that as it may, you'll be pleased to know that OLE programming with Delphi is very simple. The illustration shown here is a sample OLE client application which literally took a minute to implement. Here, one of WordArt's special effects is being displayed (WordArt is part of Microsoft Word).

To create this effect, an OLEContainer was added to the form and its
OLEClass property was then set to **WordArt**. At run-time, double-clicking on
the component automatically starts up the WordArt OLE server. Delphi
contains a number of OLE-specific routines to incorporate in your
applications. For example, the **RegisterFormAsOLEDropTarget** routine will
register a form as a target for OLE drop objects. Again, space doesn't
permit the OLEContainer object's capabilities to be covered in any detail -
you're urged to read up on this information for yourself.

The DDE Components

To a large extent, the DDE (Dynamic Data Exchange) protocol designed by
Microsoft has become less important in recent years. This is partly due to
the fact that the interface was never particularly easy to use - it was
essentially an asynchronous protocol with time-outs, meaning that an
application communicating with a DDE server had to be continually
checking for time-out errors, the death of the server, completion of the last
command and so on. Although Microsoft went some way towards
addressing the deficiencies in DDE with the introduction of their **DDEML**
library, it never really caught on in a big way. At the time of writing, OLE
2.0 looks like being the way of the future. Although OLE 2.0 is far more
complex to program in than DDE, it has the advantage that calls are
synchronous, enabling the application software to be somewhat simpler than
it might otherwise be.

Having said this, it isn't yet time to consign DDE to the scrap heap. When it comes to communicating with the Windows Program Manager, DDE still reigns supreme. If you ever write a software installation package, the chances are that you'll want to add groups and icons to the Program Manager window. To do this, you have to communicate with Program Manager via DDE.

> In fact, Microsoft have released the internal format of **Program Manager** group (*.GRP) files, so in theory, an application could modify **Program Manager's** group information directly. However, doing so would be bad practice and would almost certainly break under future versions of Windows.

Delphi provides four components for implementing DDE links. These are as follows:

Component	What it Does
DDEClientConv	For communicating with a DDE server over a DDE link. When using this component, your application acts as a DDE client.
DDEClientItem	Defines the topic of a DDE link with a server.
DDEServerConv	For communication with another (client) application over a DDE link. When using this component, your application acts as a DDE server.
DDEServerItem	Defines the topic of a DDE link with a client.

Again, a full discussion of the DDE components is beyond the scope of this book. However, the code fragment below should illustrate how easy it is to implement DDE capabilities in a Delphi application.

The DDEClientConv Component

To have a go at adding a Program Manager group, first create a new form and add a DDEClientConv component to it. Set the **DDEService** property of the component to **ProgMan** - this nominates the DDE server with which we're trying to communicate.

By default, the **ConnectMode** property will be set to **ddeAutomatic** so that, as soon as the form is created, a DDE link to the Program Manager is established. Typically, an install application would do better to establish a link at the appropriate moment using the **OpenLink** method, so set the **ConnectMode** property to **ddeManual**.

Now add the following **OnClick** handler to the form:

```
procedure TForm1.FormClick(Sender: TObject);
begin
   DDEClientConv1.OpenLink;
   DDEClientConv1.ExecuteMacro(
      '[CreateGroup(Delphi For President)]', False
   );
   DDEClientConv1.CloseLink
end;
```

Now run the application and click on the form. That's it! That's all you need to do to add a new group to the Program Manager - simple, wasn't it? In days gone by, doing that in a robust manner would have taken a lot of code.

VBX Page

As has been mentioned elsewhere, it's possible for Delphi to use existing VBX controls (the custom controls used by Visual Basic for Windows). For illustrative purposes, a number of VBX controls are included with Delphi and you'll find that they've already been installed onto the VBX page of the Component Palette.

Four controls are included: a cute 3D switch control, a gauge, a picture control and a remarkably powerful 2D/3D chart control. The picture control incorporates a built-in bevel feature. All four are shown in action on the next page:

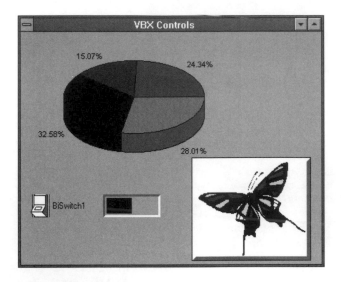

Samples Page

Delphi includes a number of sample components which build on the functionality of the standard components. The Samples page of the Component Palette is shown below:

The Gauge Component

A Gauge is typically used in install applications or anywhere that you wish to show the progress of some operation. It has to be said that the Gauge component supplied with Delphi is not very wonderful - it's rather inflexible and doesn't have the same nice 3D look as the other components. If you want to use a gauge in your application, you'd do better to use the BiGauge component that's on the VBX page.

Progress

Assigning an integer to this property controls the progress of the gauge.

Kind

This property determines the type of gauge component that appears:

Property	Behavior
gkText	A simple rectangle containing a percentage progress string.
gkHorizontalBar	A horizontal bar with the progress display moving to the right.
gkVerticalBar	A vertical bar with the progress display moving upwards.
gkPie	A circular or elliptical pie chart with progress represented by a slice which gets bigger.
gkNeedle	A needle, rotating clockwise on a dial.

ShowText

This controls whether the progress is displayed as a text percentage on the gauge (as well as any graphical indication).

The ColorGrid Component

The ColorGrid provides a handy way for the user to select from a limited range of colors (up to 16) whenever the full power of a ColorDialog is not needed. Delphi itself uses this approach - see the Editor colors page of the Environment Options dialog for an example. The ColorGrid allows for fast selection of foreground color (by left-clicking) and background color (by right-clicking) and it has the advantage that color information can be stored as a simple integer index, rather than having to deal with 32-bit **TColorRef** values.

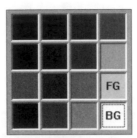

GridOrdering

This property controls the way in which the ColorGrid is drawn. You can choose from five alternatives:

Property	Behavior
go16x1	1 row, 16 columns
go8x2	2 rows, 8 columns
go4x4	4 rows, 4 columns (default)
go2x8	8 rows, 2 columns
go1x16	16 rows, 1 column

The SpinButton Component

SpinButtons are like tiny scrollbars which consist of nothing but the up and down arrow. They're often linked to an associated Edit box allowing some numerical value to be incremented or decremented by clicking the arrows. Delphi provides a component which does this 'all in one' - see the SpinEdit component described below.

The SpinButton component suffers from the drawback that it only comes in a vertical flavor - you can't get it to align itself horizontally which is rather a shame. However, a rather nice feature allows you to select alternative bitmaps for use as the up and down arrows, allowing you to create interesting effects with larger-than-life spin buttons.

The SpinEdit Component

As mentioned above, the SpinEdit component is basically a vertical spin button with associated Edit box. An **Increment** property specifies the numerical step for each push of the up or down buttons. Again, it's a pity that you can't move the up/down buttons to the left hand side of the Edit box (they're always on the right hand side) but since Borland thoughtfully provide full source code to all the sample components, you should be able to tackle this after reading Chapter 10!

The DirectoryOutline Component

The DirectoryOutline Component lets you visually navigate around in a hierarchical tree of directories. There are various formatting options available allowing you to display the tree in a number of different ways. You can also configure the bitmaps that are used with the display. If you select a larger font size, the bitmaps will (by default) stretch in size to match the larger text display.

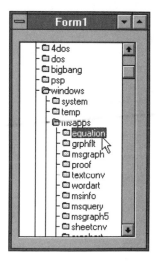

The Calendar Component

This neat little component allows you to drop a calendar right into your form. By assigning to the **Day**, **Month** and **Year** properties, you can easily alter the display under program control.

Form1						
Sun	Mon	Tue	Wed	Thu	Fri	Sat
1	2	3	4	5	6	7
8	9	10	11	12	13	14
15	16	17	18	19	20	21
22	23	24	25	26	27	28
29	30	31				

Summary

Delphi contains a rich set of controls which can be used to build sophisticated, state-of-the art user interfaces. There are times when you might think that one component is identical to another, but closer inspection will prove otherwise. For example, the RadioGroup component is far easier to program than if you were to implement the same effect with lots of individual radio buttons. The BiPict control on the VBX page has a handy, built-in bevel facility and so on. As always, you're encouraged to familiarise yourself with all the controls that Delphi has on offer - you can't choose the right one for the job if you don't know what's available!

Of course, there will be times when you just *can't* find an appropriate component. Then is the time to roll up your sleeves and enter the fascinating world of component writing - creating your own reusable components. This is the subject of our next chapter...

Chapter

10

Creating Your Own Components

Throughout this book, you've been acting as a component *user* - making use of the existing components that are built into Delphi. However, in this chapter, you'll be acting as a component *writer*, working through the process of creating a new component.

Any components which you develop can of course be used in your own applications. Equally, if you think that your new components have a broad appeal, you may feel inclined to market them to other Delphi developers. This is one of the great strengths of the Delphi development system. Even though you can incorporate new components (**.VBX** files) into Visual Basic, those components have to be created using a C/C++ or Pascal compiler - you can't create the **.VBX** files using Visual Basic itself. With Delphi, however, the process is much more self-contained - you use Delphi itself to build new Delphi components.

During the course of the chapter, you'll learn how to create a new component which is based on an existing component but which has properties tailored to your particular needs. We'll also work through the process of building a complete graphical component from scratch, and cover the following topics:

- The different types of component.
- Deriving a new component.
- Using the Component Expert.
- Modifying existing components.
- Creating a graphical component.

Types of Component

Life as a component writer is rather more complicated than you've been used to as a component user. Delphi components are written in Object Pascal, and some experience with Object Pascal must be assumed. It's recommended that you don't get down to the business of component writing until you feel comfortable with Delphi software development in general (those already familiar with Turbo Pascal might like to read Appendix A first - it details the new features of Delphi's Object Pascal).

There are two basic types of component in Delphi: **visual components** and **non-visual components**. Visual components are the most common.

Visual Components

A visual component, or control, has a design-time appearance that's similar to its run-time appearance - it looks more-or-less the same whether you're designing your application or running it. Examples of visual components include Buttons, EditBoxes, NoteBooks, Memos, TabSet and so on.

Non-Visual Components

When your application is running, a non-visual component looks nothing like its design-time representation. For example, a MainMenu component doesn't look like a menu when it's on a form. It's just a place-holder that stores the appropriate menu structure and allows access to the Menu Designer. Similarly, the various common dialogs - such as OpenDialog, SaveDialog and FindDialog - are all non-visual components. Other examples of non-visual components are PopupMenus, Timers (which actually have no run-time appearance whatsoever) and OleContainers.

Creating a New Component

When you create a new component, it must merge seamlessly with other Delphi components if it's to work properly within the environment. You can do this by modifying one of the existing components that we've been using throughout the book, or by starting with one of the abstract components which Delphi provides as an alternative. You must choose your starting point carefully, based on the desired functionality and on what's already available.

As you've probably guessed, new components are actually classes which inherit from some existing class - new characteristics are added and old characteristics are modified, as appropriate. You need to have a good working knowledge of Object Pascal and object-oriented techniques to do this properly. The object-oriented philosophy is fundamental to the business of component writing.

Modifying an Existing Component

It's important not to re-invent the wheel - you should endeavor to derive your new component from an existing component whenever you can. For example, suppose you wanted to create a MyEditBox component which differs in some small way from a standard EditBox. Rather than rewriting the source code for the EditBox component, you should make **TMyEditBox** a descendant of the existing **TEdit** class and modify the new class.

Starting with an Abstract Component

Often, you'll want to create an entirely new type of component altogether. In this case, the situation is more complex - you really need a reasonable working knowledge of the class hierarchy used by the Visual Component Library (or VCL for short). A somewhat cut down illustration of the VCL object hierarchy is shown here. For simplicity, not all the available controls are shown, and only the control part of the hierarchy has been illustrated. Nevertheless, you can see that it's still quite a complicated picture!

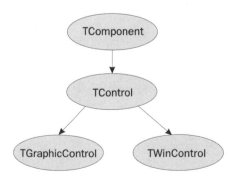

TComponent

Let's suppose that you want to create a non-visual component, such as a new type of dialog box - an About box would be a good example. Turning an About box into a standard component would give a consistent look-and-feel across all your applications. Elsewhere, we've talked about how to turn an About box into a standard form - this is a little different though. Here, we're talking about building a new component which we can access from the Component Palette, not just a pre-defined form.

Because an About box is a non-visual component, it doesn't make sense to derive it from one of the existing visual components. Naturally enough, the VCL provides an abstract class called **TComponent** which is ideal for building non-visual components.

> **If you look again at our object 'family-tree' diagram, you'll see that the menu and common dialog objects are derived from the TControl object rather than TComponent. It's not clear why this is so, but it's likely to be a historical hang-over from an earlier version of the VCL library. Certainly, if you read the *Delphi Component Writer's Guide*, you'll see that this also advises you to use TComponent as a starting point for non-visual controls.**

If you have any of the existing dialog components selected on a form, you'll notice that there are no properties like **Width**, **Height** or **Visible** displayed in the Object Inspector - that's because it doesn't make sense for a non-visual component to have these properties. If you derive a new class from **TComponent**, it'll have a sensible set of non-visual properties which you can tinker with at will.

TWinControl

If you're creating a new visual component that isn't based on any existing component, you'll most likely make it a descendant of the **TWinControl** class. This means that your new component will automatically have the following published properties: **Left**, **Top**, **Width**, **Height**, **Visible**, **Enabled**, **Cursor** and **Hint**.

> These properties aren't actually implemented in **TWinControl**, but in its immediate ancestor **TControl**. **TWinControl** simply adds a Windows handle, the ability to receive input focus, and the ability to contain other controls.

TGraphicControl

In addition to visual and non-visual components, you'll also need to understand what's meant by a **graphical control**. Unlike an ordinary visual component, a graphical control cannot receive the input focus. In other words, it can't become the active window as you tab around inside a form. Perhaps more significantly, a graphical control isn't a window at all as far as the Windows API is concerned. For this reason, graphical controls don't have an associated **handle** property - the property that's normally used to store the Windows-style handle for a component - but, they do consume fewer resources.

If you want to create a completely new graphical control, you should derive it from the **TGraphicControl** class. **TGraphicControl** simply adds a protected, read-only **Canvas** property to use as a drawing area and a protected, virtual **Paint** method for doing the drawing.

Using the Component Expert

Delphi provides a facility called the Component Expert which will help you to get off to a flying start when creating a new component. Just select New Component... from the File menu and you'll see a dialog similar to the one below:

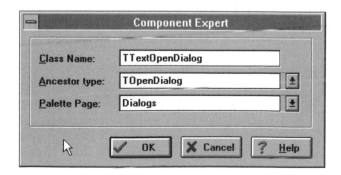

You should first select an ancestor type for your dialog, taking into account the sort of component that you want to create. To do this, use the Ancestor type: combo box to select from the list of all currently-registered component classes. Then, choose the Component Palette page on which you want your new component to appear, using the Palette Page: combo box. Finally, type in a name for your new component. You should try to make the component name as descriptive as possible. Also, remember that, as a rule, class names begin with the letter **T** - this helps to make the code more readable. When you're done, click OK and Delphi will open a new Code Editor page, containing a skeletal unit which will provide the implementation for the new component - we'll refer to this as the **component unit**. For the above screen shot, here's what the initial component unit looks like:

```
unit Unit2;

interface

uses
        SysUtils, WinTypes, WinProcs, Messages, Classes,
        Graphics, Controls, Forms, Dialogs;

type
    TTextOpenDialog = class(TOpenDialog)
    private
          { Private declarations }
    protected
          { Protected declarations }
    public
          { Public declarations }
    published
          { Published declarations }
    end;

procedure Register;

implementation

procedure Register;
begin
    RegisterComponents('Dialogs', [TTextOpenDialog]);
end;

end.
```

As you can see, the skeletal component unit is quite small - the Component Expert has very little work to do to provide us with a good starting point. As requested, the class definition of **TTextOpenDialog** has **TOpenDialog** as its immediate ancestor.

Component Registration

While you're looking at a component unit, we'll take the opportunity to introduce you to the concept of **component registration**. Before your new component is recognized by Delphi, and before it appears on the Component Palette, it must be registered. Every component unit must include an interface routine called **Register**, as in the component unit listed above. When Delphi starts up, it calls the **Register** procedure for every registered component unit - this is what causes the various components to appear on the Component Palette.

For our simple example, the **Register** procedure simply calls **RegisterComponents** with two parameters: the name of the Component Palette page on which we want our control to appear, and the class of the component itself. Here's the declaration for the **RegisterComponents** procedure, taken from the file **CLASSES.PAS** in the Run Time Library (RTL for short):

```
procedure RegisterComponents (const Page: string;
            ComponentClasses: array of TComponentClass);
```

The second parameter to **RegisterComponents** is an array of **TComponentClass**es (an array of classes which are descendants of **TComponent**). The square brackets around **TTextOpenDialog** in the component unit above are being used to build such an array on-the-fly (see Appendix A for a full explanation of this facility). We could pass several component classes to **RegisterComponents** at once. In fact, many of the units in the VCL do this, because they implement a number of components in a single file.

The **Register** routine is only called once by Delphi, but within that single call, you can register as many different components as you like. This doesn't mean that all components implemented in a particular component unit have to be placed on the same page of the Component Palette. Rather, you can make several calls to **RegisterComponents** within the **Register** routine, like this:

```
procedure Register;
begin
    RegisterComponents ('Dialogs', [TTextOpenDialog]);
    RegisterComponents ('Specials', [TSpec1, TSpec2]);
end;
```

This example adds one component to the Dialogs page, and two more to the Specials page of the Component Palette.

Modifying a Non-Visual Component

As you've probably realized by now, the simplest way of creating a new component is to derive it from an existing component, making any necessary modifications to the new class. In this section, we're going to follow through with the TTextOpenDialog component that we mentioned earlier. What we'll end up with is a new component which looks and feels just like the built-in OpenDialog component, but with one exception: when invoked, it's already set up to open text files (files with an extension of .TXT). Admittedly, this is no big deal - it's not a quantum leap in functionality. However, it will give you a feel for the mechanics of component construction.

Saving and Compiling a Component Unit

Let's begin, then, with the skeletal TTextOpenDialog code that we looked at earlier. Change the **unit** declaration at the beginning of the component unit to look like this:

```
unit TextOpen;
```

Now save the unit (using Save File As... from the File menu) with the name **TEXTOPEN.PAS**.

> **Although it's not particularly important what file name you choose, it is recommended that you don't save your new component units alongside Delphi's built-in component units. If you do so, you'll lose all your work should you absent-mindedly delete Delphi from your hard disk, or upgrade to a newer version of the development system. Instead, you should probably create a new directory, separate from your \DELPHI directory, in which to store all your custom components.**

Having saved the component unit, you need to include it in a dummy project to compile it and to check that it's installed correctly. In order to do this, create a new project and use the Add File... option on the File menu to add **TEXTOPEN.PAS** to the dummy project. You should now be able to compile the project (you must specify Build All from the Compile menu, or **TEXTOPEN.PAS** won't be compiled). If all has gone well, you'll find that you've got a new file called **TEXTOPEN.DCU** in your component directory.

This is the object code for the new component. You can now discard the dummy project.

> This is not a terribly convenient way of doing things. Unfortunately, the Delphi environment doesn't give you the ability to compile a single unit - it will only compile projects. For this reason, we have to make use of a dummy project to get our unit built.

Installing a Component

Now select Install Components... from the Options menu, and you'll see the following dialog appear:

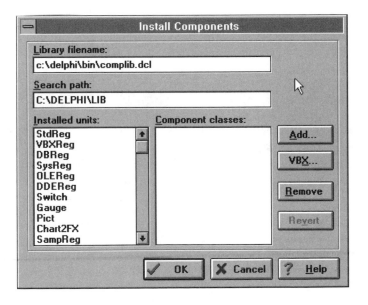

So far, we've only talked about the need to register and compile a component. However, it's also necessary to install the component unit. Delphi has the notion of a **Default Component Library** which corresponds to a special file called **COMPLIB.DCL**. This file contains the code for all installed component units.

> It's actually possible to have more than one component library, as we'll see in Chapter 11. For the purposes of this chapter, however, we'll concentrate purely on COMPLIB.DCL.

Click the Add... button in the dialog above and another dialog will appear, prompting you for the name of the component file: click the Browse... button and select TEXTOPEN.PAS unit at the location where you stored it.

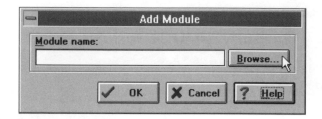

When you return to the main Install Components dialog, you'll see that the name Textopen has been added to the Installed units: list on the left, and that the path to your component unit has been added to the Search path: box. When you click OK to exit this dialog, Delphi will close any currently-open project and rebuild the component library. This may take a few moments, depending on the size of the library. Once done, you'll find your custom component residing on the Dialogs page of the Component Palette, complete with a fly-by hint, looking for all the world like one of the built-in components that ship with Delphi. When you do this for the first time, you should get quite a kick out of it!

*The built-in
TOpenDialog component*   *The newly-installed
TFileOpenDialog component*

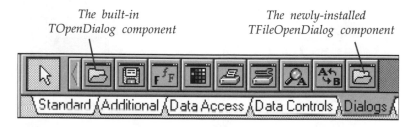

If you now open a new project, you'll find that you can add a TextOpenDialog to a form and use it just as you would the standard OpenDialog. If you're particularly observant, you'll also notice that adding a TTextOpenDialog component to the form causes Delphi to add TextOpen to the list of units in the uses clause of the form unit - but you won't see this happen until the next time you compile the project.

Setting up a Palette Bitmap

As it stands, the appearance of our new component is identical to that of its immediate ancestor. This is the default behavior if we don't supply Delphi with a **Delphi Component Resource** (**.DCR**) file. A **.DCR** is a standard Windows resource file which contains a bitmap for displaying its associated component on the Component Palette. When you install a component into Delphi's component library, Delphi looks for a **.DCR** file at the same location as the component unit and source code. If one is found, Delphi reads any bitmaps from it and incorporates them into the library.

As mentioned earlier, a component unit can contain more than one component. Where this is the case, you need to store multiple bitmaps in the **.DCR** file, one for each component. The bitmaps need to be given the same names as the corresponding component class. Additionally, the **.DCR** file itself needs to have the same name as the corresponding component unit. Suppose for example, that you have a component unit called Gizmos which implements two new component classes called **TGraphicGizmo** and **TTextGizmo**. For this situation, you'll need a file called **GIZMOS.DCR** which contains two bitmaps named **TGRAPHICGIZMO** and **TTEXTGIZMO**. (It's traditional to specify resource names in uppercase, but not essential.)

To manipulate **.DCR** files, you can use Delphi's Image Editor, accessible from the main development environment via the Tools menu. The Image Editor understands the format of **.DCR** files and can be used to create a new **.DCR** file from scratch, or modify an existing one:

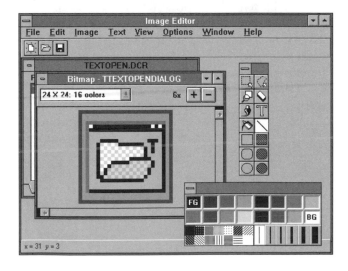

If you are deriving a new component from an existing one, as we're doing here, you may prefer to take the existing component's bitmap and modify it to suit your purposes. In the illustration above, a small T has been added in the top-right corner of the OpenDialog bitmap, indicating that this is the *Text*OpenDialog that we're dealing with. (The color of the depicted folder was also altered so as to make the difference between the two components more obvious.)

> As an alternative, if you happen to have Borland's Resource Workshop, you can use it to create and edit .DCR files. It turns out that a .DCR file is, in fact, nothing more than a standard, Windows-compatible, .RES file.

Try creating a **TEXTOPEN.DCR** file as outlined above. (Use the Image Editor to open the file **\DELPHI\LIB\STDREG.DCR** and make a copy of the **TOPENDIALOG** bitmap, change it as described, rename the bitmap to **TTEXTOPENDIALOG** and save the result as **TEXTOPEN.DCR**). Now select the Install Components dialog and remove the existing Textopen unit with the Remove button. Finally, install the unit again. This process will cause Delphi to search for the .DCR file. This time round, you'll find that the TextOpenDialog component is sporting a distinctive bitmap.

Changing Default Property Values

So far, we've built a new component, based on the OpenDialog component and given it a new bitmap. Fun though this may be, it's not much use unless we can alter the behavior of the component in some way. At the moment, it's behaving exactly like its immediate ancestor **TOpenDialog**. Let's see if we can change it to be more text-file oriented.

As you'll know from using the OpenDialog component in other situations, it's the **Filter** property which determines which files are displayed by the OpenDialog. What we want to do is alter the default value of this property so that it starts off as **Text Files (*.TXT) | *.TXT** At the same time, we'll need to change the **DefaultExt** property to **TXT** (this is the extension used if the user doesn't type one in).

To do this, open the **TEXTOPEN.PAS** file and modify the class definition so that it looks like this:

```
type
  TTextOpenDialog = class(TOpenDialog)
  private
    { Private declarations }
  protected
    { Protected declarations }
  public
    { Public declarations }
    constructor Create (AOwner: TComponent); override;
  published
    { Published declarations }
  end;
```

We've added a new constructor (**Create**), which overrides the existing constructor in **TOpenDialog**. This enables us to do custom initialization at the time that the component is created. This constructor is called when the component is added to a form at design time, and it's also called at runtime when the form is created and its individual components come into being.

Here's the code for **Create** (you'll need to add this to the **implementation** part of the unit):

```
constructor TTextOpenDialog.Create (AOwner: TComponent);
begin
    inherited Create(AOwner);
    Filter := 'Text Files (*.TXT)|*.TXT';
    DefaultExt := 'TXT';
end;
```

As you can see, it's really very straightforward. It's absolutely essential that the new constructor should first call the old constructor inherited from **TOpenDialog**, so that the latter can perform any initialization required by the ancestors of the new class. The **inherited** keyword tells Delphi that we're talking about the inherited **Create** method, rather than the new one. Without this keyword, we'd end up with an infinitely-recursive routine! Once the inherited constructor is called, we're free to make changes to the component properties - namely, **Filter** and **DefaultExt**. Try compiling the above code (by including it in a dummy project), then re-install the **TextOpen** unit into Delphi's component library (having removed it first).

Now, if you open a new project and place a **TTextOpenDialog** onto the default form, you should be rewarded with a component whose **Filter** and **DefaultExt** properties are already set up to accept text files - simple!

Using the default Keyword

As you might expect, a Delphi form file (***.DFM**) contains information on the property settings for the form itself, together with a list of all the components and the property settings for each component. In order to reduce the size of form files (which results in faster form loading, as well as giving you more disk space), Delphi will only store a property value if it differs from the default value. To change the default value, you must tell Delphi what the new default value is - it can't determine this information for itself by examining overridden constructor calls, for instance.

> If you're interested in examining the contents of a form file, Delphi has an undocumented technique for directly examining and editing them. Just choose **Open File...** from the **File** menu, choose **Form file (*.DFM)** from the file type filter box and hey-presto, you can select any existing form and load it up into a **Code Editor** window. This is especially useful if you want to make some change that affects a lot of properties. For example, you can use the **Code Editor's Replace** option to change some word in all the properties of a form in one quick operation - this is a real time-saver!

Suppose, for example, that you wanted the **FileEditStyle** property of the TTextOpenDialog to be **fsComboBox** by default, rather than **fsEdit**. This change would give the user immediate access to a history list of previously-opened files. To make this change, we'd need to redeclare the **FileEditStyle** property in the **published** part of the class definition, using the **default** keyword to set the default value. This is what the revised class definition would look like:

```
type
  TTextOpenDialog = class(TOpenDialog)
  private
    { Private declarations }
  protected
    { Protected declarations }
  public
    { Public declarations }
    constructor Create (AOwner: TComponent); override;
  published
    { Published declarations }
    property FileEditStyle default fsComboBox;
  end;
```

You'd also have to modify the **Create** constructor to change the **FileEditStyle** property to **fsComboBox**. It must be emphasized that specifying default values for a property doesn't change the property - it merely tells Delphi what the default value is going to be. When storing a form file, Delphi can discard any property information which is already set to its default value.

> Bear in mind what happens when Delphi loads a form: when a component is created, its constructor is called first. In our case, this will set the **Filter, DefaultExt** and **FileEditStyle** properties to the default values specified above. Then, and only then, will Delphi load any non-default property values from the form file and apply them to the component. Of course, specifying a default value for a property doesn't mean we can't change it at design time if we want to!

Creating a New Graphical Control

At this point, you should have a pretty good idea of what's involved when you derive a new (non-visual) component from an existing one, modifying the new component's properties to suit your needs. What's even more interesting, of course, is the process of building an entirely new type of component. As already noted, a new non-visual component (a descendant of **TComponent**) starts out with only **Tag** and **Name** properties. So, rather than do a lot of work to produce a non-visual component that's in any way useful, we'll create a new visual component instead. More specifically, it'll be one we can use for drawing, rather than a proper window, so it'll need to inherit from **TGraphicControl**.

If you look at the **TShape** component, you'll see that it gives you a variety of different shapes that you can draw. But, a surprising omission is the lack of a pie-drawing capability - corresponding to the Windows API **Pie** function - an elliptical arc whose center of curvature and two end endpoints are joined by straight lines. Let's have a go at providing such a capability.

We'll begin by deriving our new shape, **TPie**, from the abstract **TGraphicControl** class, using the Component Expert:

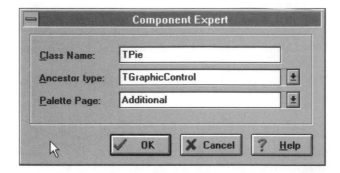

Once Component Expert has done its stuff, you should end up with a component unit which looks like this (notice that we've changed the unit name to **Pie**):

```
unit Pie;

interface

uses
    SysUtils, WinTypes, WinProcs, Messages,
    Classes, Graphics, Controls, Forms;

type
    TPie = class(TGraphicControl)
    private
            { Private declarations }
    protected
            { Protected declarations }
    public
            { Public declarations }
    published
            { Published declarations }
    end;

procedure Register;

implementation

procedure Register;
begin
    RegisterComponents('Additional', [TPie]);
end;

end.
```

Save this unit as PIE.PAS, compile it and install it into the component library. You'll find that Delphi has chosen to use the same palette bitmap for it as for **TGraphicControl**: a circle, square and triangle:

This should be no surprise, since we saw the same behavior earlier when we derived a component from the **TOpenDialog** class - by default, if you don't supply a palette bitmap for a new component, then it will inherit the palette bitmap of its immediate ancestor. If you want, you can go ahead now and create a new **.DCR** file which contains a suitable pie-shaped bitmap.

What might surprise you, though, is this: if you try double clicking on the **Pie** component, absolutely nothing will appear on the current form! The Object Inspector will change to reflect the fact that a **Pie** component is selected, indicating that the control was added to the form, but the new component is completely invisible! What's the explanation for this weird behavior?

If you think about it, the reason is obvious. A non-visual component, such as **TOpenDialog** or **TTextOpenDialog**, has no run-time visual representation. Delphi, therefore, obliges us by copying the palette bitmap onto the form, to serve as an icon. However, a graphical control certainly should have a run-time representation - this is the whole point of it. However, nothing appears on the form yet because we haven't told Delphi how to draw a **Pie**.

Drawing a Pie

Just as you need to override the **Create** constructor to perform component-specific initialization tasks, so you need to override the **Paint** method of a visual component in order to provide code to do the drawing.

First, add the following procedure declaration to the protected part of the **TPie** class definition:

```
procedure Paint; override;
```

This tells Delphi that we're overriding the **Paint** method. Now add the following **Paint** body to the **implementation** part of your component unit:

```
procedure TPie.Paint;
begin
    Canvas.Ellipse (0, 0, Width, Height);
end;
```

> Yes, we're supposed to be drawing a pie rather than an ellipse, but our main objective at the moment is merely to make our component visible on the form! We'll revisit the **Paint** procedure later to add the pie-drawing code.

All this does is call the **Ellipse** routine with the current **Width** and **Height** properties for the component (because we've derived **TPie** from the **TGraphicControl** class, it's inherited a lot of useful properties such as **Height**, **Width**, **Left**, **Top** and **Visible**). Unfortunately, if you re-compile the component unit, you still won't see the expected ellipse when you add a **Pie** component to a form!

The Object Inspector will reveal the reason for our component's continued invisibility - both the **Width** and **Height** properties are set to zero by default! If you edit these properties to some non-zero value then, hey presto, an ellipse will appear in all its glory:

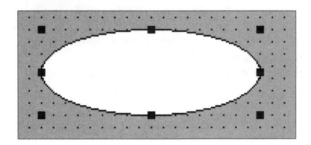

Initializing a Pie

From our efforts with the **TTextOpenDialog**, we know exactly how to initialize a **Pie**.

First, we need to add the following declaration to the **public** part of the **TPie** class definition:

```
constructor Create(AnOwner: TComponent); override;
```

Now, we just have to add the **Create** body to the **implementation** part of the unit:

```
constructor TPie.Create (AnOwner: TComponent);
begin
    inherited Create(AnOwner);
    Width := 30;
    Height := 30;
end;
```

With these changes installed, you'll find that double-clicking a **TPie** component will immediately make it visible on the form. The assignments to **Width** and **Height** give us a reasonable initial size for the component.

Adding New Properties

At this point, we have a useful ellipse-drawing component, but we've still got some way to go before we're done. For starters, we need **Brush** and **Pen** properties which specify how to draw the interior and the outline of a **Pie**.

Add a couple of new fields to the **private** part of the **TPie** class definition:

```
{ Private declarations }
FPen: TPen;
FBrush: TBrush;
```

These fields will be used to store the currently-selected pen and brush for our component. Notice that both fields are private - in order to provide access to them, the recommended approach is to implement an **access property** for each one. To do this, add the following method declarations to the **private** section of the **TPie** class:

```
procedure SetBrush (Value: TBrush);
procedure SetPen (Value: TPen);
```

Now add two new properties to the **published** section of the class:

```
property Brush: TBrush read FBrush write SetBrush;
property Pen: TPen read FPen write SetPen;
```

Now, the **Brush** property will look to the Object Inspector (and to any other application) just like a simple field of type **TBrush**. However, any assignment to this property will actually result in a call to **SetBrush**, while any attempt to read the current value of **Brush** actually reads the current value of **Fbrush** instead. The same arguments apply to the **Pen** property.

335

> It's good practice to hide your private data fields behind access properties in this way. It provides the calling application with all the convenience of direct access to fields while, at the same time, giving you complete control over the internal implementation. Just as importantly, any assignment to access properties allows the component writer to intervene, possibly redrawing the component after modifying a field - we'll see how this works shortly.

To complete the **Pen** and **Brush** properties, add the bodies of the two private methods to the **implementation** part of **PIE.PAS**:

```
procedure TPie.SetBrush (Value: TBrush);
begin
    FBrush.Assign(Value);
end;

procedure TPie.SetPen(Value: TPen);
begin
    FPen.Assign (Value);
end;
```

At this point, if you compile and re-install the **Pie** component, you'll see that the **Brush** and **Pen** properties have appeared in the Object Inspector. However, any attempt to modify these properties at design time will cause a General Protection Fault. This is because we haven't yet initialized these properties. We need to do this in the component's **Create** method. Add the following code to the end of **Create**:

```
FPen := TPen.Create;
FBrush := TBrush.Create;
```

You should now find that you can modify the **Pen** and **Brush** properties in the normal way in the Object Inspector.

Responding to Property Changes

We also need to provide a mechanism which responds to **Pen** and **Brush** changes, redrawing the associated **Pie** component as needed. To begin with, add the following line to the **published** section of the class definition:

```
procedure StyleChanged(Sender: TObject);
```

Now add the following code for the **StyleChanged** routine to the **implementation** part of the unit:

```
procedure TPie.StyleChanged(Sender: TObject);
begin
    Invalidate;      { Force component to repaint }
end;
```

This routine will cause the component to repaint itself as required. But, how do we ensure that this code is called each time the **Brush** or **Pen** properties are changed? Fortunately, since the **TBrush** and **TPen** objects have an associated **OnChange** event, this is very easy to do. Simply add the following two lines of code to the end of the **Create** procedure, and the **TPie.StyleChanged** routine will be called by Delphi whenever some changes takes place in either the **Pen** or **Brush** property. Sneaky, huh?

```
FPen.OnChange := StyleChanged;
FBrush.OnChange := StyleChanged;
```

The Paint Procedure Revisited

Now we have to make use of the current **Pen** and **Brush** settings. This is done by the following two statements which set up the **Pen** and **Brush** properties - put them immediately before the call to **Ellipse** in the **Paint** routine:

```
Canvas.Pen := FPen;
Canvas.Brush := FBrush;
```

If you re-install the Pie component, you'll find that you can change the **Brush** and **Pen** properties to your heart's content, any changes being reflected immediately in the appearance of the component:

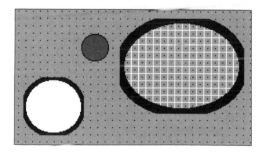

Drawing a Pie

Yes, yes, we know. It still isn't a pie, right? In order to implement a pie shape, we need to add a few more properties to the **TPie** class. These properties - **Radius**, **StartAngle** and **StopAngle** - determine, respectively, the angles of the two straight lines which bound the pie and its radius of curvature. What we really want is three access properties, just like the **Pen** and **Brush** properties we used earlier.

Add these declarations to the **published** part of the **TPie** class definition:

```
property StartAngle: Integer
    read FStartAngle write SetStartAngle;
property StopAngle: Integer
    read FStopAngle write SetStopAngle;
property Radius: Integer
    read FRadius write SetRadius;
```

Also, add the following field and procedure declarations to the **private** part of the class:

```
FStartAngle: Integer;
FStopAngle: Integer;
Fradius: Integer;
procedure SetStartAngle(Value: Integer);
procedure SetStopAngle(Value: Integer);
procedure SetRadius(Value: Integer);
```

Here's the code for the new methods - they must go into the **implementation** part of the component unit:

```
procedure TPie.SetStartAngle(Value: Integer);
begin
    FStartAngle := Value mod 360;
    Invalidate;
end;

procedure TPie.SetStopAngle(Value: Integer);
begin
    FStopAngle := Value mod 360;
    Invalidate;
end;

procedure TPie.SetRadius(Value: Integer);
begin
    FRadius := Value;
    Invalidate;
end;
```

SetStartAngle and **SetStopAngle** ensure that the angle passed in is converted to the range **0..359** before the corresponding field is modified.

Finally, you will need to add a little geometry-twiddling code to draw the actual pie - the complete **Paint** procedure is shown below:

```
procedure TPie.Paint;
var
   Start, Stop: Real; { StartAngle, StopAngle in radians }
begin
   { Set up the canvas }
   Canvas.Pen := FPen;
   Canvas.Brush := FBrush;

   { Convert rStart, rStop to radians }
   Start := -(3.1415926 * StartAngle) / 180;
   Stop := -(3.1415926 * StopAngle) / 180;

   { Use the Pie method on the canvas to do the drawing }
   Canvas.Pie(0, 0, Width, Height,
              Round(cos(Start) * Radius),
              Round(sin(Start) * Radius),
              Round(cos(Stop) * Radius),
              Round(sin(Stop) * Radius));
end;
```

With the finished version of the **Paint** procedure in place, the Pie component will produce proper pie shapes on a form. You can even use several components together to produce a pie chart: the illustration below shows three different Pie components drawn one on top of the other:

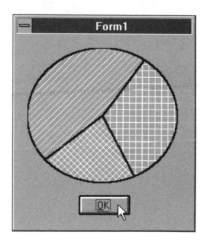

Destroying a Pie

Since a **TBrush** and **TPen** object were explicitly created inside **TPie**'s constructor, we need to ensure that they're destroyed at the proper time - that is, when the Pie component is itself destroyed. To do this, we can override **TPie**'s inherited destructor, just as we overrode its constructor.

Add a declaration for the destructor to the public part of the **TPie** class:

```
destructor Destroy; override;
```

The code for the destructor itself is quite straightforward. Just as the overridden constructor must call its immediate ancestor's constructor, so the overridden destructor must call its inherited destructor. This is necessary in order to perform any cleaning up specific to the **TGraphicComponent** class. However, whereas constructors should call the inherited constructor *before* doing anything else, destructors should call the inherited destructor *after* performing any local cleaning up. This is illustrated by the code for **TPie.Destroy** shown below:

```
destructor TPie.Destroy;
begin
   FPen.Free;
   FBrush.Free;
   inherited Destroy;
end;
```

Publishing Inherited Properties and Events

You may have noticed that our Pie component is rather lacking in the event-handling department. If you take a peek at the Events page of the Object Inspector, you'll see that a Pie component doesn't recognize any events at all! In fact, **TPie** *has* inherited a full set of event handlers from **TGraphicControl**, but before they'll appear, we have to publish them. To do this, add the following set of property statements to the **published** part of **TPie**'s class definition:

```
{Published declarations }
    property DragCursor;
    property DragMode;
    property OnDragDrop;
    property OnDragOver;
    property OnEndDrag;
    property OnMouseDown;
    property OnMouseMove;
    property OnMouseUp;
```

Artistic Postscript

As a postscript to the development of our new graphical control, below is the revised Additional page from the Component Palette, sporting the stylish bitmap which emerged after much blood, sweat and tears on our part. What - all this, and you want artistic genius too?

Summary

To some extent, we've only scratched the surface of component writing. Lots more information can be found in the Borland manuals and on-line help. This chapter has served as a gentle introduction to component writing for newcomers to Delphi. With luck, you're now feeling enthusiastic about component writing and you just can't wait to use your new-found knowledge to impress your friends and customers!

Component writing is, perhaps, the ultimate way in which you can customize Delphi. However, it's quite possible to customize the Delphi development system in a variety of ways without ever writing a single line of code. The material in the next chapter also has some bearing on would-be component authors since (amongst other things) you'll learn how to create and manage other component libraries. See you there ...

Exercises

1   You may have noticed a problem when using the Pie component
with pen widths greater than one - a problem which becomes
increasingly pronounced as the pen width gets larger. You'll see that
the component tries to place the center of the pen line on the
bounding rectangle of the component, meaning that a lot of unsightly
clipping takes place. The pen width appears to be much thinner at
the center of each side of the bounding rectangle as a result of this
clipping.

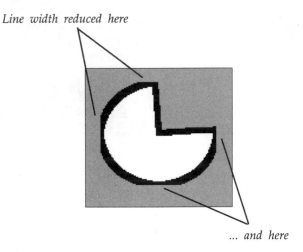

Line width reduced here

... and here

As it happens, this is a problem that's not unique to our Pie
component - try experimenting with the Shape component and you'll
see exactly the same problem. How would you go about remedying
this problem?

**Hint: remember that, as a component writer, you've got complete
control over how the component draws itself.**

2   Another problem with the Pie component concerns the conversion of
degrees to radians in the drawing code. You may have noticed that,
when you ask for a 90 degree angle, you don't always get exactly 90
degrees. Can you think of a way of improving the accuracy of these
calculations?

Chapter

Customizing Delphi

There are two issues guaranteed to spark a lively debate amongst developers - choice of programming language and choice of text editor! When developing applications in Delphi, you naturally have to work with Borland's Object Pascal, but there are a lot of ways in which you can customize the Delphi text editor - this is one of the topics covered in this chapter. We'll also look at other ways in which the development environment can be customized to suit your own personal taste. This chapter includes material on:

 Preferences.

 Customizing the Component Palette.

 Setting Browser options.

 Customizing the Code Editor.

 Setting up the Tools menu.

 Using Gallery Templates.

 Managing Component Libraries.

 Configuring the Speedbar.

Environment Options: Concepts

In Chapter 5, we covered the options that could be altered from the Project Options dialog. Here, we're going to take a closer look at the Environment Options dialog. As their name suggests, environment options affect the operation of the development environment itself, rather than the way in which a particular project is created.

To open the Environment Options dialog, select Environment... from the Options menu and the dialog below will appear:

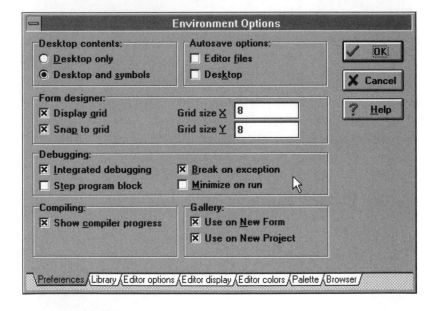

Like the Project Options dialog, there are a number of tabs along the bottom, categorizing the many options into a few individual pages. We'll look at each page in turn.

The Preferences Page

This page allows you to tune some of the more general properties of your Delphi environment.

Desktop Contents

The Desktop contents group-box determines what desktop information is saved when you exit Delphi. If you select the Desktop only option then directory information, open files and window layouts will be saved. Selecting Desktop and symbols causes browser symbol information to be saved as well, provided that such information is available from a previous successful compilation. If there hasn't been a successful compilation, or if you're compiling with browser symbol information turned off, then the Desktop and symbols option will be grayed out.

Autosave Options

The Autosave options group-box tells Delphi what information to save each time you run your application from within the environment. If your application is known to be buggy and there's a possibility of completely crashing the system, then it's a good idea to check one or more of these options. Of course, this will slow things down a little, but better safe than sorry!

Checking the Editor files check-box will save all modified source files each time your application is started, while checking Desktop will save the arrangement of your various desktop windows - some people like a particular window layout and this option will preserve one for you. Autosave options also operate whenever Delphi exits.

> **Take special care with the Editor files option. Many programmers like to make temporary, experimental changes to their source code and immediately rerun the application to see the effect. If you work this way and have Editor files checked, your temporary changes will be written out to your source file, which may not be what you want.**

Form Designer

The Form designer group-box is concerned with the operation and size of the layout grid - this has already been briefly covered in Chapter 2. If you need pixel accuracy when placing components on a form, you can turn grid-snapping off (and then optionally use the Size... and Align... facilities from the Edit menu). It's recommended, though, that you leave the grid-snapping turned on most of the time.

Debugging

The Debugging group-box controls the type of debugger that you use and its operation. These options are here (rather than in the Project Options dialog) because they apply to all projects.

If you'll be using Delphi's integrated debugger, check the Integrated debugging option - this option is on by default. The Step program block option causes the debugger to stop the first time it initializes a unit that's been compiled with debugging information - this is particularly useful when you want to debug unit initialization code. The Break on exception option stops your application when an exception is encountered (the default behavior) - if you leave this box unchecked, you can step through exception handlers without breaking out of the debugger. (For more information on exceptions, see Chapter Eight.) Lastly, the Minimize on run option simply makes Delphi close itself down to an icon whenever your application is running.

Compiling

If you check the Show compiler progress option in the Compiler group-box, a small dialog will pop up to show the progress of each compilation - Borland's Object Pascal compiler is so fast that you probably won't see much of the progress dialog unless you're working with a very large project, a very slow computer, or both! The Progress dialog shows the name of the project, the current source file being compiled, the total number of source lines compiled so far and the current source line number within the current source file:

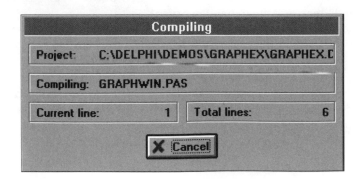

Turbo Pascal veterans may wish to check this option to remind them of previous incarnations of the compiler!

Gallery

The Gallery options turn on or off the Delphi Gallery. As the name suggests, the Gallery is a collection of predefined forms and projects. We first encountered the Gallery back in Chapter 4 where we used it to build the MDI-based SuperDoodle application. Without the Gallery, this would have been a lot more work.

Checking the Use on New Project checkbox means that each time you create a new project, you'll see a dialog like the one below. You can select a predefined project from the list of available projects or you can select the Blank project option to start from scratch.

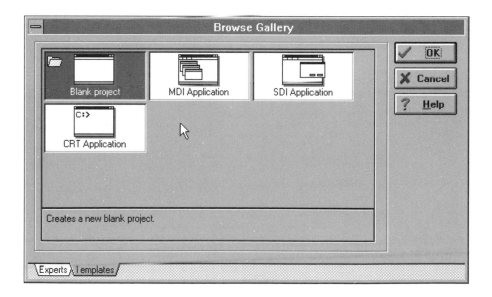

Option	What it Does
Blank project	This choice corresponds to a blank, start-from-scratch application, just as if you didn't have the Use on New Project checkbox selected.
MDI Application	A full-featured application with a Multi-Document Interface, similar to our SuperDoodle application or the Windows Program Manager.
SDI Application	A Single Document Application capable of managing only one open document at a time.
CRT Application	A special type of application which has no forms. All program output is via **Writeln** statements to a teletype-style window. This application type is provided for compatability with old code.

If you check the Use on New Form checkbox, you'll also be shown a list of available predefined forms each time you choose New Form from the File menu. Again, if you want to start from scratch, you can just click the Blank form option. However, it's recommended that you use the Gallery wherever possible. It will save you a lot of time and you can even save your own forms and projects as Gallery templates. We'll be looking at how to do that later in this chapter.

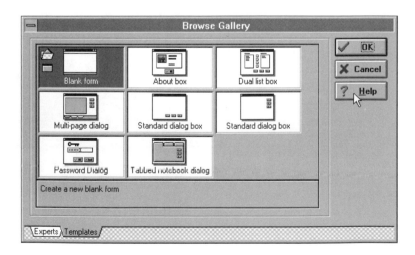

The Library Page

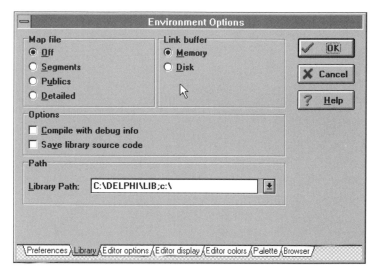

The Library page contains a number of options that relate to how Delphi builds the component library. The library is a special file which contains the compiled code and resources for all components currently accessible through the Component Palette. The default library is called **COMPLIB.DCL** and it lives in the **\DELPHI\BIN** directory. The component library is discussed more fully later in this chapter - see the section *Managing Component Libraries*.

For the options on the Library page to take effect, you must select the Rebuild Library menu item from the Options menu.

Map File

This option determines the type of map file produced for the library. This option works identically to the Map file option on the Linker page of the Project Options dialog, except that it is specific to library rebuilds.

Link Buffer

Again, this option works identically to the Link buffer option on the Linker page of the Project Options dialog, except that it is specific to library rebuilds. The same comments apply - if you run out of memory while rebuilding the library, then set this option to Disk. Running out of memory when rebuilding the library is more likely than when building an application because of the sheer size of the library - around 1.3 MBytes in its default configuration.

Options

Selecting the Compile with debug info checkbox will cause the library to be rebuilt with debugging information. This will make the library much larger, but it means that you will be able to step through the library source code during a debugging operation.

Checking the Save library source code checkbox will cause Delphi to generate a project file for the library on the next rebuild. This project file lists all the individual units which are used to create the library.

Path

This tells Delphi where to search for source files while building the library. Different pathnames can be separated by semicolons. If you get a 'file not found' error during a library build, then you should edit this environment setting.

The Editor options Page

The Editor options page allows you to control the behavior of the Code Editor. It looks like this:

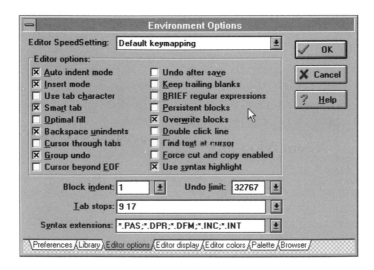

Editor SpeedSetting

The Editor SpeedSetting combo box at the top of the dialog allows you to set all the editor options in one go by selecting one of four predefined configurations. The four configurations are:

Configuration	What it Does
Default keymapping	The standard Delphi (CUA-compatible) configuration.
IDE classic	Emulates Borland DOS-based development systems.
BRIEF emulation	Emulates the Borland BRIEF editor (a popular programmer's editor).
Epsilon emulation	Emulates the Epsilon editor.

Editor options

There are no fewer than eighteen check boxes in this group box. Briefly, here's what each one does:

Option	What it Does
Auto indent mode	Each time you press *Enter*, the cursor will be placed underneath the first character of the preceding line which isn't a space or tab.
Insert mode	Causes the Code Editor to start in **insert mode** - text will be inserted at the cursor position as you type. Unchecking this option will cause the Code Editor to start in **overwrite mode** - text after the cursor position will be overwritten as you type. You can also use the *Ins* key to toggle between insert and overwrite modes while editing.
Use tab character	Causes tab characters to be inserted into the file. If unchecked, the equivalent number of space characters are used instead. Switches off the Smart tab option.

Continued

Option	What it Does
Sma<u>r</u>t tab	The *Tab* key will align the cursor horizontally to the first non-blank character on the previous line when you hit return.
<u>O</u>ptimal fill	Uses the minimum number of tabs and spaces to indent a line.
Backspace <u>u</u>nindents	When *Backspace* is pressed, moves the insertion point back to the previous indent level.
<u>C</u>ursor through tabs	Causes the arrow keys to move the cursor to the start of the next tab.
<u>G</u>roup undo	Makes <u>E</u>dit/<u>U</u>ndo (and *Alt+Backspace*) undo the last editing command, *and other editing commands of the same type*.
Cursor beyond <u>E</u>OF	Allows the cursor to be moved past the end of the file.
Undo after sa<u>v</u>e	Allows you to undo changes even after you've saved a file.
<u>K</u>eep trailing blanks	Retains any spaces or tabs at the end of a line.
<u>B</u>RIEF regular expressions	Allows BRIEF-style regular expressions when searching.
<u>P</u>ersistent blocks	Marked blocks remain selected until another block is selected, even when the cursor is moved.
Over<u>w</u>rite blocks	Replaces the selected text with whatever is typed next. (When <u>P</u>ersistent blocks is also selected, typed text is *added* to the selected text.)
<u>D</u>ouble click line	Selects the entire line when you double-click on it. If unchecked, the surrounding word is selected.
Find te<u>x</u>t at cursor	Moves the current selection into the Search/Find dialog, for faster searching.
<u>F</u>orce cut and copy enabled	Enables the <u>E</u>dit/Cu<u>t</u> and <u>E</u>dit/<u>C</u>opy menu items, even when no text is currently selected.
Use <u>s</u>yntax highlighting	Activate syntax highlighting. You can use the Editor Display page to configure syntax highlighting (see opposite).

A thorough discussion of BRIEF-style regular expressions is beyond the scope of this book. You should read Borland's documentation and try to familiarize yourself with the concept - regular expressions can be extremely useful when performing complex search and replace operations on large files. As an example of the power of regular expressions, the expression [^ryg][0-9]$ will match any occurrence of a letter, not including r, y and g, followed by a digit that comes immediately before the end of a line!

Block indent

The Block indent specifies how many spaces should be used to indent a marked block. This number can vary between 1 and 16, 1 being the default.

Undo limit

The Undo limit specifies the number of key strokes which can be undone. By default, Delphi allocates a 32,767 character buffer for recording keystrokes, the buffer being cleared each time a compilation is started.

Tab stops

The Tab stops combo box is used to specify which character columns to use as tab stops. The default setting here is 9 17, meaning that the first tab stop is in column 9, the second in column 17, and so on. This corresponds to the industry standard of 8 spaces per tab stop, but you can vary this if you wish.

It's recommended that you stick with the default value since, if you vary it, things will look messy when you load other include files and source code which use 8 spaces per tab.

Syntax extensions

Finally, the Syntax extensions combo box allows you to specify a list of file extensions for which syntax highlighting is enabled. This defaults to `.PAS`, `.DPR`, `.INT` and `.INC`, but if you want to use other file extensions for Pascal source files, you can just add them here and syntax highlighting will be enabled for those file types too.

The Editor display Page

The Editor display options relate primarily to the appearance of the Code Editor window.

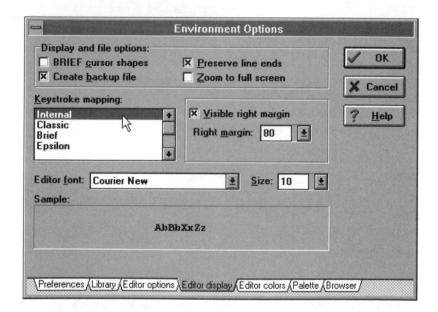

Display and file options

When you select BRIEF cursor shapes, the cursor takes on the same appearance as in BRIEF under DOS; in insert mode, you get a flashing underscore cursor, but this changes to a block cursor in overwrite mode. Some people find it helpful to have this visual feedback of editing mode.

With the Create backup file option selected, Delphi will always create backup copies of modified source files, with the extension **.BAK**. Backup files are created in the same directory as the original source file. This is a useful safety mechanism which you should probably use - if you ever make source code changes that don't work out, you can recover the original source code from the backup file.

Preserve line ends will cause Delphi to preserve any whitespace (blanks and tab characters) at the end of each source code line.

The Zoom to full screen option causes the Code Editor to occupy the whole screen when zoomed, rather than stopping short of Delphi's main window.

Keystroke mapping

In addition to the high level settings on the Editor Options page, you can also control the way the Code Editor responds to individual keystrokes via the Keystroke mapping: group-box. (A key map dictates what happens when individual keys or combinations of keys are pressed, for example, *Ctrl-E* starts an incremental search in the default mapping.) The four key mappings are Default, Classic, Brief and Epsilon. You should pick the one that you're most familiar with.

Margin Settings

While working with the Code Editor, you may have noticed a gray line towards the right-hand side of the page - the **right margin**. The right margin is placed there as a guide so that you can see when you've got to the edge of the page. Some programmers like to limit their code listings to a maximum width of, say, 80 characters to avoid problems printing or displaying on an 80-character-wide device. Using the right margin, you can see if the width limit has been reached. The Visible right margin check-box makes the right margin visible or invisible and the Right margin combo box allows you to set the right margin's location (in character positions from the left edge of the page).

> **Obviously, this is only going to work properly if you use a non-proportional (fixed width) font. For this reason, it's recommended that you stick with the default font setting of Courier New, a fixed width font that comes with Windows itself.**

Font Settings

The Editor font and Size combo boxes can be used to select the name and size, respectively, of the font used by the Code Editor. The sample box below these combo boxes shows an example of the currently-selected font. As stated above, it's recommended that you stick with Courier New, or use another fixed-width font.

The Editor colors Page

The Editor colors page is concerned with the colors used by the Code Editor during normal operation (the syntax highlighting colors) and the colors used to display special features (execution points, break points, selected text and so on).

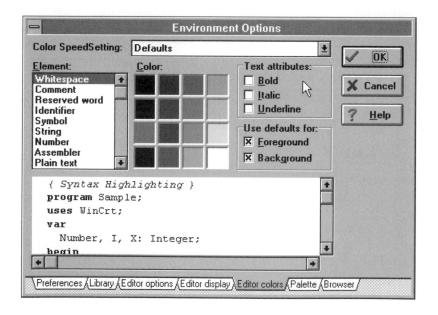

Color SpeedSetting

Firstly, at the top of the page, you'll see a number of Color SpeedSetting options which are much like the Editor SpeedSettings we saw earlier. A Color SpeedSetting is a set of predefined color settings which you can use to switch from one color scheme to another (in the same way that you can select predefined color schemes in the Windows Control Panel). Four different color schemes are provided: Defaults, Classic, Twilight and Ocean. The Defaults color scheme should be familiar to you already from your previous work with Delphi; the Classic color scheme mimics the color schemes of Borland's older DOS-based development systems; the Twilight color scheme is based on a black background; the Ocean color scheme is based on a sea-blue background.

Element and Color

Down the left side of the dialog page is a list box marked Element. Having first selected a color scheme which approximates your preferences, you can use this list box to select individual items for modification. With a particular item selected, you can click the left-mouse button in the color grid (entitled Color) to select the item's foreground color. Also, clicking the right mouse button in the color grid will select the current item's background color. Any changes you make are immediately reflected in the sample Code Editor display at the bottom of the page. The sample display is scrollable - you'll have to scroll down to the bottom to see the likes of breakpoint marks and selection blocks, changing as their colors are updated.

> An alternative, faster way of selecting a particular element for modification is to click on the element in the sample display. However, you should keep an eye on the selected item in the Element list-box to verify your choice - it's easy to get the wrong one.

Text attributes

The Text attributes check-boxes (Bold, Italic, and Underline) can be used to specify additional formatting options for the current element: reserved words, for example, are already bold, but you might like them to be underlined too.

Use defaults for

The Use defaults for group-box allows you to set the color of a particular element to the Windows foreground or background color (using the Foreground and Background check-boxes, respectively). These Windows colors can be set using the Windows Control Panel (they correspond, respectively, to

the constants COLOR_WINDOWTEXT and COLOR_WINDOW when used with
GetSysColor.) Unchecking either check box will restore the previous color
setting, as appropriate.

The Palette Page

The Palette page is concerned with the configuration of the Component Palette.
It looks like this:

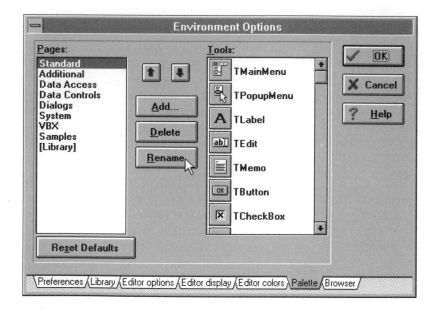

The page is split into two separate parts: the Pages list-box on the left and
the Tools list-box on the right. The Pages list shows the various pages of the
Component Palette while the Tools list shows all the components that are
installed on the selected page - as you select different pages in the Pages
list, the Tools list will change accordingly.

A quick way of getting to the **Palette** page of the **Environment Options** dialog is to right-click on the **Component Palette** itself. You'll see a small speed-menu which contains a **Configure...** item - selecting this item will take you straight to the **Palette** page. You'll also notice three other items on this speed-menu: the **Show Hints** item toggles the display of fly-by hints; the **Hide** item can be used to hide the **Component Palette** to maximize screen space - to redisplay it, select **Component Palette** from the **View** menu; the **Help** item brings up the Delphi **Help** page for the **Component Palette**.

Ordering Pages

You can use the up/down buttons located in the center of the dialog to alter the order in which pages appear in the Component Palette - it's useful to place your most-used pages at the beginning and your least-used pages at the end. To move a page, simply select it and then use the up/down buttons to move it up (towards the front of the Component Palette) or down (towards the back). When you've got the page ordering as you want it, click the OK button.

Ordering Components

Adjusting the order of components within a page is equally simple. First, select the relevant page, then select the component you want to move and use the up/down buttons as before. Click the OK button when you're done.

Deleting Pages

To remove a page from the palette, select the page and click the Delete button. You can only remove an empty page - that is, a page which contains no components. If you try to remove a page with components, an error will be displayed.

Deleting Components

To remove a component, just select the component and click on the Delete button. Although you won't be asked for confirmation, the change isn't irreversible: you can, for instance, click on the Cancel button and the status quo will be restored.

Moving Components to a Different Page

A neat feature of this dialog is that you can move components between pages. To do this, click on the component in the Components list and, with the mouse held down, drag the component to its new page in the Pages list. Releasing the mouse button will drop the component onto the target page.

Renaming Pages

To rename a page, just select the page and click on the Rename button: a small dialog will appear, prompting you to type in the new name of the page.

Adding Pages

You can add a page to the Component Palette by clicking on the Add... button. You'll be prompted to type in the name of the new page. A new page is initially empty - it's up to you to move components into it from other pages as described above.

The [Library] Page

You'll have noticed by now that there's a page which is simply called [Library]. You can't delete or rename this page - when it's selected, the Delete and Rename buttons are grayed out. So what is this page for? Quite simply, this is a special page that's used to contain all installed components, *including* those which don't currently appear on your Component Palette (it corresponds to the entire contents of your Component Library file - the one with extension *.DCL).

The [Library] page never shows up on the Component Palette, so if you drag a component onto this page, it will disappear from view temporarily. If you want to bring an invisible component back into circulation, you can just drag it back from the [Library] page to one of the normal pages.

This might seem rather odd - surely if you're not interested in a particular component, you can delete it altogether. For that matter, how do you actually add new components to the Component Palette? How are they installed into Delphi? To answer these questions, you'll have to skip to the section on *Managing Component Libraries* later. For now, just bear in mind that the Palette page of the Environment Options dialog is for working with components that you have *already* installed - it can't be used to install new components or to remove old ones altogether.

Restoring the Default Component Palette

At any time, you can restore the default layout of the Component Palette by clicking on the Reset Defaults button - you will be asked for confirmation, since this action can't be undone by clicking on the Cancel button.

Note that, if you do restore the defaults, all the components that you've installed yourself will still be available on the [Library] page.

The Browser Page

The Browser page of the Environment Options dialog, shown on the next page, allows you to control the operation and display of the Object Browser:

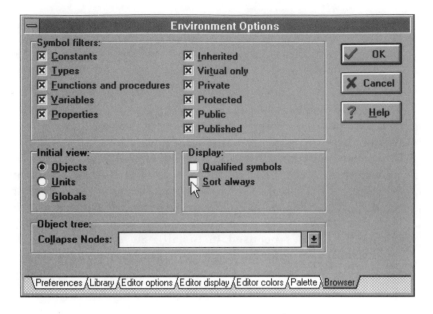

Symbol filters

The Symbol filters check-boxes determine which symbol types are displayed by the Object Browser. Initially, all these are checked and the Object Browser will, therefore, display as much information as it can - sometimes a staggering amount of information, in fact! Use these check boxes to simplify the default display. (The filters themselves are described in Chapter 6.)

Initial view

The Initial view radio-buttons determine what category of information you see when the Object Browser is first started: you can choose from Objects, Units or Globals. (Again, the available views are described in Chapter 6.)

Display

The Display check-boxes control whether or not a symbol identifier is qualified and whether the symbol display is sorted, respectively. Once again, this is described more fully in Chapter 6. Both these options correspond to menu items on the Object Browser SpeedMenu.

Object tree

This group box contains a single combo box marked Collapse Nodes - this allows you to specify which branches of the object tree will be collapsed when the Object Browser is started.

Setting up the Tools Menu

By default, Delphi's Tools menu has entries for the Image Editor, Database Desktop and BDE Config. It's possible to add your own choice of applications to the Tools menu for performing any special processing that you might wish to do as part of your application development.

For example, you're quite likely to build your application with full debugging information in the executable file so that you can run it through the Integrated Debugger or through TDW. Once your application has been debugged, you can recompile it without debugging information before shipment to customers. However, an even faster technique for creating a pared-down version of your application is to strip the debugging information from the executable file directly. Borland provide a tool which will do this, called **TDSTRIP**.

TDSTRIP is a DOS-based utility that you'd usually run from the command line in a DOS shell. Normally, it takes a single parameter giving the full pathname of the executable file. An example invocation is:

```
TDSTRIP   C:\WINDOWS\WOMBAT.EXE
```

This will strip the debugging information (if any) from **WOMBAT.EXE**. (**TDSTRIP** will remove Microsoft's proprietary debugging information as well as Borland's.)

OK, now suppose that you wanted to add **TDSTRIP** to the Tools menu so that you didn't need to keep jumping out to DOS. Here's how you'd do it: firstly, select the Tools... item from the Options menu. You'll get a dialog box showing you the list of currently installed tools. If you haven't yet installed any tools yourself, then the list will appear as follows:

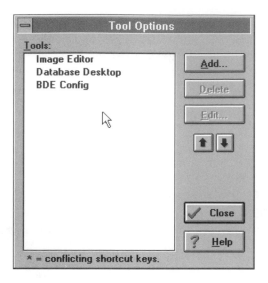

Using the various buttons on this dialog, you can add new tools, or you can edit or delete existing tools as well as move them up and down the Tools menu. If you introduce any conflicting short cuts, the offending tools will be marked with a red asterisk. (See later for a description of how to set up keyboard short cuts.)

Now, if you click the Add... button, the following dialog will appear:

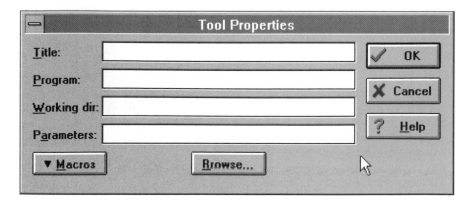

Press the Browse... button and locate the file **TDSTRIP.EXE** (it's probably in your **\DELPHI\BIN** directory). Select the file and type the Strip symbolic debug info into the Title edit-box.

How do we pass the name of our application's executable file to **TDSTRIP**? It turns out that we can pass this (and other useful information) using the built-in macros that Delphi supplies for this purpose. For example, click on the Macros button and select **$EXENAME** from the list that appears:

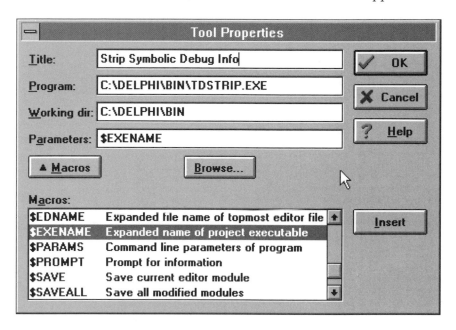

Now, click on the Insert button to insert the path name of your application's executable as a command-line parameter each time **TDSTRIP** is invoked. Click the OK button and that's all there is to it! From now on, you can strip the debug information from your application's executable file simply by selecting Strip symbolic debug info from the Tools menu. The other built in macros provide you with scope for many more customizations.

Assigning Keyboard Shortcuts

You can assign a keyboard shortcut to a menu item in the Tools menu simply by adding an ampersand character (&) in the usual way. For example, adding an ampersand sign to the beginning of the string Strip symbolic debug info would invoke this menu option in response to an *Alt-S* key combination if there were no other menu items using the same keyboard shortcut. If your chosen shortcut conflicts with what's already there, then it will be marked with a red asterisk as mentioned earlier.

Gallery Options

Delphi provides an exciting Gallery facility which can be used to give you a real head-start when creating a new application or form. We've already talked about how to activate the Gallery earlier on in this chapter. Now let's examine how you can customize the Gallery for your own use.

To begin select Gallery... from the Options menu. When you do so, you'll be confronted with a four-page Gallery Options dialog. Here's the Form Templates page:

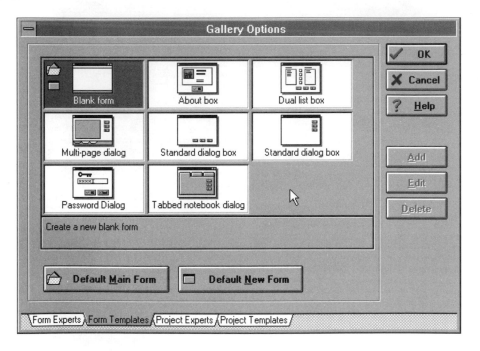

In addition to this page, there are three other pages for Form Experts, Project Experts and Project Templates. At this point, it's important for you to have a clear idea of exactly what these terms mean:

Gallery Page	What it Means
Form Experts	A Form Expert is a series of dialog pages that guide you through the creation of a form by asking you a series of easy-to-answer questions. At the end of the process, the form is automatically created according to the answers you gave.
Form Templates	A Form Template is a 'canned' form, ready for you to incorporate into a new project. Having based a new form on a template, you are then free to modify that form in any way you wish.
Project Experts	Like other types of Expert, a Project Expert is also structured as a series of dialog pages. It guides you through a number of questions and then builds a new project according to your specifications.
Project Templates	A Project Template is an 'off the shelf' project which you can immediately use as the basis for a new project. As with form templates, you may modify it as much as you wish.

Managing Form Templates

With the Form Templates page selected in the Gallery Options dialog, you can easily add, delete and modify existing form templates.

Adding a Form to the Gallery

To add a form, click the Add button on the Form Templates page and you'll see the dialog shown on the next page. Note that the Add button will be disabled if your current Delphi project doesn't contain any forms - you can only add to the Gallery from the current project.

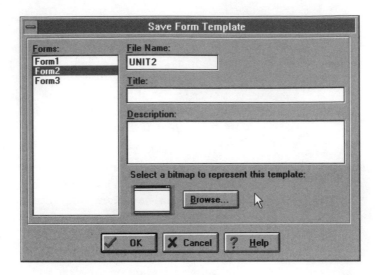

Using this dialog, you can specify which form you'd like to save into the Gallery. You can type a title for the template, a brief description, and you can press the Browse... button to locate a bitmap which you wish to associate with the template. The description information will appear when your form is selected in the Gallery just as for the forms already there.

Editing a Form Template

To edit an existing form, select the wanted form and click the Edit button. You'll see another dialog like the one below.

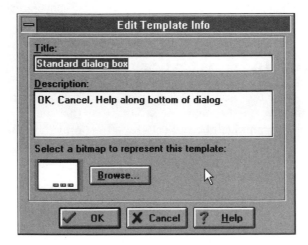

Using this dialog, you can modify the form template's Title, Description or bitmap at any time.

Deleting a Form Template

To remove a form from the Gallery, just select it and click the Delete button. You'll be asked for confirmation and then all references to the form will be removed from the Gallery.

> **Delphi won't allow you to delete or edit the Blank Form templates. Strictly speaking, this isn't really a template at all - it's there so that you can avoid picking a specific template and start from scratch to create your own custom application or form.**

Setting Default Forms

You'll notice that the Form Templates page also has a couple of buttons labeled Default Main Form and Default New Form. Here's how they work.

To set up a form as the default main form, just select the required form on the Form Templates page and then click the Default Main Form button. From now on, any time you create a new project it will automatically get a main form of the chosen type. If you have the Use on New Form option checked in the Environment Options Preferences dialog, then the chosen form will be highlighted when you see the Gallery dialog.

Similarly, selecting a form and then clicking the Default New Form button will establish that form type as the default new form. If you're using the Browse Gallery dialog, the selected form will be highlighted each time you select New Form from the File menu. If you're not using the Gallery, you'll automatically get the specified type of form.

> **To see the current selection for Default New Form and Default Main Form, just look for the small icons to the left of the main form bitmaps. These indicate the current settings.**

Managing Project Templates

With the Project Templates page selected in the Gallery Options dialog, you can add, delete and modify project templates just as easily as form templates.

Project templates can be added to the Gallery, deleted from the Gallery and edited exactly as described earlier for form templates. It's important to remember that when adding a project template to the Gallery, the *entire* current project is copied to the Gallery. Therefore, when developing a reusable project which might qualify as a project template, try to avoid incorporating any application-specific code until after you've added it to the Gallery.

Project and Form Experts

Delphi also has provision for installable Project and Form experts. A Project Expert guides you through the creation of a new project while a Form expert takes you, step-by-step through the creation of a new form. An example of the latter is the DataBase Form Expert shown below. Experts can be added and deleted just like templates.

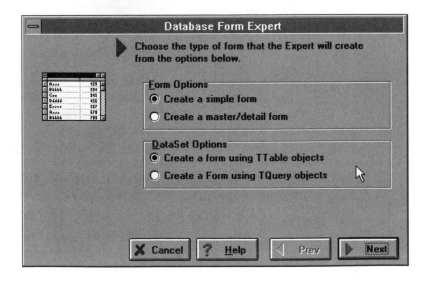

Libraries: Implementation

Throughout this book, we've concentrated on the Delphi components in the standard library, **COMPLIB.DCL**. Under normal circumstances, **COMPLIB.DCL** is the component library that's used by Delphi. However, it's perfectly possible to create a custom component library containing some or all of the components from **COMPLIB.DCL**. You might also purchase new components from other vendors, or write them yourself (as described in Chapter 10) - these new components can then be added to one of your custom libraries (or to **COMPLIB.DCL**).

> It's recommended that you leave COMPLIB.DCL as it is, so that you have something to fall back on if something nasty happens to your custom component libraries. If you wish to delete standard components from the library, or add new custom components, create a new component library first and make all the changes to that instead.

Creating a New Component Library

To create a new component library, select Install Components... from the Options menu. When you do so, you'll see a dialog like the one shown below:

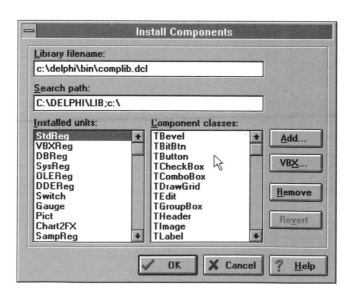

To create a new component library, just type a name for your new library into the Library filename box at the top of the dialog. Make sure that you include the full path of where you want the new component library to go, otherwise it'll be placed in Delphi's **BIN** sub-directory. Also, be sure to use the **.DCL** file extension so that the new library is recognized as a Delphi component library.

When you click on the OK button, the new library will be compiled and created at the location you specified. The new library will, by default, contain all the components and units that are contained in the currently-open library.

Editing a Component Library

Though it can be used to create a component library as we've just seen, the primary purpose of the Install Components dialog is to add and remove units from the specified component library. Notice the terminology here: **units** rather than **components**. A single Pascal unit can contain any number of component definitions - in fact, this is particularly true of the **StdReg** unit (selected in the above screenshot) which implements most of the components on the Standard, Additional, Graphics, Dialogs and File pages of the Component Palette. Here are the relevant lines of source code from the **StdReg** unit:

```
unit StdReg;

interface

procedure Register;

implementation

uses SysUtils, Graphics, Menus, Forms, Controls, Dialogs, Tabs,
     Buttons, StdCtrls, ExtCtrls, NoteBReg, TabNotBk, PageEdit, Grids,
     MnuBuild, Outline, Mask, MaskText, MaskProp, PicEdit, LibConst;
```

As you can see, this unit effectively brings together all the standard components as a single entity within the **COMPLIB.DCL** file.

> The distinction between units and components is important. The Install Components dialog can be used to add or remove units - it can't be used to add or remove individual components within those units. Having added a particular unit

to a component library, it's up to you how many of the components contained in that unit are made available on the **Component Palette** (by moving components between visible pages and the [Library] page on the **Environment Options/Palette** dialog page).

With all this in mind, the operation of the Install Components dialog is actually very straightforward. The left-hand list-box shows you what units are actually in the library, while the right-hand list-box displays all the components within the selected unit (if any). The Add... and Remove buttons can be used to add and remove units from the library. You need to be clear that, when removing a particular unit, none of that unit's components will be available - in the case of **StdReg**, that could be a lot of components! As a safeguard, the Install Components dialog has a Revert button which can be used to restore the status quo. Equally, you can just click on the Cancel button to cancel all the changes you've made since invoking the Install Components dialog.

The accompanying diagram is intended to clarify the relationship between libraries, units and components.

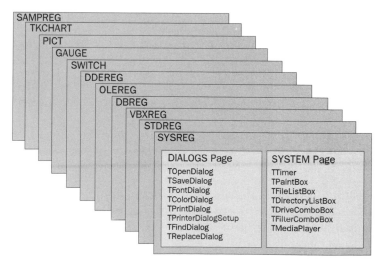

Contents of COMPLIB.DCL
The library is built from many units, each of which can implement an arbitrary number of components. Some units, such as SYSREG, register components on more than one page of the Component Palette. Delphi supports multiple libraries - switch between them with "Open Library".

To add **.VBX** files to the library, you should click the V̲BX... button which will allow you to select a **.VBX** file for installation in the library. (If your computer is anything like ours, you'll probably find lots of **.VBX** files lurking in your **\WINDOWS\SYSTEM** directory!)

Opening a Library

Once you have two or more different component libraries, you can swap from one to another by selecting the O̲pen Library... item on the O̲ptions menu. You'll see a standard OpenDialog like the one shown below:

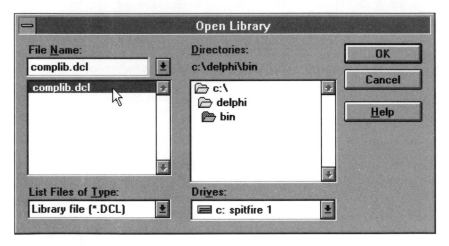

When you click on the OK button, the specified library is loaded and the Component Palette immediately changes to reflect the components therein.

Configuring the Speedbar

We've talked a lot about how you can customize the Component Palette by manipulating component libraries, arranging components on different pages, and so on. However, you can also customize Delphi's Speedbar very easily. If you want to try this, just click the right-hand mouse button on the Speedbar and you'll see the Speedbar's own speed-menu pop up, uncannily like the Component Palette SpeedMenu we saw earlier:

The Hide option will temporarily hide the Speedbar if you need extra screen space for any reason - once you've hidden the Speedbar, you can re-display it by selecting Speedbar from the View menu; naturally enough, the Show Hints item toggles the display of fly-by-hints and the Help item brings up the Delphi Help page for the Speedbar.

The Configure... option is more interesting. When selected, you'll see the Speedbar Editor appear:

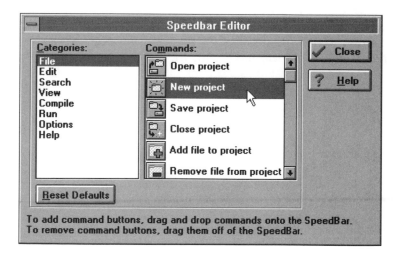

Here, the Categories list-box shows the different sets of commands available and the Commands list-box shows all the commands for the selected category - for instance, all the File commands are displayed in the above dialog.

In order to add a particular command button to the Speedbar, all you have to do is click the mouse down on the desired item in the Commands: list-box, drag it across the screen and drop it onto the Speedbar. Similarly, to remove an existing command button from the Speedbar, just drag the button off the Speedbar and let go. You don't have to drag it all the way onto the Speedbar Editor, but bear in mind that you'll only be able to drag buttons from the Speedbar while the Speedbar Editor is active.

> **If you want to add new buttons to the Speedbar and there's no room available, just use the mouse to resize the border between the Speedbar and Component Palette as described in Chapter One. Don't go mad though, or you'll end up with a huge Speedbar and no room left for your Component Palette!**

Summary

In this chapter, we've discussed some of the most important ways in which you can change the appearance and operation of Delphi to suit the way you work: configuring the Component Palette and Speedbar, adding and removing components from libraries, modifying the look of the Code Editor display, and so on. Perhaps most important of all, though, is the Gallery with its templates and experts, which can save you a great deal of time and effort.

Chapter

Database Access with Delphi

One of the most intriguing aspects of Delphi is the way in which it simplifies the creation of database applications. Delphi provides a rich set of tools and components with which you can build powerful database access software. A particular strength of Delphi is the way in which the user interface is decoupled from the mechanics of database access. To put this another way, you can write a desktop application which works with a local database. You can then easily adapt this application to work with a remote SQL server - the user interface code is insulated from changes to the underlying physical organization of the database and from changes to the source of the data itself.

In this chapter, we'll be covering the following topics:

- Delphi Data Controls
- Data access components
- Getting to grips with fields
- Using the database Form Expert

A Zero-Code Database Browser

Rather than finish up with a working application as we've done in previous chapters, we're going to break with tradition here by taking a look at the workings of an existing program, one of the demo applications that ship with Delphi. Select Open Project... from the File menu and select the **FISHFACT.DPR** project file in the **\DELPHI\DEMOS\DB\FISHFACT** directory.

When you run the application, you should be rewarded with a sight something like the one below. As you click on the vertical scrollbar alongside the grid at the bottom of the window, you'll see facts appear about many different fish. Take particular note of the information on the Clown Triggerfish - apparently, if you ever eat one of these, then it could well be your last meal!

This is a pretty snazzy little application. We're going to take it apart to see what makes it work. You might expect that with something as cute as this, there's going to be quite a bit of code in there managing the details of the user interface, updating fields as we scroll through the database and so on. Nothing could be further from the truth.

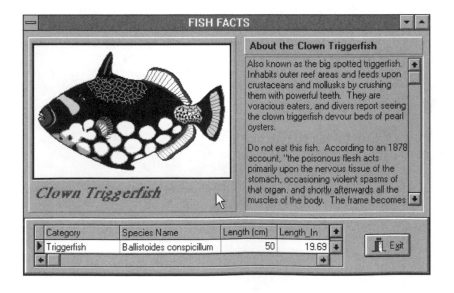

What's most remarkable about this application is that it doesn't contain one single line of code! If you look at **FFACTWIN.PAS**, the accompanying form unit, you'll see that this unit contains nothing other than the usual class definition for the form and its accompanying component. There isn't even a **OnClick** handler telling the Exit button to close the form.

Of course, we're cheating a little when we say there's no code. It should be clear that somewhere, there must be quite a lot of code! The good news is that for you, as the application developer, Borland have made the Data Controls as simple to use as possible.

Delphi Data Controls

So what do we mean by a Data Control? Delphi's Data Controls section on the Component Palette includes a set of user interface components which look much like the standard components you're already familiar with. There's a ListBox, an Edit box, a Memo component, CheckBox, Image component and so on. What's special about *these* controls is the fact that they're all data-aware. That is, they can be tied to a particular field in a database table. As the contents of that field change, so the data being displayed by the data-aware component changes too, without any programming being required on your part.

Database Terminology

We've been using a few terms such as table, field, database and so on without defining them. You may not be familiar with these terms if you've never done any work with databases before, so this would be a good time to 'bolt down' the terminology so that you're quite clear on what's what.

In the illustration on the next page, we've enlarged the grid area of the **FISHFACT** demo program. It's now large enough to display several rows of information at the same time. In database terms, each row of information is called a **record**. A record is made up of one of more **fields**. In the illustration here, we've got a Category field, a Species Name field and so on. Different fields can be of different types - the Category field contains text while the Length(cm) is numeric. There's another field (not shown here) which contains the bitmap image of fish in the database. This is an example of a **BLOB**

(Binary Large Object) field. BLOBs are very useful for storing graphics, multimedia clips or anything that's likely to be large and variable in size.

Category	Species Name	Length (cm)	Length_In	Notes
Triggerfish	Ballistoides conspicillum	50	19.69	Notes
Snapper	Lutjanus sebae	60	23.62	Notes
Wrasse	Cheilinus undulatus	229	90.16	Notes
Angelfish	Pomacanthus nauarchus	30	11.81	Notes
Cod	Variola louti	80	31.50	Notes
Scorpionfish	Pterois volitans	38	14.96	Notes
Butterflyfish	Chaetodon Ornatissimus	19	7.48	Notes
Shark	Cephaloscyllium ventriosu	102	40.16	Notes
Ray	Myliobatis californica	56	22.05	Notes
Eel	Gymnothorax mordax	150	59.06	Notes
Cod	Ophiodon elongatus	150	59.06	Notes

All of these records together constitute a **table**. We can see part of the table in the grid component shown here, and if we were to enlarge the grid even more, we might see the whole table at a glance. Obviously, in a real-world database application, a table could be very much larger than this, composed of tens of thousands of customer records.

A **database**, in turn, is made up of one or more tables. A simple database might contain only one table, but a more complex system could have several inter-related tables comprising the database. Here's a quick summary:

Term	Meaning
Database	A collection of one or more tables.
Table	A collection of one or more records.
Record	A collection of one or more fields.
Field	A single data item.

In the Grid component shown above, the currently selected record is indicated by the arrow symbol on the left hand side. You can see that in this case, the current record relates to the Angelfish. This concept of the **current record** is very important: each time the current record changes in the Grid component, all the other data-aware components update themselves to show the data in the new record. Before we look at how this happens, let's first see what Data Controls are available.

Data Control Roundup

The following table lists all the data-aware Data Controls which appear on the Component Palette and their 'non-database' equivalents.

Data-aware Control	Non-database Equivalent
DBGrid	StringGrid or DrawGrid
DBNavigator	No equivalent
DBText	Label
DBEdit	Edit
DBMemo	Memo
DBImage	Image
DBListBox	ListBox
DBComboBox	ComboBox
DBCheckBox	CheckBox
DBRadioGroup	RadioGroup
DBLookupList	No equivalent
DBLookupCombo	No equivalent

From the above, you'll no doubt have realized that most of the controls in the **FISHFACT** demo program are data-aware. The bitmap graphic is a DBImage component, the scrolling notes component to the right is a DBMemo, above the memo field is a DBText control and so on. The grid component that we've referred to several times is a DBGrid component. The DBGrid is responsible for selecting the current record in the table and the other data-aware components have each been configured to display a certain field of the current record. So how do we configure a particular component?

No programming is actually required - it's just a matter of setting up the relevant properties of each component. Two properties are important here: **DataField** and **DataSource**.

The DataField Property

If you examine the properties of each data-aware component in the **FISHFACT** program, you'll see that they've each got a property called **DataField**. The only exception to this is the DBGrid control. This **DataField** property tells the component which field it should be displaying. The DBMemo component has its **DataField** property set to **Notes** so that it displays the **Notes** field, the DBImage component has its **DataField** set to **Graphic** (because the fish bitmaps are stored in the **Graphic** field) and so on for each of the other components.

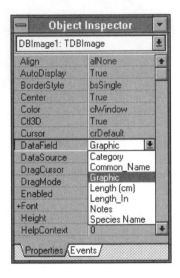

If you click on the **DataField** property of a component as shown here, you'll see a list of available fields. You can change which field is displayed simply by selecting a new field.

In the case of the DBImage control, setting **DataField** to another field will cause the control to simply display the *name* of that field rather than its contents. This is because the DBImage component can only display images. Similarly, if you set the **DataField** of a DBText control (such as the one above the Memo component) to **Notes**, then again the field name will be displayed. The **Notes** field, like the **Graphic** field is a **BLOB** and is incompatible with the DBText control. In general, if a data-aware component is asked to display the contents of an incompatible field type, then it simply displays the field *name* as an indication of the problem. However, this isn't always the case. For example if you set the **DataField** property of the DBMemo component to **Graphic**, this will be the result:

Essentially, the DBMemo control has tried to interpret the bitmap **BLOB** as a memo **BLOB**. At the end of the day, it's your responsibility to ensure that a particular data-aware component references a compatible field type.

The DataSource Property

This still leaves the question of where the data is actually coming from. If you look again at each of the data-aware components, you'll see that there's another property called **DataSource**. For every data-aware control on the **FISHFACT** form, the **DataSource** property is set to **DataSource1**. This is the name of a DataSource component. As the name suggests, the **DataSource** property identifies the source of the data by pointing at a TDataSource component. This is explained below.

Data Access Components

Up until now, we've looked only at the Data Controls. These are visual components which display the contents of fields and allow us to move from one record to another. However, Delphi also has another page of the Component Palette devoted to Data Access Components. These components are non-visual but they're crucially important - they establish the link between the data-aware controls on a form and the database itself.

The TDataSource Component

We've just discovered that the **DataSource** property of every data-aware component on the form is referencing a single TDataSource component. A TDataSource component acts as a 'channel', connecting all the data-aware components to other important, non-visual Data Access components such as Table or Query.

The most important property of the TDataSource component is **DataSet**. This property, in turn, points the TDataSource component at a source of data such as a TTable or TQuery component. A TTable component retrieves data from the Borland Database Engine (BDE) and passes it back to the data-aware components via the TDataSource component. A TQuery component does the same using SQL statements. For the sake of brevity, we'll limit our discussion to TTable components here.

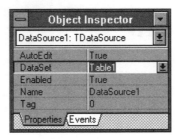

To summarize then, in the simplest possible scenario such as we see in the **FISHFACT** demo, all data-aware controls reference a single TDataSource component via their **DataSource** properties. The TDataSource component, in turn, references a TTable component via its **DataSet** property. It's the TTable component which references the actual database.

This arrangement might at first seem over-complicated, but it's actually very flexible. For example, by pointing a TDataSource component's **DataSet** property at a different TTable component, all associated data-aware components can be made to reference a different database in one quick operation.

A form can potentially hold multiple TDataSource components and multiple data sources such as TQuery, TTable at the same time. When you access a data-aware component's **DataSource** property, you'll automatically see a drop-down list of all TDataSource components on the form. Similarly, when you access a TDataSource component's **DataSet** property, you'll see a drop-down list of all possible data sources on the form. A simplified view of the database component architecture is given below:

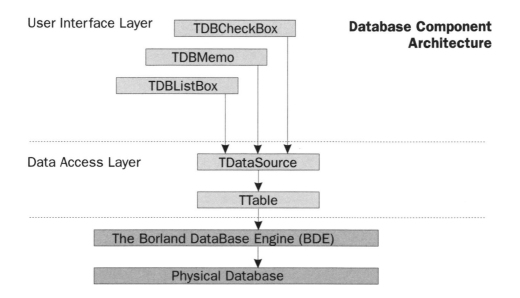

The Borland Database Engine (BDE) is responsible for managing access to both local and remote databases of many different types. A complete description of BDE is outside the scope of this introductory chapter. By default, the Delphi installation will configure the BDE to access dBASE, Paradox and the local InterBase server.

The TTable Component

Having described how the TTable component fits into the overall scheme of things, let's now examine it in more detail. The Object Inspector figure on the next page shows the properties owned by TTable. We'll look at the most important of these properties:

Active

Setting this property to **True** will open the table. Setting it to **False** is equivalent to closing the table. As you'll note from a look at the **FISHFACT** program, it's quite acceptable to have the table open for access at design time as well as at run time. Try toggling this property between **True** and **False** and watch what happens to all the data-aware controls on the **FISHFACT** form.

DatabaseName

This property specifies the name of the database which this TTable component accesses. You can specify a full pathname to the database, or else specify an alias if one exists. Just think of an alias as a shorthand way of referring to a specific database. The **FISHFACT** demo uses the pre-defined DBDEMOS alias which refers to **\DELPHI\DEMOS\DATA**. You must set the **Active** property to **False** before changing **DatabaseName**, otherwise an exception will result.

> To create, delete and modify aliases, use the Aliases page of
> the BDE Configuration utility accessible through Delphi's
> Tools menu.

Exclusive

This property determines whether your application has exclusive access to a
table. If you set this property to **True** and the table is already in use by
another application, then your program will have to wait for the table to
become free. You should not set **Exclusive** to **True** until you *must* have
exclusive access to the table. In particular, if you set **Exclusive** to **True** in
the Object Inspector window, and the **Active** property is also **True**, then the
table will be locked for use by the Object Inspector! This means that your
application will be unable to gain access.

ReadOnly

Setting this property to **True** will prevent the user from making any changes
to the currently active table. Again, you must set the **Active** property to
False before changing **ReadOnly**, or a run-time exception will result.

TableName

This property specifies the name of the wanted table within the database. As
before, you must set **Active** to **False** before modifying this property.

TableType

Modifying the **TableType** property lets you select different database table
formats such as ASCII, dBASE and Paradox. Borland recommend that you
use this property when you have more than one version of a database table
in different formats and you need to discriminate between them. It's also
useful for specifying the wanted table format when creating a new database
table. It goes without saying (or should, by now!) that you must set the
Active property to **False** before changing **TableType**.

Getting to Grips with Fields

If you've studied the **FISHFACT** demo program carefully, you may have noticed one or two strange anomalies. For example, why don't the **Notes** and **Graphics** fields show up in the grid component? Is it because the grid is smart enough to know that it can't display this type of field?

Actually, no. The fact is, these fields have been deliberately hidden so that they don't appear in the Grid component. If you take a look at the Object Inspector, you'll see that there appear to be many more components on the form than can be accounted for by what we've described so far. In the illustration below, you can see that aside from the TTable component itself, there are seven other components whose names begin with the string **Table1**. What exactly are these components?

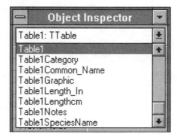

Dynamic vs Persistent Fields

You'll remember that right at the beginning of this chapter we explained that Delphi implements a mechanism which decouples the user interface part of an application from the underlying database implementation. This is a very important benefit for real world applications. Consider what would happen if you changed the internal layout of a database table. You could easily modify the physical structure of a table by reversing the order of one or more fields, adding a new field type to each record or even deleting existing fields. With any of these changes, an application would get hopelessly confused the next time it tried to access the changed database.

A field which corresponds to a physical field in the database is called a **dynamic field**. It's referred to by this name because it has to be dynamically created each time a connection to the physical database is established. Because the field corresponds directly to the database structure, it must also have the same name (from a programming perspective) as it has in the database itself. Effectively, by using dynamic fields in your application, you're 'hard-wiring' your application to a specific physical database structure. This is obviously a dangerous approach if you're likely to change the underlying database layout at some time in the future.

A better technique is to use **persistent fields**. A persistent field, as the name suggests, exists even when there is no connection to the database. A persistent field can be accessed through the Object Inspector just as if it were a component on the form. However, persistent fields are not created by placing components from the Component Palette. Unlike non-visual components, a persistent field doesn't even have a design-time representation in the form window. To all intents and purposes it's completely invisible from the viewpoint of the form window. The seven 'mystery' components in the illustration above are all persistent fields.

Why use Persistent Fields?

Persistent fields, like most things in Delphi, are objects. All persistent fields are derived from a common ancestor, the **TField** class. For this reason, Borland's documentation often refers to them as **TField** components and we'll do the same. Bear in mind though, that strictly speaking, a **TField** is an abstract class and you'll never actually meet an instantiated **TField** in the flesh.

There are derivatives of the **TField** component for every possible data type. In **FISHFACTS**, the **Graphic** field is mapped to a **TField** component of type **TBlobField**. The **Common_Name** field is mapped to a **TField** of type **TStringField** and so on. This mapping is the most important advantage of using persistent fields. We're using them to map the *physical* database structure onto a *logical* view of the database which is less intimately tied to the raw data, thus decoupling the data from its underlying form.

TFied Events

This isn't the only advantage of using **TField** components. If you look at the various **TField** components in the Object Inspector window, you'll see that **TFields** have an associated set of property handlers such as **OnChange**, **OnGet**, **OnSet** and **OnValidate**. Using these properties you can (for example) add your own specialized validation routines to a specific field.

Calculated Fields

TField components also allow you to create calculated fields - fields whose value is derived programmatically at run-time.

Hiding Unwanted Fields

We started this discussion of persistent fields by noting that not all fields showed up in the Grid component. You'll see that each **TField** component has a **Visible** property. It's this which determines whether or not a particular field appears in the grid. Try toggling the **Visible** property of the **TField** components from **True** to **False** and watch the effect on the Grid control.

Renaming Fields

TField components all have a **DisplayLabel** property. This can be used to give a field a different name as displayed in the grid component. Again, the emphasis is on divorcing an application's 'view' of a table from the real physical structure of that table. Different applications might want to use different views of the same table.

Using the Fields editor

Persistent fields are created and destroyed using the Fields editor. The simplest way of invoking the Fields editor is to double-click on a **TTable** or **TQuery** component. When you do so, you'll see something like this:

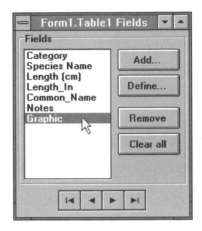

You can also invoke the **Fields editor** by first selecting the component and then clicking the right-hand mouse button anywhere on the form. You'll find that as long as a **Data Access** control is selected, an additional **Fields editor...** entry will be added to the usual **Form SpeedMenu**.

The Fields list shows all the currently defined persistent fields associated with the component. Initially, this will be an empty list because - by default - all fields are created dynamically. The four 'VCR-style' buttons along the bottom of the window is an instance of a **DBNavigator** control; you can use it to move backwards and forwards a record at a time and to jump directly to the first or last records in a table.

Changing Field Order

You can drag and drop the various fields in the Fields list in order to change their order. As you do so, you'll notice the field ordering changing in any associated Grid component - try it with the **FISHFACT** program.

Adding and Removing Persistent Fields

To add a persistent field to those already defined, click the Add... button in the Fields editor window. You'll see an Add Fields dialog from which you can select any field which hasn't yet got an associated persistent field. To create a new persistent field, just select the wanted field and click OK.

In the same way, you can use the Remove button to delete **TField** components. Since the Fields list is a multi-selection listbox, more than one field may be deleted in a single operation.

Defining Calculated Fields

You can also use the Fields editor to define new fields. Typically, you'd use this facility to create calculated fields. For example, you might create a field to show some quantity derived from performing a mathematical operation on other fields - *Net Profit = Gross Profit - Costs*, for example. For a calculated field, Delphi generates **OnCalcFields** events for which you can provide an event handler, thus allowing you to gain control and perform any needed calculations before the field's value is displayed.

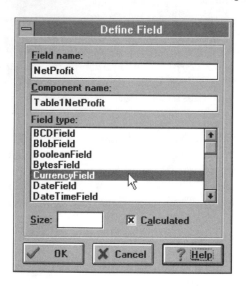

To define a new calculated field, click the Define... button in the Fields editor window. You'll see a dialog box like the one shown above. As you type in the name of your new field, you'll see Delphi concatenate the name of the associated data access control onto the front of your supplied name. Thus, **NetProfit** becomes **Table1NetProfit**. (You'll already have seen this convention used for the various persistent fields in the **FISHFACT** program.)

Next, choose a suitable field type from the Field type list box and check the Calculated box. Click the OK button and you're done. A calculated field is removed in exactly the same way as any other persistent field using the Fields editor Remove button.

Having set up a calculated field, you'll also need to set up an **OnCalcFields** event handler which performs the actual calculation. This event handler is owned by the TTable (or TQuery) component, not by the field itself.

```
procedure TForm1.Table1CalcFields(DataSet: TDataset);
begin
    { ---- add your code here ---- }
end;
```

Setting up Input Masks

Another advantage of using **TField** components is the ability to define an input mask.

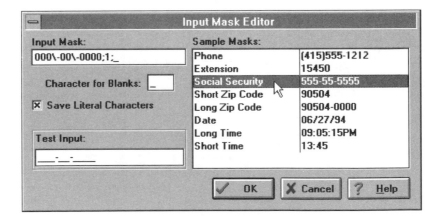

An input mask restricts user input to a specific format. For example, in the example above, input to a field is being restricted to a Social Security number format. Various other alternative formats can be selected from the Sample Masks area on the right. Alternatively, you can define your own custom input mask. to invoke the Input Mask Editor shown here, you can simply double-click on the **EditMask** field of a **TField** component.

Using the Database Form Expert

No introduction to Delphi Database programming would be complete without mentioning the Database Form Expert. We'll round off this chapter by showing you how easy to is to create a database browser application using the Form Expert. Like any other Delphi Expert, nothing takes place which you couldn't do manually, but you'll find that using the Form Expert will save you a lot of time and get your application off to a flying start.

To start the Delphi Form Expert, create a new project, select New Form from the File menu, move over to the Expert page of the Browse Gallery and click on the DataBase Form bitmap. (This assumes that you've checked the Use On New Form Gallery option in the Environment Options dialog).

You should see the first page of the Database Form Expert looking something like that shown below. Like other experts, it has Next and Prev buttons to go backwards and forwards in the question and answer process.

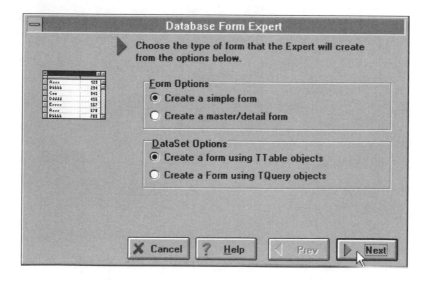

Let's specify that we want a simple form with **TTable** objects. Since this is the default, we can just click the Next button straight away. You'll then see another form asking you what table you want to use. Select the **\DELPHI\DEMOS\DATA** directory and choose the **ANIMALS.DBF** table. Then click the Next button.

On the next page, the Forms Expert will ask you which fields you want to add to the form. Let's say that we want to copy all the fields across. You can do this by using the >> button or, if you prefer, just double-click each field name until they've all been moved across. Having copied the fields across, you've now got an opportunity to rearrange them in any order that suits you. For now, just accept the fields in whatever order they happen to be in and click the Next button again.

The Form Expert will next ask you how you wish to arrange the various data-aware components on the form. The default arrangement is horizontal. Just accept this and click the Next button one last time. That completes the question and answer session - Delphi will ask for confirmation before creating the form. Click the Create button and wait for the Expert to do its stuff.

Incidentally, this exercise is an excellent example of the fact that even Experts sometimes make mistakes! If you look at the form that's been created by the Expert, you'll see that the EditBMP component, which should really be a DBImage component is actually a DBEdit component. This isn't much use for viewing the associated BLOB image that corresponds to the BMP field. To fix this, delete the existing EditBMP component and create a new DBImage component. Set its **DataSource** property to **DataSource1** and its **DataField** property to **BMP**. You may also need to set the **Active** property of the **TTable** component to **True**. Hey presto - you should end up with something suitably fearsome such as the illustration above. Not bad for a couple of minutes work!

Summary

We'd be the first to admit that this chapter has barely scratched the surface of Delphi database programming. We could easily have filled another book with information on just the database aspects of Delphi, but we hope that you've at least got a flavor for what database programming is like with this fascinating new development system. We have no doubts that we'll see a lot of exciting new database applications coming out during 1995 and that many of these programs will be Delphi based.

Delphi for Pascal Developers

This appendix is aimed at Pascal developers who already have some experience with Borland's object-oriented Pascal language. If you've used Borland Pascal development systems before, you should have little difficulty in getting to grips with Delphi. Beneath Delphi's friendly visual development environment lurks the same compiler that you're familiar with. If you merely want to use Delphi as a Pascal compiler, there's nothing to stop you doing so: you can use it to compile and build your existing Pascal projects. However, it goes without saying that this approach misses out on all the major productivity benefits that come from using a visual development tool and a rich component library.

This appendix is mainly concerned with the language changes that Borland have incorporated into the particular version of Pascal used in Delphi - **Object Pascal**. Although largely backwards-compatible with existing code, the new compiler incorporates a number of language enhancements - we'll be looking at the most important ones here. Also, we'll look briefly at what you need to think about when porting your old Pascal code to Object Pascal.

New Language Features

With Object Pascal, Borland have introduced a number of new language features, many of which relate to the Object Inspector interface. These language features generate additional categories of run-time information which are read by the Object Inspector and used to fill in the browser window with properties and events that relate to the currently-selected object.

The Class Declaration

The single most important language enhancement in Object Pascal is the introduction of the **class declaration**. Take a look at the class declaration of the Shape component which we've reproduced below:

```
TShape = class(TGraphicControl)
private
  FShape: TShapeType;
  FReserved: Byte;
  FPen: TPen;
  FBrush: TBrush;
  procedure SetBrush(Value: TBrush);
  procedure SetPen(Value: TPen);
  procedure SetShape(Value: TShapeType);
protected
  procedure Paint; override;
public
  constructor Create(AOwner: TComponent); override;
  destructor Destroy; override;
published
  procedure StyleChanged(Sender: TObject);
  property Brush: TBrush read FBrush write SetBrush;
  property DragCursor;
  property DragMode;
  property Enabled;
  property ParentShowHint;
  property Pen: TPen read FPen write SetPen;
  property Shape: TShapeType read FShape
                    write SetShape default stRectangle;
  property ShowHint;
  property Visible;
  property OnDragDrop;
  property OnDragOver;
  property OnEndDrag;
  property OnMouseDown;
  property OnMouseMove;
  property OnMouseUp;
end;
```

You can see that it looks very much like the old-style object declaration used in previous versions of the compiler and, in fact, object declarations are still supported. But, you *must* use the new style class declaration when declaring new Delphi components.

> Unlike old-style objects, class objects are always allocated on the heap, so you don't need to declare your variables as ^TShape, for instance - TShape is adequate.

A class declaration starts off with the name of the new class, an equals sign (=), the reserved word **class** and the name of the parent class (in parentheses).

> If no parent class is specified, TObject is assumed - TObject has a simple constructor and destructor called Create and Destroy, respectively.

If you have two classes whose declarations depend on each other, you can use a **forward class declaration** to tell the compiler that the full class declaration will be given later. For example, a declaration of the form

```
class TMyComponent;
```

will allow you to refer to variables of type **TMyComponent** without the compiler complaining that there is no such type.

Like object declarations, a class declaration can contain both **private** and **public** sections. There are no restrictions on access to the **public** elements of an object, whereas **private** elements may only be accessed within the module (unit or program) that contains the class declaration. Outside the defining module, **private** elements of a class are invisible.

Protected Elements

The class declaration builds on the idea of access control by adding a new **protected** section. **Protected** elements can only be accessed by descendants of the current class - this allows you to hide information from users of the class while still allowing descendant classes to exploit that information. For example, you may want to protect the fields which implement some property or other (see later).

> Note that the descendants which use a protected element don't have to be declared in the same module.

Published Elements

The most interesting part is the new **published** section. The published section of a class declaration corresponds to the Object Inspector interface for that object. This enables the Object Inspector (or anyone else who's interested) to retrieve information on an object, its properties and event handlers. There's nothing magical about the way that the Object Inspector does this - it simply makes use of the designer interface unit, **DsgnIntf** (in the file **SOURCE\VCL\DSGNINTF.PAS** in your Delphi installation directory).

Properties

Let's take a closer look at one of the property declarations in the class declaration shown earlier:

```
property Brush: TBrush read FBrush write SetBrush;
```

This declares a property called **Brush**. Because the property is in the **published** section of the class, it will automatically be made available to the Object Inspector. Additionally, since it's a property, it can be manipulated just like any normal public element of the class - property elements are also **public**.

In the above declaration, the **Brush** property is declared as being of type **TBrush** - a handle to a Windows brush object. This is followed by information which tells the compiler how to access the property. When reading the value of the **Brush** property, the compiler simply accesses the private **FBrush** field. However, the value of the property is changed by calling the private **SetBrush** method. This approach allows you to protect the private fields of a class from external access, while at the same time presenting a convenient user interface that's just as convenient to use as if we had direct access to public elements.

Doing things in this way also allows us to perform other actions behind the scenes. We've just seen that assigning to a Shape component's **Brush** property will invoke a method called **SetBrush**. Internally, the **SetBrush** method will store the new brush handle, but can also redraw the component to reflect the change of brush. These issues are covered in more detail in Chapter 10.

Events

Of course, a properly designed component has not only properties, but one or more event types that allow the component to respond to user actions such as mouse clicks, keystrokes and so on. Perhaps surprisingly, events are themselves implemented as a specialized type of property. For example, to add an **OnClick** handler to a control, you'd just include the following line in the **published** part of the class definition:

```
property OnClick;
```

Provided that your new component can trace its ancestry all the way back to **TControl**, your component will automatically get an **OnClick** event handler. To understand how this works we need to delve a little deeper - in fact, we need to look back at the definition of the **TControl** class, the 'great-grand-daddy' of all Delphi components.

```
TControl = class(TComponent)
private
    FOnMouseDown: TMouseEvent;
    FOnMouseMove: TMouseMoveEvent;
    FOnMouseUp: TMouseEvent;
    FOnDragDrop: TDragDropEvent;
    FOnDragOver: TDragOverEvent;
    FOnEndDrag: TEndDragEvent;
    FOnClick: TNotifyEvent;
    FOnDblClick: TNotifyEvent;
```

```
protected
    property OnClick:
        TNotifyEvent read FOnClick write FOnClick;
    property OnDblClick:
        TNotifyEvent read FOnDblClick write FOnDblClick;
    property OnDragDrop:
        TDragDropEvent read FOnDragDrop write FOnDragDrop;
    property OnDragOver:
        TDragOverEvent read FOnDragOver write FOnDragOver;
    property OnEndDrag:
        TEndDragEvent read FOnEndDrag write FOnEndDrag;
    property OnMouseDown:
        TMouseEvent read FOnMouseDown write FOnMouseDown;
```

```
    property OnMouseMove:
        TMouseMoveEvent read FOnMouseMove write FOnMouseMove;
    property OnMouseUp:
        TMouseEvent read FOnMouseUp write FOnMouseUp;
end;
```

This simplified class definition is extracted from the full source code to **TControl** - you can find it in **\DELPHI\SOURCE\VCL\CONTROLS.PAS**. The **TControl** class is actually very complex - we've included just the relevant information here.

TControl implements eight 'standard' events, all of which are shown here. The property definitions for these events are defined in the **protected** part of the class structure which appears to contradict what we said earlier - you must put the event property definition in the **published** area. The reason for this apparent inconsistency is simple: **TControl** is an abstract class. You can't ever create an instance of an astract class. **TControl** is simply a starting point from which 'real' controls inherit much of their functionality. Since a **TControl** is never instantiated, the property definitions belong in the **protected** area. A derived class such as **TButton** would then just add the **OnClick** property definition to its **published** part and the event then becomes available to the Object Inspector.

The procedure pointers defined in the **private** part of the class definition specify the type of the event handler and the number of parameters it expects. For example:

```
type
    TNotifyEvent = procedure (Sender: TObject) of object;
```

Abstract Methods

In previous versions of Object Pascal, you could declare a method of an object and then call the **Abstract** procedure within that method. This procedure call generated a run-time error 201. This was useful for implementing base classes (such as **TControl** mentioned earlier) where you wanted to discourage the user from instantiating an object of that base class.

The new Object Pascal built into Delphi provides a more elegant way of doing this. You can now use the **abstract** keyword as part of a method definition as shown below. Delphi won't stop you from creating an object which has an **abstract** method, but any attempt to call this method will also result in a run-time error 201. This has the benefit that you don't actually have to write the code for an **abstract** method - it just needs to be declared as such.

```
type
    MyObject = class
        procedure MyAbstractMethod; virtual; abstract;
    end;
```

Class Methods

Object Pascal allows you to associate methods - so-called **class methods** - with a **class**, rather than with any **instance** of that class; this allows you to put class-specific information inside the class, which is where it belongs. Any method in a class declaration which is prefixed with the keyword **class** becomes a class method; for example:

```
TMyShape = class(TShape)
  public
    class function GetVersionDate: String;
end;
```

Here, we're providing a function to tell us the release date of the current version of class **TMyShape** (this function could read an installation file containing release dates for all classes in the relevant library). You could then print out the version date (*without having to create an instance of the class*) using the following:

```
...
WriteLn (TMyShape.GetVersionDate);
...
```

Since class methods are independent of any particular instance of the class, they may not access instance fields.

Exception Handling

With today's sophisticated applications, exception handling features are no longer an option but a necessity when designing a serious programming language. Exception handling allows you to localize error recovery to one area and eliminates the need for repetitive checking for error conditions before and after every operation. Let's see how this works in practice (more details can be found in Chapter 8).

The try...except Block

```
function SafeDivide (A, B: Integer): Integer;
begin
  try
                                                         {Point 1}

    SafeDivide := A div B;

  except
                                                         {Point 2}

    on EDivByZero do SafeDivide := 0;

  end;
                                                         {Point 3}
end;
```

The simple routine shown above is responsible for dividing two integers and returning the result. Pascal veterans will immediately spot two oddities here - the appearance of the **try** and **except** keywords. These new keywords are used to implement the exception handling mechanism.

The **try** and **except** keywords and their associated statements are referred to as a **try...except** block. Here, there's actually only one statement (the division statement) between these two keywords but there can be as many as you like. Statements in this block execute normally (starting from **Point 1**) but, if an exception occurs, control is immediately transferred to the statement(s) following the **except** keyword (**Point 2**). If no exception occurs, execution continues at **Point 3**.

The net effect, of course, is that instead of the user being presented with a run-time error, this routine will silently return the value zero whenever a divide-by-zero error occurs. In a real-world situation, there would probably be a lot more code between the **try** and **except** keywords - code which would normally be full of lots of messy error-checking. By using an exception handling mechanism, the error checking can be done after the **except** keyword and things become very much neater.

(This concept will perhaps be more familiar to Microsoft BASIC [including Visual Basic] programmers. BASIC provides a mechanism called **ON ERR**, which allows control to be transferred to a certain point in a routine whenever a run-time error takes place. The **try...except** mechanism is very similar in operation.)

> You may also have noticed the **on** statement at **Point 2** in the source code above, which allows us to test for specific exceptions. There are a considerable number of different exception types: in this case, we're testing for a divide-by-zero exception, but you can also test for floating point math errors, file I/O errors, and so on.

The try...finally Block

In addition to **try...except** blocks, the Object Pascal language also provides **try...finally** blocks. These are particularly useful for Windows programming where it's often necessary for your application to 'clean up' after itself - deallocating temporary memory buffers, deleting custom brushes and pens, closing files and so on. For example:

```
procedure TForm1.Button1Click(Sender: TComponent);
var
  pMem: Pointer;
begin
  GetMem (pMem, 2048);
  {.......}
  FreeMem (pMem, 2048);
end;
```

In the above code, a 2 KByte block of memory is allocated at the beginning of the routine and deallocated at the end. That's fine, but what would happen if an exception (such as a floating-point error) were to occur before the **FreeMem** call was executed? Well, the call would be bypassed and the memory would remain allocated. Of course, if the run-time error resulted in the program's termination, there'd be no real problem since Windows would reclaim the memory anyway. However, if you were allocating bitmaps, pens, or brushes, these items would remain allocated even after the program terminated.

When programming with Delphi, the correct thing to do in these circumstances is to use a **try**...**finally** block, which looks something like this:

```
procedure TForm1.Button1Click(Sender: TComponent);
var
  pMem: Pointer;
begin
  GetMem (pMem, 2048);
  try
          {.......}
  finally
          FreeMem (pMem, 2048);
end;
```

With this approach, the statement(s) following the **finally** keyword will be executed even if the routine terminates with a run-time error. This guarantees that the allocated resource will be freed no matter what happens.

Run-Time Type Information

The **is** and **as** keywords are used to implement run-time type checking and typecasting respectively. For example, the following statement will determine whether an object, **xObj**, is of the given type:

```
if xObj is TForm then ....
```

This statement will evaluate to **True** if **xObj**'s class is **TForm** *or a descendant of* **TForm** - in other words, this checks whether **xObj** refers to a standard Form component or a specialized Form component.

The **as** keyword is used to perform run-time typecasting, like this:

```
with xObj as TForm do
begin
   { ..... }
end;
```

In this example, **xObj** is treated as a Form component within the block. When the **as** keyword is used, Object Pascal will perform internal checking to ensure that it's valid to treat the **xObj** as if it were a Form component (that is, that its class is **TForm** *or a descendant of* **TForm**), otherwise an **EInvalidCast** exception will be raised.

Using in to Find Files

The **in** keyword will be familiar to Pascal programmers as a test of set membership:

```
if TheInt in [1,3,5,7,9] then ...
```

However, this keyword now has an extra meaning within the context of a **uses** clause inside Delphi project files. See Chapter 5 for a fuller description.

```
uses
    Forms,
    Sdimain in 'SDIMAIN.PAS' {SDIAppForm},
    About in 'ABOUT.PAS' {AboutBox},
    DualList in 'DUALLIST.PAS' {DualListDlg},
    MultPag1 in 'MULTPAG1.PAS' {MultPageDlg};
```

The Result Variable

When developing a Pascal function, it's often useful to be able to examine the return result. Previously, it wasn't possible to do this, since specifying the name of the function in an expression was interpreted as a recursive call:

```
function GetFileHandle(fName: PChar): Integer;
begin
    GetFileHandle := _lopen(fName, 0);
    if GetFileHandle = -1 then
        MessageBox(0, 'Can''t open file', 'Error', mb_ok);
end;
```

In this example, the reference to **GetFileHandle** in the **if** statement will be interpreted by the compiler as a recursive call - obviously, not what's wanted. Moreover, the compiler will fail to compile the code anyway, complaining that no arguments have been supplied for the (supposed) call to **GetFileHandle**. In order to get around this, most Pascal programmers will use a local variable like this:

```
function GetFileHandle(fName: PChar): Integer;
var
    fd: Integer;
begin
```

```
    fd := _lopen (fName, 0);
    if fd = -1 then
        MessageBox(0, 'Can''t open file', 'Error', mb_ok);
    GetFileHandle := fd;
end;
```

There's nothing wrong with this, of course, provided that you don't mind the tedium of defining a local variable and (more importantly) remembering to set up the function result at the end of routine!

The new **Result** variable does away with these considerations. It behaves as a predefined local variable which corresponds to the function result. Unlike the actual function name, you can use it anywhere in an expression without implying a recursive call. Here's how you'd recode the above example:

```
function GetFileHandle(fName: PChar): Integer;
begin
    Result := _lopen(fName, 0);
    if Result = -1 then
        MessageBox(0, 'Can''t open file', 'Error', mb_ok);
end;
```

This gives the best of both worlds; concise and elegant code without irrelevant variables, and recursive calls when you need them.

> When porting old code to Object Pascal, it's a good idea to rename any local or global variables named **Result** or ambiguities may arise!

Changes to the Language

Object Pascal incorporates a number of useful language enhancements. In most cases, these enhancements are backwards-compatible, so they won't break any existing code. However, there are a few pitfalls for the unwary so read this section with care.

Function Result Types

With Object Pascal, Borland have relaxed the restrictions on permissible function result types. In the words of the on-line help documentation:

> Functions can now return any type, whether simple or complex, standard or user-defined, except old-style objects (as opposed to classes), and files of type text or 'file of'.
>
> The only way to handle objects as function results is through object pointers.

Open Array Construction

Some time ago, Borland introduced 'open array parameters' which allow you to pass an array type as a parameter to a function or procedure. Inside the called routine, you can use the built-in **Low** and **High** operators to obtain the lower and upper bounds of the array. In this way, you could, for example, pass an arbitrarily large array to a function which would then return the average value of all the elements of the array.

Object Pascal makes this facility even more flexible, by letting you construct an array and pass it to a routine in a single operation, like this:

```
Average := CalcAverage([5, 7, 9, 14, 234, 86]);
```

The corresponding function declaration would be:

```
function CalcAverage (Nums: Array of Integer): Integer;
```

> Since the elements of the array are enclosed in square brackets, this can look just like a set. Take care not to confuse the two.

Case Statement Optimizations

Borland have made two changes to the way **case** statements operate. Firstly, it's no longer possible to have overlapping ranges in a **case** statement. For example:

```
case Errcode of
    7:     Writeln ('Your disk is write protected');
    1..100: Writeln ('An unknown error has occurred');
end;
```

415

This code will compile fine under previous versions of Borland Pascal but won't be accepted by Delphi since **7** overlaps with the range **1..100**.

The second change concerns the way in which the compiler generates code for **case** statements. Essentially, if the various **case** constants are given in ascending order, the compiler will convert the **case** statement into a number of jumps. On the other hand, a non-sorted ordering of **case** constants will result in multiple calculations being carried out. Therefore, it's better to sort your **case** constants into ascending order if possible. For example:

```
case ErrCode of
    1:      Writeln(''This is case 1'');
    2:      Writeln(''This is case 2'');
    5:      Writeln(''This is case 5'');
    { ...... }
```

Using Your Old Code

Delphi is perfectly capable of using your old code, integrating it into a new-style Delphi project. If the old code is in the form of a **.DLL**, then you can just call the **.DLL** from Delphi. Existing units can also be integrated into Delphi applications - of course, old source code won't have any knowledge of Delphi's library structure but, provided that the **.DLL** itself has been well structured, it should be relatively easy to move it across.

But what about OWL, you ask? Well, admittedly, this could be something of a problem. You can certainly use Delphi to compile all your existing OWL source code and applications if you wish to continue using OWL, but you can't readily mix OWL code with the new Visual Component Library. We don't yet know whether Borland will provide a 32-bit implementation of OWL (because of the differences between the Win32 and Win16 APIs, it's not just a simple matter of recompiling OWL with a 32-bit compiler). Our advice is to bite the bullet and port your applications to VCL: not only will you be able to use Delphi's user interface components, giving your application a much nicer user interface, but you'll also be assured of portability to the world of 32-bits - Windows/NT or Windows 95.

This is a good time to point out the importance of 'decoupling' the user interface of an application from the nuts and bolts of the program code. Whatever sort of application you're writing, always make a clear distinction between what the application *does* and what the application *displays* on the screen. If you always bear this in mind, you can put the essence of your application into units, or even DLLs, separate from whatever user interface and application framework you might be using. If you've adopted this sort of approach with your OWL applications, then you will have greatly simplified the job of moving across to Delphi and the Visual Component Library.

Summary

Even if you're an experienced Pascal developer, you'll find there are a surprisingly large number of new language enhancements and additions in the Object Pascal dialect. Many of these changes are specifically designed to support Delphi's 'visual programming' approach, and you should therefore thoroughly familiarize yourself with what's in this Appendix to get the maximum benefit from Delphi programming. This is particularly true if you wish to try your hand at developing your own components.

Appendix

Delphi for Visual Basic Developers

This appendix is intended to serve as a quick introduction for Visual Basic developers who want to get up to speed with Delphi as quickly as possible. The really good news is this: as a Visual Basic developer, you've got a head start as regards understanding the component based (read that as 'control-based') philosophy that Delphi uses.

Like Visual Basic, there are two main steps to application development. Firstly, you lay out your user interface by choosing controls from the Component Palette, and secondly, you 'wire your application up' by writing the event-driven code, gluing your application together and causing all the different components to function as a coherent whole.

The Programming Environment

Familiar Property Names

Delphi components have a large number of associated properties with which you will already be familiar. For example, the Delphi push button control has all these properties in common with its Visual Basic counterpart:

Property	What it Does
Cancel	Specifies if this is form's Cancel button
Caption	The user-visible text of the control
Default	Specifies if this is default command button
DragMode	Determines manual or automatic drag mode
Enabled	Whether or not control is enabled
Height	Height of the control
Left	Left coordinate of the control
Name	Control name as used from program code
TabStop	True if user can tab to a control
Tag	For use by the application
Top	Top coordinate of the control
Visible	Whether or not control is visible
Width	Width of the control

Of the remaining properties, many of them have very similar names between the two different development systems - for example, **HelpContext** in Delphi, versus **HelpContextID** in Visual Basic. Sometimes you'll find a Visual Basic property that has a completely different name in Delphi - for example, **MousePointer** versus **Cursor**.

The bottom line, though, is that if you're familiar with the most common Visual Basic properties, then you should quickly understand what's going on in Visual Basic.

The same is true of events - just like Visual Basic, Delphi gives you subroutines for **Paint**, **Click**, **KeyDown** and so on. Under Delphi, these event names are prefixed with '**On**', so you'd read then as **OnPaint**, **OnClick** and so on. One thing you might be missing is the **Load** event. Traditionally, Visual Basic programmers use the **Load** event to do form-specific initialization just before a form becomes visible. Under Delphi, this is replaced by the **OnCreate** event.

Nested Properties

Another thing you'll notice about Delphi is the apparent lack of properties in the Object Inspector. For example, where has all the font size, font color and font style information gone? Under Delphi, the **Font** property is an example of a nested property. If you double-click on the small plus sign immediately to the right of the property name, the Object Inspector will 'open up' all the sub-properties belonging to that property. This is a much neater approach than Visual Basic, where you often spend most of your time scrolling around looking for the specific property you want to change.

No More On-the-fly Syntax Checking

Because of its interpreted nature, Visual Basic is silently converting your program into a tokenized form as you type it in. Every time you move the cursor to a different line, Visual Basic examines the line you've just finished with, syntax checks it, and converts it into tokens. A big benefit of this approach is that all the hard work has been done by the time you run your program - you don't have to wait for the tokenization to take place. Your program appears to start immediately.

By contrast, Delphi doesn't take much interest in what you've typed until you come to compile your application - you're quite welcome to type complete garbage if you like; Delphi won't complain until you start compiling. Having said that, the Code Editor window (in which you do most of your typing) is continually looking for keywords, numbers, identifiers and comments which it can display in the different colors selected via the Environment Options dialog.

The corollary to this is that Delphi has more work to do before your program can start running. You may have to wait a moment or two while all your application code is converted into machine code. You won't actually have to wait long though - Delphi's compiler is very probably the fastest in the business.

Language Differences

Unlike Visual Basic, Delphi is based around a real compiler. This compiler takes the program code you've written and translates it into machine language instructions that are directly executed by the processor in your PC. This translation process does not happen until you tell Delphi to compile your application. By contrast, Visual Basic translates your program - as you type it in - into an internal, tokenized form. These 'tokens' aren't machine code instructions and they need to be 'interpreted' when your program executes. The reason for converting the program into this tokenized form is to do with execution speed - it's very much easier for the interpreter to process a series of tokens than it would be for it to interpret your original program code character by character.

As a consequence of the above, Delphi differs in some important respects from what you're used to. Let's consider some of the differences.

Declaration of Variables

Because it's based around a Pascal compiler, Delphi expects you to declare *all* variables before using them. Most dialects of BASIC (and Visual Basic is no exception) allow you to begin using a variable without having previously declared it. While this is certainly convenient, it can often lead to subtle bugs in your code. Assigning to a variable called **MaxConnects** is pointless if you later refer to the same variable as **MaxConects** - something that's all too easy to do. A Visual Basic option can be used to force variables to be declared before use, but sadly, few Visual Basic programmers bother to use it.

Stronger Type Checking

Pascal has always been a strongly typed language and Delphi's Object Pascal is no exception. Type checking is the process whereby the compiler checks every operation on a variable to see if it's valid for that variable. For example, you can't use a floating point variable as an index into array.

BASIC, on the other hand, has always had very loose type checking. Visual Basic allows you to create variables of specific types by appending type specifier characters (%, $, and so on) to the variable name. Many BASICs (Visual Basic included) can be told to infer the type of a variable from the first character of the variable name.

With Pascal, everything depends on the variable declaration. When you first come to Pascal from Visual Basic, you may well feel that you're in a strait-jacket for a while, but eventually it will become easier. Languages with stronger type checking force you to think more clearly about what you're going to use a particular variable for. The following table lists some Visual Basic variables, and their Delphi equivalents.

Variable Type	Visual Basic	Delphi
Integer	`Count%`	`Count:  Integer`
Long Integer	`BigCount&`	`BigCount:  LongInt`
Single-Precision Floating Point	`SmallNum!`	`SmallNum:  Single`
Double-Precision Floating Point	`BigNum#`	`BigNum:Double,`
String	`Str$`	`Str:  String;`

In addition to the above, Delphi also supports the `Real` and `Extended` floating point type and `Comp` - an extended integer type.

You'll notice that there's no `Variant` type. By its very nature, this goes against the grain of a strongly typed language. However, if you do need to treat a memory location as holding more than one type at the same time, you can use Delphi's `union` type, or else look at the `absolute` clause as used in variable declarations.

The Dreaded Strings

There's one aspect of Delphi which will probably cause confusion, especially if you're not familiar with the Windows programming interface or API. The Windows API uses C-style strings. These are made up of a sequence of characters, terminated by a zero byte. If you call Windows API routines directly from Delphi, then you must supply strings in this format. However, Delphi itself uses Pascal strings. These are comprised of a character count followed by that many characters. You'll find that most of the time it won't be necessary to convert between the two types - you should only need to do it when making an API call. To help you with the conversion, see the string conversion routines in the **SysUtils** unit.

Nested Procedures

A nice aspect of the Pascal language is the ability to nest one routine inside another. In cases where routine B is only ever called by routine A, it makes a lot of sense to put routine B 'inside' routine A. This simplifies the structure of your code, reducing the number of outer-level procedures and makes the structure of your program clearer. A child procedure has access to the variables, types and constants defined by the enclosing, parent routine.

Run-time Issues

No More Run-time Interpreter

Because Delphi generates fully compiled machine code, your application will be a fully self-contained application to the same extent as any other Windows executable. To put this more clearly, you don't need to distribute a Delphi equivalent of the monster-sized **VBRUN300.DLL** file with your application. **VBRUN300.DLL** contains not only the Visual Basic interpreter (the assembler program which understands how to interpret the stream of tokens), but all the run-time library code for Visual Basic.

There is a down-side to this, of course. Getting rid of the interpreter is great, but what about Delphi's own run-time library code? Where's that going to reside? The answer is that it goes in your application's **EXE** file. Delphi applications are considerably larger than the equivalent Visual Basic program - the minimum size is around 170 KBytes. However, on the positive side, a Delphi application will grow quite slowly as you add more features. Since the **VBRUN300.DLL** file isn't much less than 400 KBytes in size, you can see that this represents a clear win for Delphi. If you sell your finished applications commercially, you may be able to get along with less distribution disks, and your install program can be simpler because it doesn't need to check for and/or install **VBRUN300.DLL** into the Windows system directory. The same arguments apply to the use of VBX files. Since Delphi components are linked into the executable, you have less files to worry about.

Faster Performance!

Perhaps the major win over Visual Basic is the faster performance. By its very nature, an interpreted programming language can never give performance in the same league as a compiled application. A compiled application, however, can go just as fast as the processor itself and, nowadays, that can be very fast indeed. You'll find that a Delphi application will execute considerably faster than you're used to.

Chapter

Index

The Beginner's Guide to Visual Basic 3

If you're a beginner to programming, this book is the place to start. We'll show you how easy, fun and powerful Visual Basic can be. If you're familiar with another language, you'll learn how Visual Basic does things in terms you'll understand. Along the way, you'll get all the background information you need on Windows Programming to help you develop really professional applications.

Peter Wright ISBN 1-874416-19-2
$29.95 / C$41.95 / £27.99

The Beginner's Guide to C++

The ideal start for the newcomer to the world of programming languages, this Beginner's Guide contains comprehensive coverage of the language syntax. You'll master procedural programming in easy stages, and then learn object-oriented programming - the essential programming methodology of the future.

O. Yaroshenko ISBN 1-874416-26-5
$24.95 / C$34.95 / £22.99

The Revolutionary Guide to Assembly Language

Take the Challenge. Learn how to design, develop and

debug powerful assembly language routines. Take control

of your system and increase the power of your high level

programs. Why learn unnecessary information when you

can accomplish the task with expert assistance.

"At £35.00, it's worth every penny!" (Syd Anderson, The

Association of C and C++ Users).

Vitaly Maljugin et al.   ISBN 1-874416-12-5

$39.95 / C$55.95 / £34.95

Instant C++ Programming

If you want a swift route to proficiency in C++, this no-

nonsense, fast-paced tutorial teaches you all you need to

know in an instant and gets you writing programs from

day one. The book is ideal for the programmer moving

to a new language. Lots of example code and self-check

exercises enable you to quickly become proficient in C++

and then move to object-oriented programming.

Ian Wilks   ISBN 1-874416-29-X
$19.95 / C$27.95 / £18.49